Beniamino Fortis, Ellen Rinner, Lars Tittmar (eds.)
Philosophy and Jewish Thought

Jewish Studies

Beniamino Fortis holds a PhD in philosophy. He studied in Venice, Florence, and Berlin. His research interests are picture theory, aesthetics, and contemporary Jewish thought.

Ellen Rinner studied art history, modern German literature, and philosophy in Berlin and Paris. She did her doctorate research in cultural history and theory at Humboldt-Universität Berlin and was a research associate at the Selma Stern Center for Jewish Studies in Berlin. Since 2022, she has been a research associate at the Chair for Transcultural History of Judaism at the Department of Cultural History and Theory at Humboldt-Universität Berlin. Her research interests include cultural and memory studies, art and visual history, aesthetics, and Jewish studies.

Lars Tittmar studied philosophy and sociology in Hamburg and Berlin. He did his doctorate research in philosophy at Freie Universität Berlin and was a research associate at the Selma Stern Center for Jewish Studies in Berlin. In 2023 he was a research fellow at the Franz Rosenzweig Minerva Research Center in Jerusalem. His research interests are Frankfurt School Critical Theory, social philosophy, philosophy of history, utopian thinking, aesthetics and the work of Jean Améry.

Beniamino Fortis, Ellen Rinner, Lars Tittmar (eds.)

Philosophy and Jewish Thought

Theoretical Intersections

[transcript]

The publication was made possible by co-financing for open access monographs and edited volumes of the Free University of Berlin.
The publication of this work was supported by the Open Access Publication Fund of Humboldt-Universität zu Berlin.

Bibliographic information published by the Deutsche Nationalbibliothek
The Deutsche Nationalbibliothek lists this publication in the Deutsche Nationalbibliografie; detailed bibliographic data are available in the Internet at https://dnb.dnb.de/

This work is licensed under the Creative Commons Attribution 4.0 (BY) license, which means that the text may be remixed, transformed and built upon and be copied and redistributed in any medium or format even commercially, provided credit is given to the author.
https://creativecommons.org/licenses/by/4.0/
Creative Commons license terms for re-use do not apply to any content (such as graphs, figures, photos, excerpts, etc.) not original to the Open Access publication and further permission may be required from the rights holder. The obligation to research and clear permission lies solely with the party re-using the material.

First published in 2024 by transcript Verlag, Bielefeld
© Beniamino Fortis, Ellen Rinner, Lars Tittmar (eds.)

Cover layout: Maria Arndt, Bielefeld
Copy-editing: Joan Dale Lace
Proofread: This publication has been peer-reviewed.

https://doi.org/10.14361/9783839472927
Print-ISBN: 978-3-8376-7292-3
PDF-ISBN: 978-3-8394-7292-7
ISSN of series: 2942-9730
eISSN of series: 2942-9757

Contents

Preface
Beniamino Fortis, Ellen Rinner, Lars Tittmar 7

The Legitimacy of Jewish Modernity: Gershom Scholem's Critique and Reconstruction of Jewish Enlightenment and Science of Judaism from the Spirit of Mystical Gnosticism
Christoph Schmidt 11

Thinking within the *Lehrhaus* Collective: Franz Rosenzweig on Jewish Thought and the Everyday
Benjamin Pollock 33

The Tail or the String of the Kite? Hans-Georg Gadamer, Steven S. Schwarzschild, and Jewish Hermeneutics
Massimo Giuliani 49

Idolatry and Freedom: Erich Fromm's View
Beniamino Fortis 63

Standstill in Utopia: Walter Benjamin's Philosophy of History and the Ban on Images
Lars Tittmar 85

The Approach of an Inverse Theology: A Commentary on the Aesthetic Dimension of the Jewish Prohibition of Idolatry, particularly in Adorno's and Benjamin's Philosophical Thinking
Mario Cosimo Schmidt 107

"A Singular Dossier of the Undiscovered": Intersections between Hans
Blumenberg and Aby Warburg
Ellen Rinner 121

"One Ought to Pray, Day and Night, for the Thousands": Etty Hillesum's
Approach to Prayer and Hasidic Thought
Silvia Richter 143

Literary Aspects of Philosophical Writing: The Case of Maimonides' Guide of
the Perplexed
Michael Zank 157

Authors 183

Preface

Beniamino Fortis, Ellen Rinner, Lars Tittmar

The relationship between philosophy and Jewish thought has often been a matter of lively discussion. But despite its long tradition and the variety of positions that have been taken in it, the debate is far from closed and keeps meeting new challenges. So far, research on this topic has mostly been based on historical references, analogies, or contacts among philosophers and Jewish thinkers. The contributors to this volume, however, propose another way to advance the debate: rather than adopting a historical approach, they consider the intersections of philosophy and Jewish thought from a theoretical perspective.

Every essay in this volume represents a contribution to the discussion about how two such different ways of thinking as the philosophical and the Jewish can relate to each other. But while some chapters aim to give insights into the way philosophy affects Jewish thought, others are more focused on the role of Jewish conceptions and motifs in the development of philosophical reasoning. In other words, the essays collected in this volume seek to answer the following complementary questions: What can Jewish thought gain from philosophy? And: What can philosophy learn from Jewish thought?

In both cases an encounter is implied – or better, recalling the term that appears in this volume's subtitle, both cases presuppose an intersection. This, however, can take two opposing trajectories. On the one hand, thinking processes developed in the field of philosophy can be used as keys to reading Jewish phenomena, which are thus reinterpreted in a new light and invested with new philosophical significance. On the other hand, ideas derived from Jewish sources can be thoroughly rethought and reshaped to be then integrated into secular contexts and contribute to the development of philosophical reflections. In short, philosophy can fruitfully affect Jewish thought and this, in turn, can play a significant role in several philosophical traditions. Both aspects are at issue in the following essays, which, from different perspectives, investigate the different modes of intersection.

Christoph Schmidt's chapter opens this volume with a thorough inquiry into the relationships between philosophy and Jewish thought in Gershom Scholem's conception. More precisely, Schmidt reads Scholem's investigations into Jewish mysticism against the backdrop of the neo-Kantian methodology that characterizes Ernst Cassirer's *Philosophy of Symbolic Forms*. The interaction between Scholem's understanding of Kabbala and Cassirer's philosophical method allows the Jewish tradition to be interpreted as a plurality of possible responses to the Revelation on Mount Sinai.

The Jewishness of Franz Rosenzweig's philosophy is the main topic in **Benjamin Pollock**'s chapter. By examining how Rosenzweig understands, presents, and practices a form of Jewish thinking during the time he spent at the Freies Jüdisches Lehrhaus in Frankfurt, Pollock delineates a novel account of what "Jewish thought" can be.

Secular and Jewish hermeneutics are at issue in **Massimo Giuliani**'s contribution, which ponders and reevaluates Steven Schwarzschild's critique of Hans-Georg Gadamer's rehabilitation of authority and tradition. Both concepts play a decisive role in Jewish hermeneutics too, which is conceived of as *shalshelet ha-qabbalah* and claims to have divine origin (*Torah min ha-shanmaim*). But while Gadamer rehabilitates authority and tradition *against* the idea of *raison critique*, Schwarzschild recognizes a dialectical relationship between them.

In his first major book *Escape from Freedom* (1941), Erich Fromm analyzes human freedom as essentially dialectical in nature. The reflections developed in this work, moreover, seem to exert a strong influence on Fromm's interpretation of idolatry, expounded in *You Shall Be as Gods* (1966) twenty-five years later. On this basis, **Beniamino Fortis**' article focuses on how a philosophical conception like Fromm's account of freedom provides theoretical guidelines for dealing with a typical issue in Jewish thought: that is, the origin and meaning of idolatry.

The chapters by **Lars Tittmar** and **Mario Cosimo Schmidt** are dedicated to the central role the Jewish ban on images (*Bilderverbot*) plays in the field of critical theory. While Tittmar focuses on the connection between utopian thought and *Bilderverbot*, which allows Walter Benjamin to situate the utopian chance in the present rather than in the future, Schmidt concentrates on the aesthetic implications of the biblical law, analyzing them through a detailed comparison between Adorno's and Benjamin's conceptions.

Despite the worldwide attention that Etty Hillesum's diaries have received since their publication in 1981, little work has been done to date onto examining the influence of Jewish thought on Hillesum's intellectual profile. In her essay, **Silvia Richter** tries to bridge this gap, by investigating Hillesum's Jewish identity and analyzing the contribution of Jewish sources to her conceptions of God and theodicy.

Ellen Rinner's essay proposes a comparative perspective between Aby Warburg's anthropological cultural science and Hans Blumenberg's philosophical anthropology. Warburg, who placed himself and his method of cultural study in the "tradition of German-Jewish intellectuality," is still a largely overlooked influence on Blumenberg's metaphorology. However, the paths of these two eminent figures in the intellectual landscape of pre- and postwar Germany never crossed directly: In 1933, Warburg's Hamburg library was forced into exile, and by the time Blumenberg began his philosophy studies there in 1945, it had already found a permanent home in London. In light of this disrupted tradition, the essay aims to show that a transdisciplinary perspective can reveal a hitherto undiscovered form of afterlife – to use Warburg's term – of Jewish thought.

In his study on Moses Maimonides' *Guide of the Perplexed*, **Michael Zank** explores the connection between Jewish thought, philosophy, and its literary form. Rather than addressing questions of genre or style, he examines the broader relationship between philosophical thought, language, and writing – namely, the relation between the appearance of truth in our minds and the linguistic or symbolic forms in which it invariably appears to us. By tracing the reception of the *Guide* through the centuries, he highlights the intrinsic connection between Maimonides' philosophy and the specific literary form it takes, thereby raising the question of its translatability.

To conclude, it is safe to say that, despite the variety of topics covered in this volume, each of them represents a significant theoretical intersection between philosophy and Jewish thought.

The Legitimacy of Jewish Modernity: Gershom Scholem's Critique and Reconstruction of Jewish Enlightenment and Science of Judaism from the Spirit of Mystical Gnosticism

Christoph Schmidt

I Introduction

"It is in fact a new Bible [...] That's what it is. To write a Jewish Zarathustra [...] whoever could do such a thing." (Scholem 1995: 54)[1] Thus the diary entry of the young Scholem on November 16, 1914 in reference to his Nietzsche lecture, intoning a motif central to his later engagement with Jewish mysticism: the motif of life. "But that someone experiences life – that is the rarest and most unheard of phenomenon [...] that life might appear to us in our sleep or in broad daylight in a vision: that would indeed be a mystical experience." (ibid: 227)

In fact, in his diaries Scholem formulates the first approaches to a history of Jewish mysticism, which he initially depicts as a combination of general philosophy and Jewish mysticism but is already anticipating as a transition from Nietzsche to Buber – i.e. from philosophy to mysticism – which he will develop into an inner-Jewish history of mysticism. "I would choose Buber because through him the albeit unrepresented Jewish mysticism would be addressed and he is [= compared to Nietzsche] the specifically mystical manifestation." (ibid: 228)

Not only will Scholem go on to correct his position on Martin Buber in the course of formulating this history, but the basic motifs – from the idea of life to

---

1   The following considerations are an elaboration of my essay: "Sein eigenes Gesetz sein... – Politisch – theologische Voraussetzungen und Konsequenzen der Theorie der Kabbala der symbolischen Formen bei Gershom Scholem" (Schmidt 2009; cf. Schmidt 2000). All translations of quotations in the text are my own.

the reconstruction of Jewish mysticism as an answer to the modern philosophy of life – are already manifest in these drafts.

This essay will first demonstrate how Scholem, in the crisis situation of modern Jewish culture, reformulates the conception of life encapsulated in post-Nietzschean philosophy (cf. Simmel 1918, 2003a; Bergson 1916)[2] into the messianic conception of life in Jewish mysticism. Secondly, it will describe the significance of the messianic mystical life for a comprehensive critique of modern Jewish philosophy of the Enlightenment and the Science of Judaism. Thirdly, it then shows how Scholem later revises this critique by integrating the conception of life into a theory of mystical symbolism. Fourthly, if the post-Nietzschean philosophy of life stands as the model for Scholem's messianic mysticism of Jewish life in Sabbatianism, which motivates the political-theological critique of the Jewish Enlightenment and the Science of Judaism, then the theory of Kabbalistic symbolism appears as a rehabilitation of the (neo-Kantian) philosophy of the Enlightenment, whose affinity to Ernst Cassirer's *Philosophy of Symbolic Forms* (Cassirer 1925)[3] is unmistakable. We are talking about a return to the idea of the Jewish Enlightenment and the Science of Judaism in the sense of an alternative, ethical messianism of pluralistic forms of life based on the theory of the mystical symbol. Fifthly, in this manner Scholem is actually seeking to reestablish the legitimacy of the Jewish modern era from the spirit of Gnosticism, which opposes any political-theological claim to sovereignty over tradition. Sixthly, in contrast to Hans Blumenberg's well-known construction of the *Legitimacy of the Modern Age* (Blumenberg 1996)[4] as an overcoming of Gnosticism, Scholem shapes his implicit justification of Jewish modernity as an implicit dialogue between philosophy and mysticism, drawing on the essence of Gnosticism.

---

2   Note Scholem's sharp criticism of Simmel: "This man has succeeded in dissolving himself entirely into a terminological system" (Scholem 1995: 385).

3   In the diaries, Scholem's statements about Cassirer are, of course, negative: "All these colloquia on the history of philosophy, all this business about the history of philosophy is completely unnecessary and pointless to me" (ibid: 424).

4   As far as I can see, Scholem does not make any explicit statements about Blumenberg and his thesis of modernity as a successful second overcoming of Gnosis. However, Scholem's reestablishment of modernity from the spirit of Gnosticism seems like a critical response to Blumenberg, especially in the context of the debate the latter initiated on secularization and political theology.

II Life as a Mystical-Messianic State of Emergency

At the heart of Scholem's studies on Jewish mysticism we always find the extreme, borderline, and exceptional case of the suspension or destruction of the symbolic-halachic order through the messianic theology of Sabbatianism. This destruction reveals itself above all in the most radical forms of its antinomian messianism, which – as in the case of the Frankists – reveals the vitalist core of this theology in the "longing of its adherents for a renewal of the life of the nation" (Scholem 1963a: 90). "This way of life [...] is the way of nihilism, which means to free oneself from all laws, rules and religions, to discard any guise and to despise everything." (ibid: 94)

For Scholem, this recourse to Sabbatian theology always leads to a diagnosis of a radical crisis in the Jewish way of life in modern secularized culture, which he interprets as a direct consequence of this messianic and destructive state of emergency. The idea of an unbound freedom of life forms the core of the messianic strategies of the radical Sabbatians, who actually discredit the law of Jewish tradition – in remarkable kinship with the apostle Paul – as the law of death. "The place to which we are going suffers no law, for all this comes from the side of death, but we are going to life." (ibid: 98) In these words Jacob Frank proclaims his messianic politics to his fellow messianic comrades-in-arms, while Scholem sums up the teaching thus: "Frank taught the necessity of dispelling all 'guises' and repudiating everyone in order to find the anarchic life in the depths of the destruction of all laws [...]." (Scholem 1936: 11)

The Sabbatian messianism and the mystical nihilism that developed from this messianism not only describe the historical expression of an absolute state of emergency and a radical crisis of the traditionally Jewish – i.e. religious-national way of life – but also "disclose" a fundamental structural problem of religious tradition in general, which Scholem repeatedly defines as "the formlessness of the original experience" or as the "mystical form of the formless." (Scholem 1973a: 20–21)

Insofar as the messianic destruction of the halachic order is directed against the God of the legal order deemed obsolete as the God of the extant global era of exile, and invokes the genuine – still hidden – "completely other" God beyond this global era, the destruction highlights this fundamentally structural problem. This destruction is actually a dialectic consequence of the intrinsically "formless" absolute, its "excessive transcendence," so to speak, insofar as the hidden, unknown, nameless, and unrepresentable – i.e. formless – God reveals himself as a Being beyond thought and language. The completely other God presents Himself then as the "Nothing" that is unattainable by language and thought, which in Sabbatian-messianic practice strikes outwards as a destructive and negativistic power. In other words, the Sabbatian state of emergency proves to be the revelation of the genuine – i.e. unknowable – God before the traditionally positive representations of the God of the law. It thus reveals the fundamentally Gnostic structure of the deity at the moment when the symbolic order collapses.

"The formlessness of the original experience can also lead to the dissolution of all form in interpretation. It is this perspective, destructive yet not unrelated to the mystic's original impulse, that allows us to recognize the borderline case of the nihilistic mystic as that of an all-too-legitimate legacy of mystical aftershocks" (ibid).

III Life between the Philosophy of Life and Heretical Mysticism

Before Scholem went on to develop this symbolic state of emergency into an expression of the crisis of modernity with its theological prerequisites for a comprehensive theory of kabbalistic symbolism, he referred this basic structure back to the then current historical context of the crisis of culture in the philosophy of life:

(1) At first glance, the radical-messianic Kabbalah seems like a transposition of the prevailing philosophy of life after Nietzsche, which for its part – as in the case of Georg Simmel, for instance – understands itself as a reflex to the crisis of the Enlightenment and the so-called "tragedy of culture" (cf. Simmel 1918, 2003a, 2003b, 2003c). The forms of culture created by life – according to Simmel – would ultimately always have to solidify in such a way that life would have to turn against these forms rendered stable by reason and law and blow them apart. In fact, the famous Nietzschean dualism of Dionysian life and Apollonian form adopted by Simmel appears in Scholem as a template for the theological dualism of the two Gnostic deities, which in this case aims to destroy Jewish enlightened culture and its expressions in the Science of Judaism.

(2) Drawing on the categories of this metaphysical constellation of Jewish Gnosis, Scholem undertakes his radical critique of modern Jewish philosophy and Enlightenment, the Science of Judaism, and the Jewish Reform movement of his time as one-sided constellations of the rationalization, formalization, and spiritualization of Jewish life.

(3) The Science of Judaism as an epochal event of a fundamental repression of the (national-religious) life thus serves Scholem at the same time as a reconstruction of the genesis of the Jewish Enlightenment in the 18th century from the spirit of nihilistic messianism. In this sense, the Jewish Enlightenment of the 18th century appears like a mirror of the neo-Kantian Enlightenment at the beginning of 20th century: while the first emerged from the crisis of Sabbatian mysticism of life and its destruction, the latter will face a destruction through the philosophy of life and radical mysticism of life.

The immanent crisis of messianic theology is thus not only an expression of the crisis of the messianic idea of freedom as it is supposed to be represented in the symbol of life, but can hardly hide its simultaneous origin in the philosophy of modern life.

> The messianic freedom in salvation and the substance of Enlightenment, which concerns the essence of this freedom, crystallize around the symbol of life. The mystic encounters life in the mystical experience. This life [...] is that which grows and changes freely and is not shackled by any law or authority, the unrestrained outpouring and the incessant annihilation of all forms that emerge from it, which determine this concept of life. (Scholem 1973a: 451)

This depiction of the immanent relationships of radical mysticism actually appears like a transposition of the then prevalent life philosophy, which tried to portray Nietzsche's dualism of Dionysian life and Apollonian form as a cultural philosophy and sociology – i.e. as an existential ontology. Scholem not only transposes the mystical category of life from Nietzsche's antithesis of the two mythical deities Dionysus and Apollo into the language of Jewish Gnosis as a dualism of the two deities, the gods of life and of law. As in the philosophy of life, where the discovery of life as the ultimate reason for being becomes the goal of an eschatological liberation of life from the rational shackles of culture, so the heretical life of Jewish mysticism characterizes the core of messianic practice and therewith the beginning and end of the messianic politics of the redemption from captivity in exile.

From Henry Bergson's vitalistic metaphysics (Bergson 1949) through to Georg Simmel's philosophy of life and Ludwig Klages' critique of logocentrism (Klage 1929/1932, 1930), life is elevated to a philosophical prime category that protests against the rational constitution of culture in order to free itself from its ossified forms of life. Bergson describes this uprising as a "coup d'état" of life against its symbolically rational encrustation, citing the "sudden appearance of the will" (Bergson 1949: 132–133)[5] to indicate the possible decisionist politics of this metaphysics of life. In any case, life designates the absolute ground before any symbolic-legal order; it is the event of the "break[s] with the symbols" (Bergson 1916: 49), which reveals itself only to intuition or a kind of "intellectual intuition."

Georg Simmel, following Nietzsche and Bergson, also elevated life to the basic principle of his cultural philosophy. Life creates from itself the forms it needs to live, but which very soon, when confronted with the dynamics of life, appear alien, as laws, limits, and contradictions. Apparently, Simmel understood above all the neo-Kantian philosophy of culture, with its orientation towards the law of reason as the principle of form, limits, and opposites, and leading on from there, life as a tragic conflict in which limits, form, and shape are finally swept aside.

> To put it as briefly and generally as possible, it is this: that life at the level of the spirit, as its unmediated expression, creates objective structures in which it expresses itself, and which in turn, as its vessels and forms, want to absorb in themselves its other currents, while their ideal and historical fixity, circumscription and rigidity sooner or later come into opposition and antagonism with the eternally variable, boundary-blurring, continuous life. (Simmel 1918: 160–161)

Life as the ground and counterinstance of form, law, and symbol thus becomes first of all a metaphysical prelude to the great liberation of the intrinsically Dionysian or anarchic being, which will finally "burst" all boundaries and fetters of form, as, for example, in the contemporary avant-garde art, where the genius of life expression – think of Wassily Kandinsky, Arnold Schönberg, and Hugo Ball – dares to suspend the traditional constitution of art. Against the various constitutions that life gives itself in the shape of philosophy, art, law, and politics, the subject, genius, and mystic of life reveals itself in a teleology and eschatology of life, which breaks its way to reality in the sense of a fulfillment and unveiling of life as the "coming of the kingdom." The messianism of life oscillating between erotic-Dionysian and political anarchy thus follows the sovereign decision of a Messiah who incarnates the originally anarchic

---

5 "Das plötzliche Auftreten des Willens ist wie ein Staatsstreich, den unser Verstand vorausahnt [...]."

Dionysian reality of life of the community of believers when he suspends the legal order and constitution (cf. Benz 1964; Taubes 1947; Löwith 1983; Lubac 1979; Moeller van den Bruck 1931; Bloch 1974).

This messianic political theology that has always made itself felt in the philosophy of life and the mystical life is revealed here. Scholem used it in order to protest against rationalist Science of Judaism and its foundations in the Jewish Enlightenment and to avenge the symptoms of a fundamental "forgetting of life," to which they have given rise. At the moment, when mysticism becomes practical and political in the messianic subject, it demands – in defiance of the strategies of self- and life-abandonment through reason, law, and morality – the opposite – i.e. the true accomplishment of the redemption of life and self and their national-religious community here and now. The Science of Judaism in its rationalist form, according to Scholem, represents the Jew who "wants to liberate himself from himself" so that "the Science of Judaism is the burial ceremony for him, something like the liberation from the yoke that weighs on him." (Scholem 1997: 8)

In a paradoxical way, Scholem connects the mystical messianic longing of life for redemption with the longing for death in the Science of Judaism, in Reform Judaism, and in the Jewish Enlightenment as a whole, insofar as the rationalization and spiritualization of the Jewish way of life is actually nothing other than the "other side" of the longing for redemption, the completion, so to speak, of the destructive energy inherent in messianic mysticism. The Jewish Enlightenment and the modern Jewish culture of reform and secularization are supposed to represent – thanks to a retrospective projection of the life-mystical criticism of the neo-Kantian Enlightenment – the late configuration of the Sabbatian practice of salvation itself, which is no longer conscious of itself, the form of its activist theology rendered moribund, as it were, by reason and law.

With his recourse to the mysticism of life, Scholem, like life philosophy in the 1920s, aims at a comprehensive destruction of (Jewish) philosophy and Enlightenment in its current form as the forgetting and repression of life, in order to use this destruction as a starting point to trace the historical genesis of the Enlightenment out of the crisis of Jewish theology in the era of its mystical messianic revelation. Herein belongs Scholem's fascinating reconstruction of the biography of the Frankist Moses Dobruschka and his connections to the Enlightenment and the French Revolution (cf. Scholem 1974b), which, as it turns out, cannot really hide the fact that there is little historical evidence per se for the comprehensive inner connection between Sabbatianism and Enlightenment that he suggests.

In any case, the two tendencies – the rationalization of Jewish theology on the one hand and the mystical foundation in theology of life on the other – are combined in Scholem's addition of the heretical theology of Abraham Miguel Cardoso (Scholem 1963b).[6] By means of this theology, the Kabbalah researcher actually performs a kind of seamless transposition of the philosophy of life into the Gnostic dualism of the two deities, in order henceforth to disregard the life-philosophical presupposition of his own historical diagnosis in the sense of an entirely immanent Jewish intellectual history constructed on its mystical foundation alone.

Scholem, in order to destroy the rational destruction of life by Jewish Science and Enlightenment via this immanent historical construction of Jewish mysticism, puts on the mask of the "anarchist heretic" himself, so to speak, which means: he reduces the philosophical Enlightenment to the life denied by it as the true original principle of religion and nation. Like the Sabbatian, he descends into the depths of the "Sitra Achra" of Enlightenment culture in order to unveil, behind the rational way of life of Kantian law and reason, the active anarchic principle of the lawlessness of true life. This life always reveals itself as the true inner side of its alienated outer form – that is, it is the hidden aspect of the true God of life, that has been suppressed by the God of law and reason. Cardoso's distinction between the exilic God of reason, which derives the world and history from the prima causa, and the true God of life, as revealed in the Torah, codifies Scholem's transposition of Nietzsche's aesthetic dualism (Dionysus and Apollo) in the Gnostic dualism of these two deities, in order to undertake from here the methodical destruction of the modern philosophical culture of Judaism as Enlightenment, Science and Reform, described now from the perspective of a Secessio Judaica and only immanent Jewish historiography as phenomena of a catastrophic loss of self. This change of perspective results in a new dialectic constellation of the crisis:

(1) When Scholem interprets the Enlightenment, Reform and Science of Judaism as the final articulations of Jewish mysticism, as its heretical emptying, then these phenomena, with their political-cultural effects of emancipation and assimilation, demonstrate a complex system of crisis phenomena that develop as a result of this mysticism.

---

6   First published in: "Der Jude", Sonderheft zu Martin Bubers 50.Geburtstag, Berlin 1928, pp. 123–139. Cf. Scholem 1974a, with original texts from Cardoso.

(2) In this way, the crisis of modern Jewish culture is in fact "enlightened" from an inner-Jewish context (= of Sabbatian messianism), but the phenomenon of the crisis is at the same time shifted back into the immanent Jewish history – i.e. the crisis as such is an inner-Jewish crisis and thus requires a more precise analysis of the crisis of mysticism in order to understand "the saving element" alongside "the growing danger."

(3) Here Scholem uses the elaboration of the mystical context of the crisis in the mysticism of life to develop a theory of the Kabbalah from the spirit of the problem of its symbolism as revealed by the crisis, which enables a comprehensive restoration of Jewish culture and its history. The most interesting point of this Kabbalah of symbolic forms is, of course, that it actually presents itself as a reconstruction of the neo-Kantian Enlightenment, specifically of Ernst Cassirer's *Philosophy of Symbolic Forms*. Thus, it is already revising the sharp division between philosophy and mystical theology of the first phase again in the sense of a new relationship – however implicit – between the two.

IV From Mystic Experience to a Theory of the Mystical Symbol: Authority and Mystical Interpretation

As we have seen, the messianic destruction of the halachic order of symbols and the ineffable way of being of God initially form the extreme poles and correlates of Scholem's diagnosis of the mystical crisis as it emerges from a post-Sabbatian perspective translated from a post-Nietzschean philosophy of life. But the original "formlessness" of the mystical experience, which becomes evident in Sabbatian messianism, is itself always a historically mediated constellation, whose possibility itself remains to be explained from within the logic of the history of mysticism. The messianic break with the history of the exilic life order is itself mediated historically and thus as a historical phenomenon within the history of mysticism – i.e. it is to be reconstructed from the dialectic of the tradition of revelation founded by Moses and practiced in the tradition of commentary and interpretation.

Scholem now develops a model of tradition that starts from Moses' revelation and confirms it in tradition through mystical experience – i.e. formulates it "in a language, in images and concepts that were created before him and for him" (Scholem 1973a: 16). But this situation begins to change when the mystic feels inclined to modify this language in terms of an emergent crystallizing "own experience," so that the given language and his own experience begin to diverge. This creates a "crack" or a "tear" in the language of the tradition, so that one's own experience of divine being and the language mediated by the tradition (with its images) are no longer congruent, and a first awareness of utterability and thus of the difference between sign and signified emerges. "It is precisely this element of the indefinable, of the absence, of the capacity for expression, that constitutes the greatest difficulty of the mystical experience. It cannot be translated simply and completely into clearly defined images or concepts." (ibid: 19–20)

The revelation of God, His speech, or His voice are increasingly presented as the absolute meaning before the word that circumscribes any concrete meaning. Thus, the initial tear widens into an abyss between the word of God and its meaning articulated by the mystic. God in His excessive transcendence and as the absolute and ineffable origin of language now remains radically meaningless. "The word of God must be infinite [...] the absolute word is meaningless in itself, but it is pregnant with meaning." (ibid: 22) With the emerging awareness of this symbolic difference, however, not only is the infinite meaning of God's word in the biblical text newly forged and deepened, so that in its depths the text discloses infinite meaning, but now the mystic himself gains also a completely new competence. He is "no longer just a factor [...] in the process of upholding tradition, but also in the process that develops it and drives it forward." (ibid: 17) Beyond the difference between the pre-established order of symbols and the concrete situation of interpretation, mystical subjectivity is constituted through the modification of this given order as "own experience," which in case of doubt will invent new symbols and rules. If the mystical subjectivity is initially the effect of the semiotic difference that settles in the folds of language, its actual potential is realized only in the case where one's own experience fully emancipates itself from the given structure of language, and turns against this order of symbols and laws that has been pre-stabilized by tradition. The mystic suspends the legal and symbolic order in the name of "his own law" (ibid: 20) – i.e. in the name of precisely this own, messianically founded experience.

This moment of mystic and messianic realization is thus made possible by the heretical act of interpretation as an internal historical event: It is the hour of birth of the Jewish mystical subject, now sovereign, rising above legal authority in a messianic state of exception. In this way, Jewish tradition becomes the event of its self-overcoming, which derives the sovereign subject from the absolute being of God, which in its excessive transcendence and formlessness verily reveals itself as nothing and thus in its potentially destructive power.

Sabbatai Zvi, the mystical Messiah, represents thus the fundamental epochal change from the objective legal order to the sovereignty of the subject, which the political philosopher Leo Strauss describes for modernity as a whole (cf. Strauss 2001). In place of the sovereignty of the law, which gives authority to the subject, comes the sovereignty of the subject, which now overrules the law or establishes it as the work of the subject. Even if the Enlightenment neutralizes the power of the sovereign through the law of the subject's reason, this law, based only on the subject's reason, loses its effective power at the first profound conflict over the meaning of the law and is potentially overruled by a sovereign verdict. Leo Strauss therefore intended that only a law that is valid above all subjective power – divine or platonic – can overcome this cyclical logic of subjective power and law.

But Scholem's real point is this: Instead of looking for a way that could restore the lost objective validity of the rule of law for the modern age and overcome the age of subjectivity, he takes this modern crisis as the point of departure for the understanding of the whole of tradition and of the ancient, objective law ordained by God in the Law of Moses. Whereas Moses until now seemed to possess an authority directly from the law decreed by God, Sabbatai Zvi and Jacob Frank stand for the subjectively mystical experience that undermines this authority and thus reminds us of its own formless origin, now Moses' law is itself understood as function of a subjective interpretation of the ineffable voice of God.

In this sense, Scholem presents a Hasidic Midrash of the revelation of Sinai as a back-projection of this idea of interpretation onto the Mosaic revelation:

In a most succinct and impressive way this whole problem of authority and mysticism is summed up in a saying handed down by one of the great saints of Hasidism, Rabbi Mendel Torum of Rymanow (died 1814), a saying which I shall here endeavour to interpret. What, it may in fact be asked, is truly divine about the revelation as it was given to Israel at Sinai, a revelation which, well understood, is an exceedingly sharply defined piece of doctrine and a call to the human community, a revelation that is extremely articulated in all its elements and in no way represents a mystical solution that remains infinitely interpretable? Already in the Talmud there is a discussion about this question of Israel's experience in receiving the Ten Commandments. What actually could they hear, and what did they hear? According to some of them, all the commandments came to them through the unbroken medium of the divine voice. According to others, they only heard the first Two Commandments – "I am the Lord your God" and "You shall have no other gods before

Me" (Ex.20:2/3) – directly from God's mouth. [...] According to Rabbi Mendel of Rymanow [...] not even the first two commandments come from an immediate revelation to the whole community of Israel. Everything that was revealed to them, what Israel heard, was nothing but that aleph with which the first commandment begins in the Hebrew text of the Bible, the aleph of the word "anochi", "I". This seems to me a most remarkable and thought-provoking sentence. In Hebrew, the consonant aleph represents nothing less than the laryngeal onset of the voice [...], which precedes a vowel at the beginning of a word. The aleph thus represents the element from which every articulated sound originates, and in fact the Kabbalists have always understood the consonant aleph as the spiritual root of all other letters, which in its essence encompasses the entire alphabet and thus all elements of human speech. To hear the aleph is really akin to nothing, it represents the transition to all audible speech, and it certainly cannot be said that it conveys in itself a specific sense of a clearly defined character. With his bold statement about the actual revelation, Rabbi Mendel reduced this revelation to a mystical revelation, that is, to a revelation that in itself was infinitely meaningful, but without any specific meaning. It represented something that, in order to establish religious authority, had to be translated into human language, and that is what Moses did in the sense of that saying. Any statement that justifies authority would therefore only be a valid and high-ranking, but necessarily still human, interpretation of something that "transcends" it. (Scholem 1973a: 46–48)

The final consequence with which Scholem summarizes this logic here – that "it [is] the mystical experience that gives birth to and releases authority" – must, however, be described as his own interpretation and conclusion, insofar as the Torah itself takes as its starting point that the people of Sinai actually only "saw the voices" (!), while Moses spoke with God face to face. The idea that Israel only heard the onset of a voice is therefore highly compatible with the very traditional view that only Moses received and understood the revelation directly, while the people could only hear a more or less vague sound or noise. In this respect, Scholem goes beyond Mendel Rymanov's own conclusion, as if, with this Hasidic version, the tradition as a whole should now be understood as a work of interpretation. All the more significant in this context is the statement by the theologian Franz Rosenzweig, which Scholem quotes here in an accompanying footnote: "Revelation [...] has only itself as its immediate content, with *va-yered* [= he descended, in Exodus 19:20] it is actually already finished, the interpretation begins with *va-yedaber* [= he spoke, Exodus: 20:1], not to mention '*Anochi*'

[= the 'I' at the beginning of the Ten Commandments]." (ibid: 265, emphasis added) In any case, through Rosenzweig's understanding, the principle of interpretation would indeed have been projected back onto Moses' revelation, so that it would have been elevated to the last principle of traditional revelation as well. The crisis that broke out in Sabbatianism could thus be overcome through this backward projection onto tradition.

The full implications of this back-projection, however, emerge from Scholem's second implicit conclusion. In other words, the whole point of this now hermeneutically and semiotically grounded theory of symbolism lies not only in this "first" back-projection of heretical suspension onto the founding act of religious authority by Moses, but also precisely in the consequence for the authority of the one who suspends the symbolic constitution in the name of a new messianic revelation. The very claim to absoluteness of the heretical subject himself is now defused and challenged in his claim to exclusivity by the anchoring of his "own experience" in the nameless "nothingness" of revelation that is to determine his decision. Both claims to absolute authority, then, the orthodox one to the objectivity of the law, and the modern one to the absolute, antinomian subjectivity, are rejected by the back-projection of the heretical crisis onto the whole of tradition. Both are always already relativized as interpretations of the meaningless beyond any absolute grasp.

Thus, through the historicizing of the crisis, Scholem succeeds in achieving a reintegration of the messianic revolution, achieving in fact a considerable limitation of damage to the catastrophe of the destruction of the Jewish way of life, as Scholem laments for modern Jewish culture in the shape of the Enlightenment, Reform, and Science.

V The Reconstruction of the Enlightenment as an Ethics of the Kabbalistic Symbol

If the early Scholem initially inscribed the post-Nietzschean philosophy of life in a mysticism critical of reason and the Enlightenment, the later integration of the mysticism of messianic life aims at a comprehensive theory of symbols that finally ties in with the neo-Kantian philosophy of the Enlightenment, as set out by Ernst Cassirer in his *Philosophy of Symbolic Forms*. In other words, Scholem's Kabbalah of symbolic forms ultimately represents a rehabilitation of the idea of a comprehensive Jewish Enlightenment that dialectically inscribes life and form in an ethics of pluralistic life forms.

Georg Simmel's philosophy of life already fashioned life in a dialectical relationship to the form that emerged from it, and thus always tried to overcome in his own way the "state of emergency" of an intrinsically formless life. His later philosophy of life appears like a Nietzschean concept of life from a restored Hegelianism – i.e. he thinks of life in its dialectic as a power that always reaches beyond itself, which can never be fixed or finalized in an ultimate constellation, but is always articulated in a new constellation (cf. Simmel 1918: 160–170). Life in itself is transcendence and thus always presents itself in an open structure.

In this context, Ernst Cassirer's *Philosophy of Symbolic Forms* (1925) appears above all to have given the impetus for reformulating the problematic of life and form, mysticism and symbol, myth and concept. The affinity between Cassirer's and Scholem's theory of symbols is unmistakable. Cassirer formulates this problem as follows:

> The pure immediacy of life [...] can [...] be seen entirely or not at all: It does not enter into the representations that we seek from it, but remains as something fundamentally different, opposed to and outside of them. The original content of life cannot be grasped in any form of representation, but only in pure intuition. [...] The decision is whether we want to understand the substance of the spirit in its pure originality [...] – or whether we want to devote ourselves to the fullness of the diversity of these mediations. (ibid: 48–49)

In fact, Cassirer in this context develops a theory of the genesis of symbolic consciousness from its originally mythical constellation, i.e. the supposed identity of symbol and symbolized in myth. The mystic becomes aware of the fundamental difference between the symbol and the symbolized through the modification of his own experience compared to the shaping of tradition, in order to recognize the fundamental legitimacy of the various symbol orderings through this difference.

> It [= the myth] cannot reveal and express itself in any other way than in it [= its own world of images] – but the further it progresses, the more it begins to become something "external" to this expression, for which its actual expressive powers are not entirely adequate. Here lies the basis of a conflict that gradually becomes more and more acute and which, while splitting the mythical consciousness within itself, at the same time truly reveals its raison d'être and depth in this split. [...] The progress consists in the fact that certain basic traits, certain spiritual determinations of the earlier stages are not only

developed and expanded, but that they are renounced, that they are verily absolutely destroyed. (ibid: 290, 289)

In other words, the crisis of the mythical symbol is always faced with the alternative of a destruction of the symbol, destructive to both life and culture, or its pluralization in a hermeneutic ethics of the symbol, as Cassirer finds modeled in Nicholas Cusanus' *Theology of the Coincidentia Oppositorum*:

> The content of faith itself, insofar as it is always and necessarily human conceptual content, has become a "conjectura" [= supposition]: It is subject to the condition that one being and one truth can only be expressed in the form of "otherness". No single form of belief can escape this otherness, which is based in fact and in the essence of human knowledge itself. So now there is no longer a generally valid and generally binding "orthodoxy" opposed to a plethora of mere "heterodoxies", but the otherness that is heteronomous recognized as the basic element of doxa itself. The truth, which in its essence remains unassailable and incomprehensible, can only be known in its otherness. [...] From this basic point of view, Cusanus has constructed a truly magnificent "tolerance", which is anything but indifference. Because the majority of forms of belief are not just tolerated as a mere empirical coexistence, but are demanded speculatively and epistemologically justified. (Cassirer 1994: 31–32)

With this recourse to Nikolaus Cusanus, in whom Cassirer sees in fact the founding philosopher of an alternative and pluralistic version of modernity, the horizon opens up to a symbol theory beyond its classic modern alternative between Hegel's absolute identity of self-consciousness and an absolute vitalism of the purely intuitive and therefore destructive life of radical life philosophy. Cassirer here is actually presenting an ethics of pluralistic forms of life as a model for a different Enlightenment, which apparently found its mystically underscored reformulation in Scholem's reflections on the Kabbalah and its symbolic forms.

Like the philosophy of Cassirer's symbolic forms, the Kabbalah of symbolic forms postulates an original "otherness" in the formlessness of the original experience and thus enables an analogous constellation of plural interpretations, which in itself already establishes an ethics. In fact, Scholem not only demands a coexistence of the divergent mystical forms of life for Jewish mysticism, but he also always makes them a requirement for the interreligious context. In this sense, he poses the question:

> [W]hy [...] actually does a Christian mystic repeatedly see Christian visions and not those of a Buddhist. Indeed, why does a Buddhist see the figures of his own pantheon and not Jesus or the Madonna? Why does a Kabbalist meet the prophet Elijah on his way to Enlightenment and not a figure from a foreign world? The answer, of course, is that the expression of their experiences translates immediately into traditional symbols from their own world, even if the objects of that experience are fundamentally the same, and not [...] entirely different. (Scholem 1973a: 26–27)

With this symbolic integration of the Sabbatian crisis, Scholem finally effects a rehabilitation of the philosophical Enlightenment which he attacked so violently in the first phase of his life-mystical rebellion against the Jewish culture of Enlightenment, Science, and Reform. In fact, he not only rejects the inner-Jewish secession from post-Nietzschean philosophy caused by the retreat into Jewish mysticism, but he actually opens up the horizon for a possible alternative dialogue between philosophy and Jewish mysticism on a symbol-theoretical basis.

VI The Legitimation of Jewish Culture out of the Spirit of Gnosticism

What is actually involved here is a rehabilitation of Jewish philosophy and Enlightenment, however implicit, from the spirit of Jewish Gnosticism. With this implicit return to a paradigm of neo-Kantian Enlightenment from the spirit of Jewish Gnosticism, Scholem's Kabbalah actually seeks to re-establish the legitimacy of Jewish modernity in the face of its vulnerability to crises.

This new foundation of a Jewish legitimacy of modernity is in fact diametrically opposed to the legitimation that Hans Blumenberg (1996) sketched in his monumental work on the legitimacy of modernity. In contrast to Blumenberg, who intends to overcome Gnosis and its "completely different" God, and thus of theology as a whole (with its excesses of political theology) by the Cartesian subject, Scholem aims at the rehabilitation of mystical Gnosis as a condition for the possibility of a pluralistic ethics. This ethics revises and at the same time integrates the orthodox, secular, and Reform-oriented definitions of the divine "formlessness" in their claim to truth. Gnosis means, from the perspective of a critical awareness of the way in which the symbol works, that insofar as every symbol simultaneously reveals and conceals God's nature, every symbol is legitimate in principle (1), and that insofar as every authority is now in principle an authority based on interpretation, there is no authority in the classical – orthodox or heretical – decisional sense, no absolute law and no absolute messianic decision. Thought through to the end by the two deities, Gnosis separates between the absolute being of God and God as being and cause of the respective orderings, the infinite God beyond language and at the same time the "finite" God of his utterances. In this way, Gnosis actually becomes a prerequisite for a theology of another Enlightenment and thus for a pluralistic ethics, which is based on the unity of the ensemble of the various theologies – from Orthodoxy to Reform, from Halacha to Kabbalah, indeed from theology to the secular philosophy of culture – referred to in the various forms of life. Being beyond the symbol remains ontologically open to its historical meaning of being, designating "God," "life," "being," or even "nothing," so that this legitimacy of modernity, unlike the radical negation of all theology in the philosophy of Blumenberg, actually makes possible not only a relationship between the theologies, but also and especially between theology and philosophy.

Ultimately, the Kabbalistic Gnosis reconstructed by Scholem appears as a counterpart to the negative theology of Nikolaus Cusanus, as Ernst Cassirer describes it in his book *Individuum und Kosmos* (1994) as another source for a possible genealogy of modernity. While the completely different god of Kabbalah and Cusanian mysticism resists any codification as the absolute origin of an "orthodox" system, his light only appears in the infinitely colored facets of his refractions and interpretations. Both Kabbalah and Cusanian theology are in fact indebted to a specific appropriation of the negative theology of Maimonides, which facilitates the evolution of this medieval Enlightenment into a neo-Platonically mediated version of mysticism and a skeptical enlightenment and ethics of pluralistic life-forms.

VII Conclusion: The Messiah as a Symbol of a Deconstruction

This closes the circle of Scholem's adoption of philosophy for mysticism. The transformation of the post-Nietzschean philosophy of life into Sabbatian mysticism and messianology was at the same time a reckoning with the philosophy of the Enlightenment, which introduced both as limit and problem the reintegration of this messianic mysticism into a comprehensive theory of the symbol. By means of this theory, Scholem actually effects a return to the paradigm of the Enlightenment on a changed theological basis, in order to facilitate a different, as we would say today, "post-secular" dialogue between theology and philosophy (cf. Habermas/Ratzinger 2004),[7] but also to jettison the political problem of the messianic dynamic.

In the end, Sabbatai Zvi not only proves to be a possible harbinger of the positive, symbolically mediated character of modernity, but he must now paradoxically be appointed as the messiah of modernity, who – to borrow Walter Benjamin's theological political fragment – frees modern Judaism from all political messianism.

In fact, if one considers how often Scholem points out that the messianic is indeed the seduction of life par excellence, but at the same time can only manifest itself in destruction on account of its claim to be absolute, then Sabbatai Zvi's destroying work of redemption is not only exemplary for the theological-political aporia of Jewish messianism, but for eschatological modernity as a whole. The idea of an absolute political utopia realized in history can only find itself in the nihilism of destruction or in totalitarian rule.

In contrast to Scholem's vehement insistence that the messianic in Judaism, unlike in Christianity, is a public event,[8] the whole restoration work of his reflections on the symbol in tradition is based on the counter-thesis that the messianic as a public political event denotes the catastrophe in itself. From the perspective of the symbolic, metaphysical restoration of this work of destruction, the work of destruction of Sabbatai Zvi assumes the positive meaning of a necessary destruction inherent in the essence of messianic mysticism, which now, from a retrospective perspective, can simultaneously be seen as "therapy" and "healing" from all messianic politics.

In this way, however, the act of destruction itself becomes a symbol of the very impossibility of the messianic in real political history – the third event, as it were, of a destruction of the temple, namely the "temple of modernity" or rather of its specific subjectivity, which in precisely the political messianism and its political theology of the realization of the Kingdom of God on earth wants to assert its own being "here and now" and yet in its violence and destruction is always refuting itself. At the juncture where the halachic order or

---

7   Jürgen Habermas later worked through these perspectives in Habermas 2022.

8   Cf.: "Judaism, in all its forms and configurations, has always adhered to a concept of salvation that saw it as a process that takes place in public, on the scene of history and in the medium of community, in short, which is decisive in the world of the visible and cannot be thought of without such a manifestation in the visible" (Scholem 1963c: 7; see also Taubes 1996).

the taboo established by Jewish philosophy in the Middle Ages against any messianism finds itself endangered, where the exilic life after the destruction of the Second Temple is threatened by the mystical spirit of Messianism, that is the point at which now – after the Sabbatian destruction – a new order is to be established which not only has its own viability for modernity as a symbolic form of life, but it is necessary to commemorate in the drama of Sabbatai Zvi the destruction of messianism as a symbol which thus – like the destroyed Temple in 70 A.D. – makes it possible to codify the restoration of the orders of life as an unmistakable warning sign. The new pluralistic symbolic orders of life, which replace the absolute orthodox order, need their own founding symbol, which Scholem established in his monumental biography of Sabbatai Zvi (Scholem 1973b). Thus, however, the ruin of messianic subjectivity becomes at the same time an alternative messianic symbol of the ethical order of Jewish culture in the spirit of a critical Jewish Enlightenment.[9]

---

9   Cf. Scholem 1963c. Here Scholem unfolds, among other things, the tension between messianism and apocalypticism in order to work out the difference between utopian hope and the destructive intrusion of another eon. It is precisely this tension that creates the abyss that the messianic activist wants to bridge through his concrete actions in order to conjure up the real inner-worldly destructive powers. Scholem aims here at a critique of the moralization and historicization of the messianism of the Enlightenment and the science of Judaism when he plays out the apocalyptic as an unforeseeable event against them: "In ihnen [= den moralisierenden Deutungen des Messianismus] kündigt sich ein Moralismus an, der späteren Umdeutungen des Messianismus im Sinne einer vernünftig besonnenen Utopie willkommen sein musste. Im Grunde aber kann der Messias nicht vorbereitet werden." (ibid: 27) At the same time, however, he incessantly repeats the warning "against human action that fails to bring redemption" (ibid: 32). This warning condenses into an insight into the modern ambivalence of political Zionism between the seduction of a political messianism and its impossibility: "It is no wonder that the readiness for irrevocable commitment to the concrete, which does not want to be brushed off, a readiness born of horror and doom, which Jewish history has found only in our generation, when it began the utopian retreat to Zion, is accompanied by overtones of messianism, without, however, being able – conspiring to history itself and not to a meta-history – to commit itself to it." Political Zionism, which has tended to draw on Sabbatai Zwi since its beginnings, is the current political constellation of messianic aporia between utopia and apocalypse, which Scholem is obviously trying to circumvent with his ethical-moralizing messianism of plural forms of life in order to take on – of course only implicitly and regardless of how critically underpinned – the messianism of the Enlightenment.

Bibliography

Benz, Ernst (1964): Ecclesia Spiritualis – Kirchenidee und Geschichtstheologie in der Franziskanischen Reformation, Stuttgart: Kohlhammer.

Bergson, Henri (1916): Einführung in die Metaphysik, Jena: Diederichs.

Bergson, Henri (1949 [1911]): Zeit und Freiheit. Eine Abhandlung über die unmittelbaren Bewusstseinstatsachen, Meisenheim am Glan: Westkulturverlag Anton Hain.

Bloch, Ernst (1974): Das Prinzip Hoffnung I-III, Frankfurt a.M.: Suhrkamp.

Blumenberg, Hans (1996): Die Legitimität der Neuzeit, Frankfurt a.M.: Suhrkamp.

Cassirer, Ernst (1925): Philosophie der symbolischen Formen, II. Teil: Das mythische Denken, Berlin: Bruno Cassirer.

Cassirer, Ernst (1994 [1927]): Individuum und Kosmos in der Philosophie der Renaissance, Darmstadt: Wissenschaftliche Buchgesellschaft.

Habermas, Jürgen (2022): Auch eine Geschichte der Philosophie, Vol. 1: Die okzidentale Konstellation von Glauben und Wissen, Vol. 2: Vernünftige Freiheit, Spuren des Diskurses über Glauben und Wissen, Frankfurt a.M.: Suhrkamp.

Habermas, Jürgen/Ratzinger, Josef (2004): "Vorpolitische moralische Grundlagen eines freiheitlichen Staates." In: Zur Debatte. Themen der katholischen Akademie Bayern 34/1, pp. 1–7.

Klages, Ludwig (1929/32): Der Geist als Widersacher der Seele, Leipzig/Munich: Johann Ambrosius Barth.

Klages, Ludwig (1930): Vom kosmogonischen Eros, Jena: Diederichs.

Löwith, Karl (1983 [1953]): Sämtliche Schriften, Vol. II: Weltgeschichte und Heilsgeschehen. Die theologischen Voraussetzungen der Geschichtsphilosophie, Stuttgart: Metzler.

Lubac, Henri de (1979): La Posterite soirituelle de Joachim de Flore, Paris: Lethielleux.

Moeller van den Bruck, Arthur (1931): Das dritte Reich, Hamburg: Hanseatische Verlagsanstalt.

Schmidt, Christoph (2009): "Sein eigenes Gesetz sein... – Politisch-theologische Voraussetzungen und Konsequenzen der Theorie der Kabbala der symbolischen Formen bei Gershom Scholem." In: id., Die Theopolitische Stunde – zwölf Perspektiven auf das eschatologische Problem der Moderne, Munich: Fink, pp. 163–204.

Schmidt Christoph (2000): Der häretische Imperativ – Überlegungen zur theologischen Dialektik der Kulturwissenschaft in Deutschland, Tübingen: Niemeyer.

Scholem, Gershom (1936): Zum Verständnis des Sabbatianismus. Zugleich ein Beitrag zur Geschichte der Aufklärung, Berlin: Schocken.

Scholem, Gershom (1963a [1937]): "Erlösung durch Sünde." In: id., Judaica 5, Frankfurt a.M.: Suhrkamp, pp. 7–116.

Scholem, Gershom (1963b [1928]): "Die Theologie des Sabbatianismus im Lichte Abraham Cardosos." In: id., Judaica 1, Frankfurt a.M.: Suhrkamp, pp. 119–146.

Scholem, Gershom (1963c): "Zum Verständnis der messianischen Idee im Judentum." In: id., Judaica 1, Frankfurt a.M.: Suhrkamp, pp. 7–74.

Scholem, Gershom (1973a [1957]): "Religiöse Autorität und Mystik." In: id., Zur Kabbala und ihrer Symbolik, Frankfurt a.M.: Suhrkamp, pp. 11–48.

Scholem, Gershom (1973b): Sabbatai Zwi. The Mystical Messiah 1626–1676, Princeton, NJ: Princeton University Press.

Scholem Gershom (1974a): Studies and Texts Concerning the History of Sabbatianism and Its Metamorphoses (in Hebrew), Jerusalem: Bialik Institute.

Scholem, Gershom (1974b): "Karriera Shel Frankist: Moshe Dobrushka WeGilgulaw." In: id., Studies and Texts Concerning the History of Sabbatianism and Its Metamorphoses (in Hebrew), Jerusalem: Bialik Institute, pp. 141–218.

Scholem, Gershom (1995): Tagebücher 1913–1917, Frankfurt a.M.: Jüdischer Verlag.

Scholem, Gershom (1997): "Überlegungen zur Wissenschaft des Judentums." In: id., Judaica 6: Wissenschaft des Judentums, Frankfurt a.M.: Suhrkamp, pp. 7–52.

Simmel, Georg (1918): Lebensanschauung. Vier metaphysische Kapitel, Berlin: Duncker & Humblot.

Simmel, Georg (2003a [1911]): "Philosophische Kultur." In: id., Gesamtausgabe XIV, Frankfurt a.M.: Suhrkamp, pp. 159–459.

Simmel (2003b [1918]): "Der Konflikt der modernen Kultur." In: id., Gesamtausgabe XVI, Frankfurt a.M.: Suhrkamp, pp. 181–207.

Simmel (2003c [1917]): "Der Krieg und die geistigen Entscheidungen. Reden und Aufsätze." In: id., Gesamtausgabe XVI, Frankfurt a.M.: Suhrkamp, pp. 7–58.

Strauss, Leo (2001 [1935]): "Hobbes' politische Wissenschaft in ihrer Genesis." In: id., Gesammelte Schriften III, Stuttgart/Weimar: Metzler, pp. 3–192.

Taubes, Jacob (1947): Abendländische Eschatologie, Bern: Franke.
Taubes, Jacob (1996 [1982]): "Der Messianismus und sein Preis." In: id., Vom Kult zur Kultur. Bausteine zu einer Kritik der historischen Vernunft. Gesammelte Aufsätze zur Religions- und Geistesgeschichte, Aleida Assmann/ Jan Assmann et al. (eds.), Munich: Fink, pp. 43–49.

Thinking within the *Lehrhaus* Collective: Franz Rosenzweig on Jewish Thought and the Everyday

Benjamin Pollock

How are we to understand the relationship between philosophy and Jewish thought? At first glance, Franz Rosenzweig appears hopelessly unable to make up his mind about how to answer this question and thus about how his thought might contribute to a volume like this one. To his close friends and first readers in 1919, he insists his *Star of Redemption* is a "Jewish book," and nearly breaks off friendships with those who don't find the book's Jewishness readily apparent.[1] But he opens his 1925 essay "The New Thinking" by backtracking, explaining that the *Star*, "in general, is not a 'Jewish book,' at least not in the sense that buyers who were so angry with me, think of a Jewish book [...] It is merely a system of philosophy" (Rosenzweig 1979b: 140).[2] After completing the *Star*, while beginning to formulate his thinking in terms of the healthy human understanding, Rosenzweig urges his audience – in a 1921 *Lehrhaus* course entitled *Anleitung zum jüdischen Denken* – "to summon the courage for Jewish thinking, thus for the use of the healthy human understanding" (Rosenzweig 1979d: 598).[3] But when Rudolf Hallo draws the conclusion that Rosenzweig's thought is Jewish, Rosenzweig again retorts impatiently on February 4, 1923:

> I believe just as little as you in the special Jewishness of the new philosophy. Where you get that, I don't know. [...] You apparently don't know I already

---

1   See Rosenzweig's letters to Hans and Rudolf Ehrenberg from the summer of 1919, cp. Rosenzweig 1979, pp. 634–643. See also Rosenzweig's letters to Margrit and Eugen Rosenstock during the same summer, e.g., June 27, June 29, and July 1, 1919 (https://www.erhfund.org/gritli-not-chosen/).

2   All translations of Rosenzweig's quotes in the text are my own, unless otherwise stated.

3   Cass Fisher notes that it is in preparation for this course (i.e., late 1920-early 1921) at the *Lehrhaus*, that Rosenzweig begins to situate his thinking in reference to the healthy human understanding. Cf. Fisher 2016: 349–350.

sketched out my philosophy in a ... presentation where even the title is "philosophy of the healthy human understanding." (Rosenzweig 1979a: 888–889)

Does Rosenzweig's philosophy qualify as "Jewish thought" or not? Does his thinking according to the healthy human understanding stamp that thinking as Jewish or precisely as transcending the confines of Jewishness? In what follows, I will examine how Rosenzweig understands, presents, and practices a form of "Jewish thinking" during his *Lehrhaus* period. My hope is that by working through what led Rosenzweig into an apparent about-face regarding the Jewishness of his philosophy, we may arrive at a novel account of what "Jewish thought" can be.

On November 1, 1920, Rosenzweig writes to Margrit Rosenstock-Huessy about his plans for the second term at the *Lehrhaus* under his leadership: "As for [...] my lecture [course], what does Eugen say to the title, 'Einführung in den Gebrauch des gesunden Menschenverstand (Auszug aus der gesamten Philosophie)'? In the first hour, I would then reveal: 'Auszug' here is not just extraction, but also – Exodus."[4] Notice first of all the movement Rosenzweig ascribes to the course he has planned: it will lead students *into* the use of the healthy human understanding and *out of* the realm of philosophy. Rosenzweig appears especially proud of his play on words: "Auszug" from philosophy is not just an extraction – i.e., a taking out (*Aus-ziehen*) – but an exodus: a redemptive liberation from slavery modeled on the movement of the ancient Israelites.

By the time the *Lehrhaus* term is advertised, Rosenzweig has changed the course's title – citing "external reasons"[5] – to *Anleitung zum jüdischen Denken*. But the course's first lesson makes clear that the new title does not entail a change in approach.[6] Rosenzweig opens the course by announcing that "we want ourselves to think here, to think Jewishly." He then immediately asks:

"Is there Jewish thinking? Is thinking not something universally human? Certainly it *should* be. But has it been up to now? [...] Philosophy was not uni-

---

4   Rosenzweig to Margrit Rosenstock-Huessy, November 1, 1920 (https://www.erhfund.o rg/gritli-not-chosen/).

5   See Rosenzweig to Margrit Rosenstock-Huessy, February 13, 1921 (https://www.erhfun d.org/gritli-not-chosen/).

6   Indeed, Annemarie Mayer sums up Rosenzweig's "Anleitung" course as follows: "Jüdisches Denken verstand er als einen Auszug aus der gesamten Philosophie zugunsten des gesunden Menschenverstandes" (Mayer 1987: 59).

versally-human. Universally human was, is, and will be the healthy human understanding." (Rosenzweig 1979d: 597)

Rosenzweig opens his course on Jewish thinking, we see, by introducing four categories of thought: Jewish thinking, universal human thinking, the healthy human understanding, and philosophy. He implies that the first three form a kind of set, against which stands philosophy, as if Jewish thinking itself were precisely universal human thinking according to the healthy human understanding.

Philosophy, unlike a Jewish or universal human thinking according to the healthy human understanding, Rosenzweig proceeds to explain, removes itself from actual life, to its own detriment, but also to the detriment of life itself. This is because living human beings depend on thinking in order to confront questions that arise in the course of life. Rosenzweig states that life "never has a good conscience so long as thinking turns its back on it. For as long as the healthiest human understanding is not yet *totally* healthy, it is still automatically disarmed by certain questions." (ibid) We'll have to see what kinds of questions Rosenzweig has in mind as "disarming" human understanding in the course of life. But the questions philosophy asks regarding the essence of things – what they "really" are – Rosenzweig claims, express philosophy's disdain for actual life, for they imply that actual things, actual persons, actual relationships must be left behind or transcended if we are to arrive at the truth about them. The healthy human understanding, to the contrary, seeks "to retie the torn threads between the everyday and the holiday, to turn away from the wrongful separation of actuality and ideal ... . To reconcile life with thinking" (ibid: 598).

"Is this Jewish thinking?" Rosenzweig asks. He answers: "Yes. And the opposite to it? Greek thinking. Thinking about the 'really.'" In the lives and writings of Jewish thinkers across the ages, Rosenzweig claims, "Jewish thinking has waged a (mostly unsuccessful) struggle against the learned Greek, from Philo and Saadia to Cohen." Here Rosenzweig issues a challenge to his audience:

"We seek [...] to summon the courage for Jewish thinking, thus for the use of the healthy human understanding, at the risk that our *extraction* out of Greek philosophy will become an *exodus*. The courage thus to formulate thoughtfully what was self-evident to our ancestors so long as they did *not* philosophize (*only* so long). And what is also self-evident to us, so long as we just don't philosophize." (ibid)

Jewish thinkers across the centuries, Rosenzweig suggests here, are human beings within whom Jewish thinking and Greek thinking, healthy human understanding and philosophy, wage battle. And Rosenzweig seeks to awaken his audience to identify with such Jewish thinkers as their ancestors, thereby inspiring them with the courage to use the healthy human understanding and wage their own battle with their inner Greek. Unable to resist the play on words he spilled to Gritli beforehand, Rosenzweig suggests such a battle on behalf of the healthy human understanding against philosophy is nothing less than a reliving of the experience of liberation from slavery from the Jewish mythic past, now reconceived as a movement out of philosophy and into a realm of healthy thinking and living.

Rosenzweig stresses the link to tradition entailed by such Jewish thinking: in thinking according to the healthy human understanding, Rosenzweig urges his audience to "formulate thoughtfully what was self-evident to our ancestors" in those moments when they overcame the urge to philosophize. Note, finally, that Rosenzweig doesn't just call for the affirmation of life here. What should be self-evident must be "formulated thoughtfully": questions *do* arise in life, before which – recall – we risk being "disarmed" in life. Without the thoughtful expression of the healthy human understanding – of Jewish thinking – life is left defenseless, and subject to philosophy's response to such questions.

What exactly is the thinking according to the healthy human understanding which Rosenzweig identifies with Jewish thinking? As Rosenzweig was soon to spell out in detail in the 1921 *Das Büchlein vom gesunden und kranken Menschenverstand*, the healthy human understanding is a form of thinking that trusts in the linguistic conventions of interpersonal life – in the names for things we inherit from the past, in the reciprocal address between persons in the present, and in the language we share in pointing to a common future (cf. Pollock 2021). "Here you live from trust," Rosenzweig explains in the *Anleitung* course.

> You can only enter this chain, if you trust. Trust first in the tradition which you find; second, in your own need for speech; third, in the future – which can be the next moment – that there will be answer for you. But this is nothing other than totally everyday knowing. (Rosenzweig 1979d: 603)

Note that the trust which Rosenzweig urges as the key to the healthy human understanding is trust in forms of language which tie us together with others within time – through tradition to our past, in the interpersonal address of the present, and in hope for response in the face of the future (cf. Franks 2006).[7]

The *Büchlein* spells out extensively how Rosenzweig understands the opposition between healthy human understanding and philosophy. The healthy human understanding "trusts in the actual" (Rosenzweig 1991: 32), Rosenzweig reiterates here: it trusts the language one uses in everyday life, and trusts that when life produces experiences of wonder that make one pose questions, "he need only wait, only continue to live in order for the standstill of his wonder to resolve itself." (ibid: 29) The *Büchlein* explains the traditional philosophical quest to discover what things "really" are as an unhealthy – but perfectly understandable – response to a particularly fundamental source of wonder: the realization that the language we use in our day-to-day lives – to identify blocks of cheese we wish to purchase, to address persons we love, to declare someone's guilt or innocence in a court of law – has no evident foundation beyond our own commitment to the linguistic conventions of our community. In such moments we are driven to ask what innocence and guilt really are, who that person really is whom I think I love, and even – what the essence of cheese really is. The process in which such questions can arise is most easily seen in the case of court judgment. Rosenzweig imagines a judge, "instead of judging," getting

> caught in the net of the question, "Is there then something like a crime? [...] Since indeed I myself first [...] append to this most complex fact [...] the designation of crime: is the act a crime? What is it really?" It is clear what drives him to such questions: knowledge of his own part in the designation of the act. In that he reflects on this his own part, the result, the naming of the crime, becomes uncertain. He believes [...] he "could have" "also" not named it thus. He can "conceive" perhaps that at one time it will not be so called. The firmness of the designation, the trust in the name, begins to wobble. He now [...] asks the desperate question-of-doubt about this action, which seeks something firm, something that remains, an "essence," [...] the question: what is? (ibid: 45–46)

---

7   See also Hilary Putnam's introduction to the 1999 publication of Nahum Glatzer's translation of the "Little Book" into English, as *Understanding the Sick and the Healthy* (Putnam 1999: 3).

It is indeed unsettling to find no clear ground holding up our linguistic conventions beyond our own responsibility to uphold their use. The problem with philosophy, Rosenzweig explains in the *Büchlein*, is that it tries to overcome this inherent and unavoidable instability of human life by attempting to remove its elements from the context of our everyday, temporally grounded linguistic conventions, examining them, as Rosenzweig writes, "on the needlepoint [*Nadelspieß*] of the detemporalizing question 'what-is-that'" (ibid: 31) really, in the hopes of discovering a stable, substantial ground to support them. But such a divorce of thinking and knowing from actual life leads, according to Rosenzweig, not to a grasp of universal truth grounding life *absolutely*, but rather to skeptical paralysis: "acute *apoplexia philosophica*." (ibid: 57) There is no end to the what-is and why questions we can ask, and the very questioning itself threatens to enslave us.

The *Büchlein* suggests that the therapy required for such cases of skepticism entails re-instilling trust in our linguistic conventions, fragile as they may be, but at once recognizing in them forms of expression that are directed towards an ultimate condition of interhuman understanding. "Language doesn't [...] want to be, it cannot at all be the essence of the world," Rosenzweig writes. "It is the seal of the human being." (ibid: 73) Immediately qualifying this evident instability of our quintessentially human linguistic practices, however, Rosenzweig asks:

> Only of the human being? Then the mistrust would be justified, which the sickened understanding brings over against the word. Yes, at one point the human being began to name. [...] How many words cluster around one thing, and hardly two mean precisely the same, where even in the same language two people don't understand each other. Indeed, the word of the human being alone does nothing. Were there not certainty, that the beginning which the always-singular human being posits with his word, would be posited-forth up to the ultimate goal of a universal language. (ibid: 74)

The trust in the actual which the healthy human understanding assumes, Rosenzweig conveys here, is trust that the linguistic conventions to which we commit in our everyday interpersonal relationships unfold towards a "universal language," an ultimate form of shared communicability and mutual recognition. The healthy human understanding thus replaces philosophy's quest to find an essential, substantial, eternal grounding in the here and now with a thoughtful trust in the temporal unfolding of our language-bound relationships towards the goal of comprehensive interpersonal understanding.

For reasons I will spell out shortly, I want to highlight how this account of the ultimate horizon of our linguistic practices in the *Büchlein* aligns both with what Rosenzweig had designated in the *Star* as "the ideal of perfect understanding which we represent under the language of humanity" (Rosenzweig 1996: 123), as well as with his assertion, in his *Jehuda HaLevi* postscript, that any act of translation presupposes the ultimate unity of all language and "the command resting upon it for all-human understanding" (Rosenzweig 1979g: 3). The act of translation, Rosenzweig argued there, should be directed towards the actualization of universal mutual understanding. But this process is to occur not in some independent universal language – he scoffs at Esperanto – but rather within each and every language: "one should translate so that the day of the harmony of languages comes, which can only grow within each individual language, and not in the empty space 'between' them." (ibid: 4)

What do such claims about translation have to do with a Jewish thinking which Rosenzweig has identified with the healthy human understanding? Just as translation advances towards the ideal of the ultimate language of humanity by working within a given individual language, so the healthy human understanding is a form of thinking which – while universally human – develops within the particular linguistic conventions of a given community. Trust in the names one has been taught by tradition to use to designate things, trust in the temporal unfolding of personal relationships through language, trust in a shared horizon of mutual understanding must develop as trust in the linguistic conventions of one's *own* community. I will return to this idea at the end of the essay

Rosenzweig does not identify healthy human understanding as "Jewish thinking" in the *Büchlein*. But we find him advocating for, and even practicing the thinking of the healthy human understanding *as Jewish thinking* throughout his time at the *Lehrhaus*. Indeed, almost immediately upon taking up its directorship Rosenzweig appears to have identified the *Lehrhaus* community as the context for thinking according to the healthy human understanding. In a well-known letter from August 1920, Rosenzweig tries to explain to his *Doktorvater*, Friedrich Meinecke, why he is no longer interested in an academic position. He describes how he now sees the pursuit of knowledge as something that must take place within the context of everyday life and not in a separate institution devoted to knowledge alone:

> The little, often very little "demands of the day," as they step out at me in my Frankfurt position – the wearisome, insignificant and yet necessary surrounding of myself with people and relationships – this and no longer the writing of books has become the beloved content of my life, really and with all the annoyances bound up with it. Knowing is for me no longer its own purpose. It has become a service for me. A service to *human beings* [...] For me, not every question is worth asking. I am no longer filled by scientific curiosity and aesthetic hunger for stuff [...]. I ask only yet where I *will be* asked – asked by *people*, not by scholars, not by "science." [...] *Its* questions are no questions to me. But the questions of human beings have become that much more pressing to me. To stand up to them and to answer them as well as I know how – [...] that is what I called "knowing as service." (Rosenzweig 1979a: 680–681)

In the same breath that Rosenzweig here rejects the pursuit of knowledge for its own sake – referring directly to academic scholarship but surely including philosophy in what he calls knowledge as "*Selbstzweck*" – he urgently affirms thinking in the context of everyday life. Recall that questions arise in the midst of life, and if they are not met with a thinking according to the healthy human understanding, the only answers they are liable to find are the life-transcending answers of philosophy. Rosenzweig thus commits himself to thinking in the service of life in the *Lehrhaus* context. The questions of the human beings surrounding him "have become that much more pressing," and it is these questions and these alone that, when posed to him, he seeks to answer. We know that this approach to answering not from on high but from on the same plane as questioners became the very principle of Rosenzweig's leadership at the *Lehrhaus*. Indeed, Rosenzweig once claimed the director of the school needed to approach teaching and learning as a common person, an "*am ha'aretz*," in order to ensure that the discourse at the *Lehrhaus* remain grounded in the everyday:

> *Am Ha'aratzus* had to be made pedagogically fruitful. This was the most noble task of the director. He himself had to be enough of an *Am Ha'aretz*, in order not to despise the pedagogical possibilities like an expert. He must have the inner readiness to transform himself at every moment from a teacher to a student, but also the reverse. So, being at once teacher and student among the teachers, and co-teacher and co-student among the students, he himself

becomes not just the director, but the focal point of the Lehrhaus. (Rosen-zweig 1979a: 913)[8]

I want briefly to note a few examples of how Rosenzweig's approach to Jewish thinking as healthy human understanding guided him, not only in his leadership, but also in his lectures and essays from the *Lehrhaus* period. In his famous open letter to Buber, "The Builders," Rosenzweig describes how a traditional Jewish life that long included theological questions and answers gradually became, over the course of the 19th century, *dependent* on the viability of answers to such questions.

> Would a Jew earlier have believed, if he wasn't asked, that he kept the law [...] only for this reason, that it was imposed upon Israel by God at Sinai? Certainly, if one asked him, perhaps this reason would have forced itself to the front of his mind. [...] Philosophers have always preferred this answer. [But] from Mendelssohn onwards our whole people has undergone the torture of all these truly painful questions, and the being-Jewish of each individual now danced on the needle-point of a Why [*Nadelspitze eines Warum*]. [...] For the question-less ones living, this justifying-ground of the law was only one among others, and scarcely the strongest. (Rosenzweig 1979f: 703)

It is striking to note the parallels between the premises of Rosenzweig's discussion of Jewish life and thought here and those of his account of the healthy human understanding in general. Questions can and do arise in the midst of life. But philosophy responds to such questions both by isolating them from their living context and by making them the ultimate adjudicators of life's value and direction. In the *Büchlein*, recall, philosophy is said to set the objects of our everyday life "on the needlepoint [*Nadelspieß*] of the detemporalizing question 'what-is-that'" really. Using almost identical language, Rosenzweig here criticizes Jewish philosophers for making "being Jewish [...] dance on the needle-point [*Nadelspitze*] of a Why." When healthy, life lives on with questions – it doesn't make its unfolding in time dependent on the attainment of absolute answers in the here and now. Just as he does in the *Büchlein*, Rosenzweig thus rejects the philosophical demand to determine what is essential in Judaism:

---

8   Rosenzweig to E. Strauss, M. Buber, R. Koch, and E. Simon on July 17, 1923. On the model of the *Am-Haaretz* at the Lehrhaus (cf. Simon 1965: 399).

> Only where the condition of Jewish life was otherwise set in question, only there did past times set the border [between essentially and inessentially Jewish ...]. Modernity made the answer constitutive, in that it made the putting-in-question permanent, here too [in the case of practice] as with the question of essence in the case of teaching. The future may no longer recognize that border. (ibid: 705–706)

Just as we would expect from a thinker committed to the healthy human understanding, Rosenzweig rejects determinations of what is essential for Jewish life, in learning and practice, and instead calls for living Jewish life as a whole.

Rosenzweig issues a similar call in his lecture "Bildung und kein Ende." Here he announces that the key to renewing Jewish life – just as it was the key to living thoughtfully according to the healthy human understanding – is precisely *trust*:

> Only readiness and nothing else can we bring over to the Jewish man in us. [...] Nothing else but this simple decision to say once: "nothing Jewish is foreign to me." [...] Trust is the word for the readiness, the readiness which doesn't ask after recipes, doesn't have between its teeth a [...] "how can I do this." Trust doesn't worry about the day after tomorrow. It lives in the today, it goes with careless feet over the threshold, which leads from today into tomorrow. [...] And just for this reason the whole belongs to him. (Rosenzweig 1979c: 499–500)

Rosenzweig's call to his *Lehrhaus* audience here is precisely the call of the healthy human understanding to trust in the everyday temporal context of life – here, Jewish life – not to be held up by the presumption that only with recipes, only in the answer to questions, can one find the ground upon which to go on.

Allow me, lastly, to note a text in which the struggle of Jewish against Greek thinking comes to the fore: "Apologetic Thinking," Rosenzweig's review of Max Brod's *Heidentum, Christentum, Judentum* and Leo Baeck's *Wesen des Judentums*. In a letter to Baeck in the wake of the essay, Rosenzweig writes on August 11, 1923 that "apologetic thinking ... merely sets forward a method of everyday thinking into the scientific region" (Rosenzweig 1979a: 918). In the essay, Rosenzweig argues that Jewish thinking *about* Judaism – what Judaism is – only happens when Jewish thinkers are pushed to the border of Jewish life in response to attacks from without:

> One does not become a Jewish thinker in the undisturbed circle of Judaism. Here thinking would not become thinking about Judaism, which was just the most self-evident-of-all, more a Sein than a "tum," but rather a thinking *in* Judaism: learning. [...] Anyone who was tasked with reflecting *on* Judaism had somehow, if not in his soul then at least intellectually, to be torn at the border of Judaism. (Rosenzweig 1979e: 679)

Rosenzweig's criticism of Brod and Baeck is precisely that, in meeting their adversaries at the border of Judaism, they allow their own depictions of Judaism to be determined by the questions their opponents pose. Here we meet, once again, the problematic question of essence:

> They let their theme be determined by the attacks. The theme is one's own essence. One could think that it would now come to its highest consciousness, but precisely the apologetic character of the thinking prevents that. Insofar as the thinker looks into his innermost, he indeed sees this innermost, but for this reason he is still far from seeing – himself. For he himself is not his innermost but is to the same extent also his outermost, and above all the bond that binds his innermost to his outermost, the street upon which both reciprocally mingle with one another. (ibid: 686)

Much as he claimed that 19th century orthodoxy found the answer to its Why question within the tradition – the empirical fact of the giving of the Torah at Sinai – but had isolated and elevated it from out of its traditional living context, so Rosenzweig suggests that Brod and Baeck answer the question of the essence of Judaism with what is indeed most "innermost" to them as Jews. But in doing so, they isolate what is thus innermost from its place within the whole living Jewish person. Instead of guiding their Jewish readers in an exodus out of the realm of philosophy and back into Jewish life, Baeck and Brod seek to answer the question of essence on its own ground.

I propose the texts we've reviewed from Rosenzweig's *Lehrhaus* period provide us with a rich account of Jewish thinking as healthy human understanding, an account which first occurs to Rosenzweig when he takes up the leadership of the *Lehrhaus* in the summer of 1920, which he first articulates in the *Anleitung zum jüdischen Denken* course in early 1921, and which he develops in practice and in writing throughout his *Lehrhaus* years. Nevertheless, as I noted at the beginning of my remarks, when Rudolf Hallo suggests Rosenzweig's thought be designated as "Jewish," he rejects such a designation with the argument that he has formulated his thinking as "healthy human understanding"!

It is time to return, then, to the question with which we began: Is the form of thinking according to the healthy human understanding Rosenzweig advocates in the early 1920s "Jewish thinking," or is it a thinking that is "universally human"? The path we've taken through Rosenzweig's account of the healthy human understanding gives us components out of which we can offer an answer to this question. But I'd like to work towards this answer, first, by citing one last text of Rosenzweig's, a letter to Margrit Rosenstock-Huessy from February 13, 1921, written in the midst of the *Anleitung zum jüdischen Denken* course. "The headline 'Jewish thinking' was like a blow to the head for you," he writes, referring to the change in the course's title and Gritli's apparent reaction to it. He proceeds to remind her:

> Originally I had wanted to name it "Einführung in the use of the healthy human understanding," and for external reasons gave it up. Nevertheless, I can only do it before Jews. In the individual case before each human being. But by a greater audience, before the public, only before Jews. Because only there do I have the possibility of connection in common = experiences [*Erlebnisse*]. (In war I also had them a little before others.) It belongs to this kind of thought-leading [*Vordenken*], that one is also *Mitleber*. (The abolition of the Lecture Chair!) In any given case, I can always (eventually) be *Mitleber* for the individual person. For the community only if I belong to it. For this reason, I can only have an impact among Jews. There alone will my impact be immediately law-renewing. Whether elsewhere, that it not my business. Perhaps through you two.[9]

In this remarkable letter, Rosenzweig makes a basic distinction between thinking or philosophizing in relation to another individual, and doing so in the context of a collective. Rosenzweig suggests he can only lead a collective in the practice of the healthy human understanding – no matter how "universal" such thinking may be – if that collective is Jewish. Why? In order to guide a collective in such thinking, Rosenzweig claims he must share experiences with them which provide for the "possibility of connection in common." What does he have in mind here? I suggest Rosenzweig is referring to the very linguistic conventions, the trust in which is entailed by the healthy human understanding.

---

9   Rosenzweig to Margrit Rosenstock-Huessy, February 13, 1921 (https://www.erhfund.or g/gritli-not-chosen/), emphasis added.

But just as the act of translation aspires to actualize the ideal of universal human understanding through the expansion of particular given languages and not "between them," so the linguistic conventions of the healthy human understanding – however universal they may be – are always the linguistic conventions of one's own community. Rosenzweig sees no reason to think that the kind of thinking he promotes within the Jewish community would *not* find an audience beyond the bounds of that community. Perhaps Gritli and Eugen, as individuals, will find something worthwhile in his account and carry it over into their Christian community. But this isn't Rosenzweig's concern. His concern is to teach those with whom he is a living companion – a "*Mitleber.*" To the extent to which he shares a tradition of linguistic practices with his fellow German Jews, he abolishes the lecture chair and guides them in thinking (*Vordenken*) from out of their shared context of everyday life. Such thinking is "Jewish thinking," because it thoughtfully formulates responses to questions that arise in the context of Jewish collective life; because it draws upon a tradition of such thoughtful formulations given by Jewish ancestors; and because it guides questioners by way of such responses out of the enslavement to philosophical essences and back into a healthy but thoughtful collective life in time, lived in commitment to the linguistic conventions of Jewish life. But the horizon towards which such life according to Jewish linguistic conventions strives is the ideal of perfect mutual human understanding in a universal language towards which all other human communities also strive through their own respective linguistic practices and, in this sense, the healthy human understanding Rosenzweig advocates is indeed universally human.

Depending on how his interlocutors understand the "Jewishness" of his philosophy, Rosenzweig will thus at times have to affirm it and at times deny it. For his Jewish thinking is precisely the universal human thinking of the healthy human understanding.

Bibliography

Fisher, Cass (2016): "Absolute Factuality, Common Sense, and Theological Reference in the Thought of Franz Rosenzweig." In: Harvard Theological Review 109/3, pp. 342–370.

Franks, Paul W. (2006): "Everyday Speech and Revelatory Speech in Rosenzweig and Wittgenstein." In: Philosophy Today 50/1, pp. 24–38.

Mayer, Annemarie (1987): "Judentum – Christentum – Menschtum: Eine Einführung in Leben und Denken Franz Rosenzweigs unter besonderer Berücksichtigung seiner Lehrhaustätigkeit in Frankfurt." In: Werner Licharz (ed.), Lernen mit Franz Rosenzweig, Frankfurt am Main: Haag + Herchen, pp. 47–66.

Pollock, Benjamin (2021): "'The All and the Everyday': Franz Rosenzweig and Ordinary Language Philosophy." In: Iyyun: The Jerusalem Philosophical Quarterly 69, pp. 249–279.

Putnam, Hilary (1999): "Introduction." In: Franz Rosenzweig: Understanding the Sick and the Healthy: A View of World, Man, and God, translated by Nahum Glatzer, Cambridge, MA: Harvard University Press, pp. 1–20.

Rosenzweig, Franz (1979): Der Mensch und sein Werk. Gesammelte Schriften I.1: Briefe und Tagebücher 1900–1918, Dordrecht: Kluwer.

Rosenzweig, Franz (1979a): Der Mensch und sein Werk. Gesammelte Schriften I.2: Briefe und Tagebücher 1918–1929, Dordrecht: Kluwer.

Rosenzweig, Franz (1979b): "Das neue Denken." In: Franz Rosenzweig: Der Mensch und sein Werk. Gesammelte Schriften III: Zweistromland. Kleinere Schriften zu Glauben und Denken, Dordrecht: Kluwer, pp. 139–161.

Rosenzweig, Franz (1979c): "Bildung und kein Ende (Pred. 12, 12): Wünsche zum jüdischen Bildungsproblem des Augenblicks insbesondere zur Volkshochschulfrage." In: Franz Rosenzweig: Der Mensch und sein Werk. Gesammelte Schriften III: Zweistromland. Kleinere Schriften zu Glauben und Denken, Dodrecht: Kluwer, pp. 491–503.

Rosenzweig, Franz (1979d): "Anleitung zum Jüdischen Denken." In: Franz Rosenzweig: Der Mensch und sein Werk. Gesammelte Schriften III: Zweistromland. Kleinere Schriften zu Glauben und Denken, Dordrecht: Kluwer, pp. 597–618.

Rosenzweig, Franz (1979e): "Apologetisches Denken: Bemerkungen zu Brod und Baeck." In: Franz Rosenzweig: Der Mensch und sein Werk. Gesammelte Schriften III: Zweistromland. Kleinere Schriften zu Glauben und Denken, Dordrecht: Kluwer, pp. 677–686.

Rosenzweig, Franz (1979f): "Die Bauleute." In: Franz Rosenzweig: Der Mensch und sein Werk. Gesammelte Schriften III: Zweistromland. Kleinere Schriften zu Glauben und Denken, Dordrecht: Kluwer, pp. 699–712.

Rosenzweig, Franz (1979g): Der Mensch und sein Werk. Gesammelte Schriften IV.1: Jehuda HaLevi. Fünfundneunzig Hymnen und Gedichte, Deutsch und Hebräisch, ed. Rafael Rosenzweig, Dordrecht: Kluwer.

Rosenzweig, Franz (1991): Das Büchlein vom gesunden und kranken Menschenverstand, ed. Nahum N. Glatzer, Frankfurt am Main: Jüdischer Verlag Suhrkamp.

Rosenzweig, Franz (1996): Der Stern der Erlösung, Berlin: Suhrkamp.

Rosenzweig, Franz (2022 [1917–1929]): "Not Chosen, But Laid On Me By God": The Surviving Letters of Franz Rosenzweig and Margrit and Eugen Rosenstock-Huessy, Eugen Rosenstock-Huessy Fund, West Haven, VT (https://www.erhfund.org/gritli-not-chosen/).

Simon, Ernst (1965): "Franz Rosenzweig und das Jüdische Bildungsproblem." In: Ernst Simon: Brücken. Gesammelte Aufsätze, Heidelberg: Lambert Schneider, pp. 393–406.

The Tail or the String of the Kite? Hans-Georg Gadamer, Steven S. Schwarzschild, and Jewish Hermeneutics

Massimo Giuliani

In a brief, acute evaluation of the developments of modern Jewish thought in the context of the history of Western philosophy, the German-American Jewish thinker and rabbi Steven S. Schwarzschild (Frankfurt 1924-St. Louis 1989) affirmed that Jewish thought played not only a complementary, but also a driving, a guiding role in the intellectual processes that contributed, on the one hand, to the deconstruction or even the dissolution of the subject (from Freud to Derrida, via Lévi-Strauss), and, on the other hand, to the reconstruction of a form of subjectivity that, on a hermeneutical basis, represents an alternative to Heidegger's ontological and historicist approach (from Bloch to Jonas and Levinas, via Cohen, Rosenzweig, and Buber). Two main elements can be found at the core of such elaboration: the overcoming of a certain historicist interpretation of the hermeneutical circle – a circle from which the subject cannot really be emancipated, given its entanglement with the object – and a new form of heteronomy (theological and/or halakhic) developed in the name of "practical reason," that is, in the name of a concrete universal law – politically necessary in the light of the totalitarian deviations of the 20th century – prior to and beyond a "theoretical reason," prior to and beyond the "question of Being." According to the philosopher-rabbi, all of this may seem an updated confrontation between Kantism and Hegelism. Moreover, its re-elaboration in Jewish garb, based on "Jewish existence and experience," could lead to the conclusion that "Jewish philosophy is [...] a tail, so to speak, on the kite of secular philosophy" (Schwarzschild 1990b: 233), that is, of philosophy as such. On the contrary, the idea of heteronomy – stigmatized as infantile by an "enlightened vulgarization" at war with any form of tradition and authority – can act as a correction to the fragmentation of postmodern subjectivity and thus be seen as the most significant contribution of Jewish thought in getting out of the vicious circle of that "historical reason" that is forged by Heidegger's ontologism. In this regard, one may just consider the debates on the pretentions of enlightenment, not only in Heidegger, but also in Adorno, Horkheimer, and Foucault, up to the recent dialogue between Habermas and Ratzinger (2007). Now, according to Schwarzschild:

> At the outset of modernity Mendelssohn discerned Jewish particularity in the law, itself an expression of essentially rational morality. We have seen how even the Jewish Hegelians of the nineteenth century and certainly Cohen and his disciples proclaimed Kant's "primacy of practical reason." The traditionalist Jewish thinkers like Rabbi Kook and Rabbi Soloveitchik must, of course, always uphold the centrality of Halakhah. Buber's and Heschel's thought emphasizes the ethical and social demands made by the reality of the human–divine encounter. And at the present time all of Levinas' work centers on the ultimacy of the ethical God "beyond essence." [...] The claim may thus be that Jewish philosophy is not finally the tail on the kite but the string that leads it. (Schwarzschild 1990b: 233)

It is within this framework that Schwarzschild's critique of Hans-Georg Gadamer needs to be considered. Especially *Truth and Method* (Gadamer 1975) is for Schwarzschild a work in which the most representative interpreter of Heidegger's hermeneutical *kehre* or paradigm shift aims to recover, to rehabilitate, the ideas of tradition and authority. A few years later, the French philosopher Paul Ricœur synthesized this issue as follows: "Gadamer inevitably turned hermeneutic philosophy towards the rehabilitation of prejudice and the defense of tradition and authority, placing this philosophy in a conflictual relation to any critique of ideology." (Ricœur 1981: 26)[1]

Here "prejudice" means "pre-comprehension" in the most genuinely Heideggerian sense of the term, and this connects with the concepts of "tradition" and "authority" (for example, the authority of a sacred text or a political constitution) in order to establish the horizon – a metaphor beloved by Gadamer – and the hermeneutical conditions of comprehensibility of that reality that is

---

1   In this essay, Ricœur forces Gadamer's hermeneutics to interact with the critique of ideology Jürgen Habermas elaborates along the rationalistic line of the Enlightenment. Ricœur positions himself in a middle position, a sort of "French" way between the two "German".

called "historical consciousness." Schwarzschild immediately grasped the importance of this revival of Heidegger's hermeneutic circle in Gadamer's masterpiece and singled out the chapter "Rehabilitation of Authority and Tradition" (in Gadamer 1975: 278–285). The order of the two terms is not negligible – in fact, it is a crucial issue from a Jewish point of view, not *despite* but precisely *by virtue of* the fact that the two notions, tradition and authority, are at the root of the complex architecture of any Jewish hermeneutics. In fact, this latter is also based on the authoritative value of a tradition – the *shalshelet ha-qabbalah*. This is conceived of as the oral Torah (*Torah she-be-'al peh*), which, according to the written Torah (*Torah she-bi-ktav*), is derived from divine revelation, that is, from the highest possible source of authority. But while Gadamer's rehabilitation is aimed against Enlightenment's *raison critique*, Schwarzschild's Jewish hermeneutics is rather involved in a positive dialectical exchange with such modern reason and its critical approaches. It almost forms a symbiosis with it, as has always been the case in the history of Jewish philosophy, at least from the Middle Ages onward (from Sa'adia Gaon to Maimonides, among others).

Starting from these premises, the goal of this chapter is to explore the Jewish interpretation of the hermeneutic circle, that is, the specific form of pre-comprehension through which a Jew approaches the knowledge of the world. Another point at issue, then, is how the idea and praxis of authority – both ethical (exegetical-noetic) and halakhic (juridical-political) – should be understood in a tradition that is centered on the art of interpreting texts. But first it is necessary to underline the prejudice, or the pre-comprehension, that inspires Schwarzschild's critique of Gadamer – a critique that is deeply affected by the existential but also historical fact that Gadamer was a loyal student of (never) repentant national-socialist Heidegger, or in other words, that "Gadamer was, to put the best fact on it, not an anti-Nazi" (Schwarzschild 1987: 165). Of course, this fact may not or should not have direct philosophical implications. But nonetheless, those implications are precisely what Schwarzschild is looking for. For example, one of them has to do with Gadamer's evaluation of Hermann Cohen – in fact, a total devaluation, almost a nullification of Cohen's role, if one considers that he is never mentioned in *Truth and Method*. Actually, such Jewish thinkers as Spinoza, Marx, Rosenzweig, Simmel, Bergson, Husserl, Cassirer, Adorno, Horkheimer, and Marcuse can be found throughout Gadamer's work, but Cohen is completely ignored. Thus, a drastic conclusion can be drawn: that "Gadamer completes the process of the relegation of Cohen to oblivion that Heidegger began" (ibid: 166). What does this mean? Nothing personal, Schwarzschild suggests, but a radical philosophical divergence on the topics of method and truth, which are at stake when the place of the human being in the hermeneutic circle is investigated. According to Cohen, the truth we are aiming at remains an ideal that transcends any human ontological-existential dimension, while according to Heidegger – and to Gadamer, who follows in his footsteps – truth is the expression of that dimension, its original substance, and – just like a root or a seed that is destined to disappear under the tree to which it gives life – truth is eventually revealed to its searcher. In the first case, truth is a process of approximation that keeps an asymptotic form; in the second case, truth is a "gift" obtained through a sort of illumination, something one can only be awakened to. The phenomenological *epoché* helped Heidegger "discover" such a truth in oneself and made him emphasize this root as the very rediscovering of Being, that is, his ontological revolution. This led to the ontological characterization of the hermeneutic circle itself as emblematic of the co-belonging of subject and object within the dimension of being – of the truth and its searcher, of a text and its interpreter. The interpreter, in other words, "belongs" to the text and vice versa. In Schwarzschild's words: "The substance of the argument always remained in the foreground, however, and it is again the core of *Truth and Method*: truth is not rationally or methodologically constructed but ontologically and experientially unveiled. All authority derives from that phenomeno-logico-existentialist truth." (ibid: 166)

Heidegger's and Gadamer's perspective cannot but be at odds with that of Hermann Cohen. Schwarzschild, however, sides with Cohen's point of view and tries to rescue it from the oblivion it is relegated to by existentialist currents and hermeneutic schools of thought that depend on *Being and Time* (cf. Heidegger 1966) – currents and schools that, in the end, bring grist to the mill of pan-historicism. Avoiding pan-historicism was the theoretical effort Ricœur made with the help of Habermas, but in order to achieve it, the way to follow is an almost necessary "return to Kant," a return that in Germany, in the first part of the 20th century, implied the recognition of the role played by the Marburg School and above all by Hermann Cohen. Unfortunately, though, Cohen was Jewish. Schwarzschild thinks that *Wahrheit und Methode* can be read as a kind of "guide for the perplexed" of *Sein und Zeit*, at least judging by the linguistic difficulties it presents and the obscurity of many of its passages. A B/being that is resolved into B/being-there (*Da-sein*) and temporality ends up reducing the issue of truth to history, showing the impossibility of a way out of the hermeneutic circle – that is, the horizon of traditions, prejudices, and the authority that expresses and guarantees them. Where is reason in such a phenomeno-logical–existential concatenation of ideas? Or better, what is reason reduced to in a horizon, where truth is brought into the "house of B/being"? Schwarzschild asks ironically: Is every "tradition" true just because it is "traditional"? Has every "authority" to be respected and obeyed because of the mere fact of being established as "authority," without appeal to any other criterion of control or verification, without resorting to any external judgement other than prejudice? By keeping a hermeneutic perspective, for example that of text interpretation – so beloved by Heidegger and Gadamer as readers of poets, but also cherished by the Jewish tradition as a "studying community" – a three-fold question arises: "How do you distinguish between authentic revelation and false claims of revelation? [And, supposed you know the difference,] how do you distinguish between valid and invalid interpretation of that authentic revelation?" (Schwarzschild 1987: 167) Hence, a third question, a profoundly rabbinical one, can provide orientation in addressing the two previous questions: "How do we know that a given set of hermeneutic rules is valid?" (ibid: 167) As acutely noted by the philosopher-rabbi, this third question is grafted onto the first, thus showing the authentic nature of the hermeneutic circle: its heteronomy, its coming from outside, from Sinai, disproving the claim that truth, any revealed truth, coincides with the historical process in which and through which it has been acquired. It is the interpretative effort that generates truth. But at the same time, truth is not such by virtue of that effort; rather, it is "given" as law, as a command, able to order, demand, prescribe – literary, "scribe-in-advance," ancestrally, Levinas would say: an-anarchically – in an extreme effort to break the Heideggerian pan-historicism which, in the intoxication of his ontological existentialism, has forgotten that the "truth of being" is external to any being, even to the Being. The power of the anti-idolatrous precept forbidding any representation of the Divine can be recognized here, along with a key to understanding biblical anthropomorphism (as Maimonides and Rosenzweig argued in different ages). More precisely, such power can best be appreciated in the state of the "should be," in the "not-yet" of an existence given and lived in the paradox of its incompleteness, of its structural infinitude; an existence given and lived as a task never fully achieved; an existence given and lived only in an ethical perspective, in a moral horizon. Incidentally, it is not by chance that, in 1985, Schwarzschild defined Emmanuel Levinas as "at present, perhaps, the most creative, specifically Jewish philosopher" (Schwarzschild 1990b: 232).

This critique of Heidegger's and Gadamer's hermeneutic circle, based on the limits of interpretation and the possibility that the B/being is (heteronomously) governed by a "should-be" or a "must-be," brings "the question [the issue] of the historicality of reason" to the very center of the hermeneutic discourse. It is a topic – Schwarzschild maintains – that Kant addressed in his first *Critique*, in which the chapter "History of Pure Reason" (*Geschichte der reinen Vernunft*) explores "the ineluctably historical character of the cognitive (and other) categories" (Schwarzschild 1987 [1981]: 168). But is this not precisely that pan-historicism (implicit in Heidegger's hermeneutic circle) that must be overcome as amoral, as a self-centered tradition, self-appointed as "the authority"? And now the same horizon seems to be found in Kant. The meaning of "historical reason" is derived from the ability to locate reason *within* human history, without transforming it into the *ratio of* history, the law of time. In some Christian theologies: "In the world, not of the world." Here is the "meaning of reason," formulated by Schwarzschild in the neo-Kantian language of Hermann Cohen:

> All of reason, including the very notion of reason itself, is regulative: this is to say, *reason* is the notion of a non-existent canon, such that, if it existed, all the propositions made under its authority would be not only consistent with one another but also true. All historical forms of reason – that is to say, all rationalities actually used at any and all times – fall short of that regulative notion of reason. History, including the history of philosophy and of logic itself, is, if useful, progressive toward that reason; if retrogressive or even only static, it is to be rejected. In other words, a-historical reason is really post-historical reason – or, if you please, messianic reason – but as such it is a necessarily postulated possibility. As such [it is Schwarzschild's conclusion], as a necessary possibility, it also legitimately breaks the hermeneutic circle of pan-historicism. (ibid: 169)

The only way to open history to any progress is a radical break with the idea that history is itself progress, regardless of a rational evaluation of where the historical processes are going. In Jewish terms, it can be said: Only in so far as history is not the messianic age, but just time-oriented to the coming of the Messiah, it remains open to real improvements, it gets closer to the Kingdom, and perhaps even hastens its coming through the effort, the creativity, and the search for a perfect ideal that can never be fully achieved, but only approached through Torah and *mitzwot*, study and observance. In non-Jewish terms, and keeping within a German debate, Schwarzschild's critique of Gadamer is similar to that advanced by Jürgen Habermas and Karl-Otto Apel. On the one hand,

> Habermas shows that a distinction between any true speech and any "universally accepted false speech" is possible only on the regulative presupposition of an "idealized" speech of a life-form yet to be realized in the future – that without such a regulative [rationality] we are subject to always violent authority, rather than to reason. (ibid: 184)

On the other hand, in a different perspective, Apel comes to the same conclusion, criticizing Gadamer and underlining the necessity of "a community of interpretation." Its members are supposed to agree on some practical regulative principles which enable them to recognize the drift toward violence of those who enjoy the, albeit legitimate, authority.

We always live and think in a tradition that is rich in values and ideals. However, we are unable to represent and implement them completely. A margin will always remain. We are constantly in a gap, in a state between the real and the ideal, between historical facticity and ethical expectation (which can be called "redemption" from a religious point of view). This in-between state can be useful, though, as it makes us aware of where and what we really are – *benonim*, in the middle; *dor be-dorot*, a generation among the generations, a ring of a chain (*sharsheret*) in a long history of reception and transmission (*qabbalà, masorà, moreshet*) – because, as Rabbi Tarfon said: "it is not up to us to finish the work, yet we are not free to avoid it" – *Rabbi Tarfon omer: lo 'alekhà hamelakà lighmor ve lo attà ben-chorin lehibbatel mimmena* (Avot II,16).

Only on this condition, in a messianic openness of history – meaning open to progress, but ready to transcend any possible goal established in that progress – the issue of authority may be rehabilitated in terms that are neither authoritarian nor coercive; neither absolutistic nor violent, for the topic of authority is always combined with that of violence. Who can stop the violence of an authority that is legally and legitimately established (by regular elections, for example) and recognized as such? Nobody should have known better than Heidegger and Gadamer (and maybe also explained) how central such a question was in the 20th century. Authoritarianism that degenerates into violence can be stopped only by the same force that has legitimated it as authority in the first place. But the force of authority and tradition is based on the structure of their ratio, on the idea of a regulative ratio, as a law or a normative system. Hobbes' aphorism from *Leviathan* is well-known: "*Auctoritas not veritas facit legem*" (Hobbes 1996: 175–192); but, at the same time, it is true that only a stronger law, or a different law, can curb the arrogance of an authority that claims to be a law to itself. This is why, in the biblical tradition, the king was anointed by a prophet and, according to an icon idealized in Devarim/ Deuteronomy, a king "should keep with himself a copy of this Law and read it all of the days of his life" (17: 18–20). The primacy of the Law means the priority of the ideal over the real, of the ethical over the useful or the desired.

In this context, Schwarzschild refers to Leo Strauss' critique of Heidegger's philosophy, which he considers a form of "de-ethicization of being" (Schwarzschild 1987:171).[2] But he also quotes the *naturaliter Jew*, as he calls Jean-Paul Sartre. If Gadamer clarifies the Heideggerian hermeneutic circle, Sartre singles out the dizzy paradoxes of the ontological existentialism of *Sein und Zein* and, at the same time, makes a stand against the dissolution of the "dialectics of freedom" in the horizon of the historical "given," the temporal "thrownness." Schwarzschild understands Sartre's criticism and explains it as a jolt of ethical consciousness, a philosophical will to keep human history ethically open. As the rabbi-thinker writes:

> The fundamental difference between *Being and Nothingness* and *Being and Time* is, one can say, that on Heidegger's view time – history – exhaustively determines the location of man's thrownness (therefore, the absence of ethics in his philosophy) and his self-realization within that "given," whereas Sartre always struggles to extract human freedom, and therewith ethics, from the tight networks of history, causality, science. Marxist dialectics, etc. [...] so that the world [...] would be, at least in small part, a world which he himself had intentionally made. Man chooses the meaning of what he is and the situation into which he is thrown. (Schwarzschild 1990a: 170–171)

It is arguable that such a Sartrean position toward the world, in Schwarzschild's mind, is consistent with and inspired by the fundamental Jewish ethical imperative that can be read in Devarim/Deuteronomy 30, 19: "choose life!" That means that everyone can forge the meaning of their own lives, regardless of the situations they find themselves in. Through such a choice, it is possible to change the course of events, or at least to shape their ultimate sense. Schwarzschild concludes his appreciation of Sartre by quoting a powerful statement from *Being and Nothingness*: "Thus reflective consciousness can be properly called a moral consciousness" (Sartre 2003: 119). And adds:

---

2 Schwarzschild remarks – and does not forgive – the Freudian *lapsus* Gadamer makes in referring to Leo Strauss' *Persecution and the Art of Writing* (1988 [1952]): instead of "persecution", Gadamer talks about "understanding".

> Sartre was always painfully conscious of how difficult the philosophical struggle had to be for him of jumping, as it were, over the shadow of both Heidegger and (later) Marx. He admits, in his last interview, that he did not really succeed in working his way forward to a philosophical ethic until he arrived at his views on Jewish Messianic ethics at the very end of his life [...]. In other words, the search for an ethics led from *Being and Nothingness* to the *Critique of Dialectical Reason* and from there to Jewish Messianic ethics. (Schwarzschild 1990a: 171)

Another substantial point of Gadamer's hermeneutics (ontologically inspired by Heidegger) is subjected to Schwarzschild's harsh criticism, thus showing how far Gadamer is from a biblical-Jewish *Weltanschauung*. As is well-known, *Truth and Method* is divided into three parts, the first being entirely dedicated to aesthetics. The sub-chapter criticized is that devoted to "the ontological valence of the picture" (cf. Gadamer 1975: 130–138) and, in particular, to the ontological significance of the religious pictures. Gadamer argues that the picture is not a copy of a represented being but is in ontological communion with the depicted being. Word and image are not simple illustrative additions; rather, they make the represented reality achieve its authentic being.

Such an aesthetic ontologism – or ontological aesthetics – sounds to Schwarzschild's Jewish ears as a conception that is deeply indebted to the Christian "incarnationism" and ends up abolishing the gap between the real and the ideal, the "thing" and its representation, between "what is" and "what is represented" (be it depicted or sculptured). "Jewish aesthetics turn precisely on the contradictory [that is, the opposite] thesis, that God is such that he logically cannot and ethico-aesthetically, axiologically, may not be depicted (that is, God is beyond ontology, and depictive art in fact practices idolatry)." (Schwarzschild 1987: 173)

Here is one of the pillars in Schwarzschild's thought: the *Menschwerdung* (incarnation), so dear to the German idealism and to the (post-Kantian) romantics, is for him the major road that leads to idolatry. Its beautification by means of long reflections on art, genius, and ingenuity (both individual and national), on the sublimity of music (as, for example, in Schopenhauer's view), does not change the fact that incarnation is always at least conducive to idolatry. To be more precise, idolatry, in this context, means the identification of being with the good, of nature with the ethics and/or with the supernatural law, which are rather supposed to govern nature and being, giving them their true value. In aesthetics, as well as in ethics, the principle of *creatio continua* is at work. But it is conceived of as an invitation to adhere to and imitate the Creator, rather than celebrating an ontologically perfect order without any striving for improvement. Schwarzschild is convinced that Gadamer's ontological conservativism in art – which is "conservative" in an aesthetic sense, if one considers that *Truth and Method* was written in the 1960s and is based on a hermeneutics of factuality as well as on a historicistic given, all-determining origin called Being – results in an idolization of Being, which sometimes is platonically identified with beauty (the supreme aesthetic-artistic value), sometimes with the good (the supreme ethical quality), and finally is confirmed in its character as an idol. Messianic ethics – the regulatory ideal, the drive, and the *telos* of the revealed law (the goal, not the end of the law, to interpret the famous dictum in Paul's *Epistle to the Galatians*) – is not only an-iconic, but also anti-iconic, in so far as the *eikon*, the icon or the representation, claims to be worshipped in place of the *eidos*, the idea or the represented.

At this juncture, Schwarzschild quotes a Hassidic *rebbe*, Israel di Ruzhin, who died in 1850 and taught – *ex abundantia cordis*, as he was lacking profound rabbinical erudition – that "the Messianic era will be without images" (ibid: 189), meaning that when redemption is completed, the possibility will emerge that the "aesthetic-ontological difference" between *eidos* and *eikon*, idea and reality, represented and representation is eventually overcome. Perhaps the *rebbe* was just trying to say that, with the coming of the Messiah, reality will be so new and beautiful that it will no longer be in need of any representation, of any artistic mediation. Perhaps. But until then, until the advent of the Messiah, representation remains, and cannot be identified, or "confused," with the represented. Here, Gadamer's horizons cannot at all fuse with one another, and should rather remain ontologically distinct. By way of summary, Schwarzschild writes:

> I think my argument illustrates, though I admit that it does not by itself prove, that the only ultimate authority that Judaism can acknowledge is no authority that "is" (be it a person or an institution or a book – "bibliolatry") but only an authority that "ought" to be, and that that regulative authority [...] cannot but be rational – whatever form that rationality may take. (ibid: 175–176)

Finally, it is possible to try to answer the question about what characterizes the hermeneutic circle from a *Jewish point of view*, and how the idea and praxis of an authority can be understood that is ethical (exegetical-noetic) and halakhic (legal-political) at the same time, within a tradition based on text interpretation. Schwarzschild answers obliquely, by providing a contemporary example: the debate between Levinas and Derrida, whom he ironically named "Reb Derrida," revolving around the value of the Book. The main point at issue is whether Revelation is just "in history" or rather "history in itself" – in other words, whether the Torah is *eidos* or just *eikos*. The relevant essays considered are: "Violence and Metaphysics" (1978a [1964]), in which Derrida, for the first time, ponders over Levinas' thought, but also "Edmund Jabès and the Question of the Book" (1978b). These two essays are later included in the anthology *The Scripture and the Difference*. This latter title is ambivalent, as is often the case with Derrida's prose, because the French "*et*" (that is, the English "end") sounds and may be also understood as a *copula*, that is: scripture is difference, makes the difference.

Edmund Jabès left Egypt in 1957 and settled in Paris. His main work, *The Book of Questions* (1976), is a poetic-philosophical symphony in seven parts (called "books," as in the Middle Ages), all dealing with one, gigantic issue: the relationship between Judaism and S/scripture. From Jabès' point of view, every book is but a refraction of sparks of the Book, and even God – Jabès writes – does not exist, but for the Book He is in (ibid: 31). Judaism teaches the grammar that is necessary to read that Book; the Jews have been its first readers, out loud, and have been the first to learn how that Book has to be listened to, and chanted, and interpreted; they were and are the custodians of the bibliophilia as the archetype for every textuality and, in the same breath, for the protest and demythization against any scriptural claim to become biblio-latry. A text – that is, a book, a scripture – is only a pre-text or an *ur-text* for comments, explorations, exegeses, interpretations, *ein sof*, without an end. Caught in this task of custody and protest, Derrida notes,

the Jew is split, and split first of all between the two dimensions of the letter: allegory and literality. His history would be but one empirical history among others if he established or nationalized himself within difference and literality. He would have no history at all if he let himself be attenuated within the algebra of an abstract universalism. Between the too warm flesh of the literal event and the cold skin of the concept runs meaning. This is how it enters into the book. Everything enters into, transpires in the book. This is why the book is never finite. It always remains suffering and vigilant. (Derrida 1978b: 75)

Philosophy and Jewish Thought

Although Derrida's prose is often quite enigmatic, a clear, significant reflection on Jabès can be found here:

> Poetry is to prophecy what the idol is to truth. It is perhaps for this reason that in Jabès the poet and the Jew seem at once so united and disunited.

> And Reb Lima: Freedom, at first, was engraved ten times in the Tables of the Law, but we deserve it so little that the Prophet broke them in his anger.[3]

> Between the fragments of the broken Tables the poem grows and the right to speech takes root. Once more begins the adventure of the text [...]. The necessity of commentary, like poetic necessity, is the very form of exiled speech. In the beginning is hermeneutics. (ibid: 67)

From a Jewish point of view, the hermeneutic circle is foremost between the Book and its interpreter. Thus conceived, its shape is always that of a "broken circle," a "fragmented circle," consciously experienced and thought of in the necessary brokenness of the scripture – so that the scripture itself is not transformed into an idol. That circle, moreover, preserves the symbolic, empty space among the letters, because such a space is the very condition for those letters to have a meaning. That circle is formed by the never-ending dialectics between center and periphery, between "divine saying" and "human said," word and comment. Without the exiled words of the comment, the original word would be inaccessible or incomprehensible. That circle affirms the primacy of (Pharisaic) orality over (Sadducean) textuality. This is a conflict that has being going on for 2000 years, between those who, through study and *ars interpretandi* (*chiddush*), make the letter of the text alive, and those who, in the name of the spirit of the text, tend to mortify – or to ignore – the letter. As Derrida says, once again:

> The original opening of interpretation essentially signifies that there will always be rabbis and poets. And two interpretations of interpretation. The Law then becomes Question and the right to speech coincides with the duty to interrogate. The book of man is a book of question. (ibid)

Is this not an invitation to break the "divine saying" through the "human said"? Is it not a call to embracing an open circularity made of scripture and orality,

---

3   The sentence in italics is Derrida's quote from Jabès' work. Cf. Jabès 1976: 115.

of *mah-she-bi-ktav* and *mah-she-be-'al-pè* – a circularity that is typical of the Jewish tradition? Is this not an invitation to practice interpretation as the most authentic form of reading, broadly construed?

Schwarzschild writes:

> 1) "Interpretation," free reading, is required so that God (being, truth) may be (re-)constructed and 2) contrary to Levinas' Rosenzweigianism, God (and Jewish authenticity) may be not outside of, but in history (and all that history comprises). (Schwarzschild 1987: 176)

In different ways, Jabès, Derrida, and Schwarzschild deal with such circularity, and warn against the risk of an idolatrous use of the Book, and even of revelation. Here is the meaning of the "messianic difference" the rabbi-philosopher speaks about, along with the perennial message of the Jewish-Kantian legacy of Hermann Cohen.

In conclusion, it is arguable that Schwarzschild delineates a hermeneutic circle thought of in terms of a constant dialectics between the text and its reader/interpreter, a dialectics aimed at preventing the always lurking risks of solipsism and historicism. In order to break such a vicious circle, a regulative reason that governs history becomes necessary – an external question, an ethical-spiritual interest that is not prone to defend the subject *qua talis*. In more Jewish terms, it is the necessity of biblical and halakhic precepts, the *mitzwot* or, adopting Levinas' terminology, the primacy of ethics, or also the primacy of practical reason, as Kant would say. All of these are instances and criteria able to overcome the solipsism of authority and the authoritarianism of solipsistic thought, in the name of a call, or a reason, or a God that resound through history, but do not belong to history. They represent the only form of resistance against any offence to human dignity and to the world. Only on that condition, finally, Jewish philosophy can be the string, and not the tail, of the kite. "For the rest, as Hillel said [...], 'go and learn!'" (Schwarzschild 1990c: 256).

Bibliography

Derrida, Jacques (1978a [1964]): "Edmond Jabès and the Question of the Book." In: id., Writing and Difference, Chicago: University of Chicago Press, pp. 64–78.

Derrida, Jacques (1978b [1964]): "Violence and Metaphysics. An Essay on the Thought of Emmanuel Levinas." In: id., Writing and Difference, Chicago: University of Chicago Press, pp. 79–153.

Gadamer, Hans-Georg (1975 [1960]): Truth and Method, London, New York: Continuum.

Habermas, Jürgen/Ratzinger, Joseph (2007): The Dialectic of Secularization. On Reason and Religion, San Francisco: Ignatius Press.

Heidegger, Martin (1996 [1927]): Being and Time, Albany: State University of New York Press.

Hobbes, Thomas (1996 [1651]): Leviathan, Oxford: Oxford University Press.

Jabès, Edmond (1976 [1963]): The Book of Questions, Middletown, CT: Wesleyan University Press.

Ricœur, Paul (1981 [1973]): "Hermeneutics and the Critique of Ideology." In: id., Hermeneutics and the Human Sciences. Essays on Language, Action and Interpretation, Cambridge: Cambridge University Press, pp. 23–60.

Sartre, Jean-Paul (2003 [1943]): Being and Nothingness. An Essay in Phenomenological Ontology, London, New York: Routledge.

Schwarzschild, Steven (1987 [1981]): "Authority and Reason contra Gadamer." In: Norbert M. Samuelson (ed.), Studies in Jewish Philosophy, Lanham, MD: University Press of America, pp.161-190.

Schwarzschild, Steven (1990a [1983]): "Jean-Paul Sartre as a Jew." In: Menachem Kellner (ed.), The Pursuit of the Ideal. Jewish Writings of Steven Schwarzschild, Albany: State University of New York Press, pp. 161–184.

Schwarzschild, Steven (1990b [1987]): "Modern Jewish Philosophy." In: Menachem Kellner (ed.), The Pursuit of the Ideal. Jewish Writings of Steven Schwarzschild, Albany: State University of New York Press, pp. 229–233.

Schwarzschild, Steven (1990c): "Afterword." In: Menachem Kellner (ed.), The Pursuit of the Ideal. Jewish Writings of Steven Schwarzschild, Albany: State University of New York Press, pp. 251–259.

Strauss, Leo (1988 [1952]): Persecution and the Art of Writing, Chicago: University of Chicago Press.

Idolatry and Freedom: Erich Fromm's View[1]

Beniamino Fortis

> So long as the human beings remain free, they strive for
> nothing so incessantly and so painfully
> as to find someone to worship.
> (F. M. Dostoevsky, The Brothers Karamazov)

Gershom Scholem once said that "Max Horkheimer's *Institut für Sozialforschung* [is one of the] most remarkable 'Jewish sects' that German Jewry produced" (Scholem 1980: 131). Apart from obvious biographical references and ironic exaggeration, this assertion is actually not far from the truth if one considers that interactions between Jewish thought and the intellectual profile of the *Frankfurter Schule* can be appreciated at many levels in the theories of the school's major exponents. The interaction modes can be broken down into two main types, or, better put, the intersection dynamics can follow two opposite directions. Concepts, motifs, and ideas coming from Jewish sources undergo a process of theoretical adaptation to then find application to secular contexts,[2] but the opposite is also possible, and thinking processes elaborated in the context of dialectic and critical theory are used as keys to the reading of Jewish phenomena. In short, Jewish thought can contribute to philosophical reflections,

---

1   This essay was written during my research stay at the Maimonides Centre for Advanced Studies at Universität Hamburg, DFG-FOR 2311.

2   A significant example in this sense is the revival of the biblical ban on images (*Bilderverbot*), which, through a process of secularization, plays a central role for several exponents of the *Frankfurter Schule*. Cf. Lars Tittmar's and Mario Cosimo Schmidt's chapters in this volume.

but the contrary also holds, and philosophical reflections can shed new light on issues in Jewish thought.

This latter case is very well epitomized by Erich Fromm's considerations about the dialectical nature of human freedom (Fromm 1941) and the key role these play in his later interpretation of the Jewish view of idolatry (Fromm 1966). These two main topics, examined in two works, also determine the configuration of this chapter, which is accordingly divided into two main parts. A reconstruction of the dialectical structure that Fromm recognizes in the dynamics of human freedom, in the first part, will serve as a basis to show how idolatry can be interpreted as a moment of this dialectic in the second. More precisely, idolatry can be included in the dialectic of freedom as its negative moment, one of the preeminent examples of what Fromm calls "escapes from freedom."

While there is a general consensus that idolatry has to be rejected, a common definition of its features and a shared understanding of what is wrong with it are far from being reached. In fact, idolatry has been condemned for many different reasons over the centuries: because it corresponds to an act of treachery, because it is associated with lechery, promiscuity, and immorality, or because it constitutes a category mistake, to name but a few examples. In this regard, Fromm's specific contribution to the debate consists in reading idolatry through the prism of freedom dynamics as a *regressive* moment in the course of human liberation. Abolishing idolatrous ways of thinking and acting is thus required, in Fromm's view, to allow for the full development of the human being.

The Dialectic of Freedom

The dialectical nature of human freedom is the cornerstone around which Fromm's reflections in his 1941 book *Escape of Freedom* revolve. As he himself declares in the preface,

> it is the thesis of this book that [the] modern human being, freed from the bonds of pre-individualistic society, which simultaneously gave her security and limited her, has not gained freedom in the positive sense of the realiza-

tion of her individual self; that is, the expression of her intellectual, emotional and sensuous potentialities. (Fromm 1941: viii)[3]

The connections Fromm recognizes between security and limitations lead him to develop a view in which every step taken toward freedom implies a sense of uncertainty that confronts the human being with two alternative paths: the first leads to new forms of dependence and submission, the second to a higher dimension of freedom.

Along the first path, the human striving for freedom ends up being converted into its opposite, thus giving rise to a vicious circle of liberation and subjection; along the second, a possibility of breaking this circle is recognized in a radical change in the way in which freedom is conceived – that is, from negative to positive freedom, in Fromm's own terms. "Negative" freedom means the mere overcoming of limitations, a reactive drive to liberation *from something* constraining. But freedom can also develop into an active principle, into spontaneity, free expression, creativity, and the full realization of the individual. This is freedom *to do something*, "positive" freedom, which resists being caught up in a dialectical movement and is even able to stop it.

Thus, the path leading to a vicious circle is not unavoidable, and an alternative exists – as Fromm says:

> Does our analysis lend itself to the conclusion that there is an inevitable circle that leads from freedom into new dependence? Does freedom from all primary ties make the individual so alone and isolated that inevitably she must escape into new bondage? Are independence and freedom identical with isolation and fear? Or is there a state of positive freedom in which the individual exists as an independent self and yet is not isolated but united with the world, with other human beings, and nature? We believe that there is a positive answer. (ibid: 257)

---

3   The generic use of masculine nouns and pronouns was standard practice in the patriarchal perspective of the time when Fromm's books were published, in 1941 and 1966. The same remark, moreover, can be made about other texts considered here. In this essay, however, gender-inclusive language has been adopted. This means that a gender-neutral alternative has been used whenever the masculine form appears in the quoted passages with a general meaning. Thus, such terms as "man" and "mankind" have been substituted with "human being" and "humankind." Finally, the pronouns used to refer to them are "she" and "her".

Both the circle and its rupture lend themselves to being schematized in terms of different developmental moments or stages. The circle is made up of three moments that deserve the adjective "dialectical," as they give rise to a typically dialectical process governed by the contradictory dynamics of opposite poles that lead to one another. On the other hand, the rupture of the circle can be seen as a fourth moment. Calling it "anti-dialectical" is thus particularly appropriate for highlighting its ability to interrupt the succession of the previous phases.

The first dialectical moment corresponds to a primordial condition in which the human being is still completely embedded in nature as a part of it and thus entirely subject to its laws, entirely determined by natural necessity. For Fromm, this condition is characterized by the fundamental feeling of comfort and safety that can be provided by blind adherence to an established set of rules. However, *the highest degree of perceived safety is counterbalanced here by the lowest degree of freedom.*

It is precisely this lack of freedom that prompts a transition from the first to the second dialectical moment. From a state of comfortable but unconscious union with nature, the human being gradually detaches herself from natural necessity and attains a condition of conscious independence. But

> by being aware of herself as distinct from nature and other people, by being aware – even very dimly – of death, sickness, ageing, she necessarily feels her insignificance and smallness in comparison with the universe and all others who are not "she" [...], she would feel like a particle of dust and be overcome by her individual insignificance. (ibid: 21)

In other words, the newly acquired freedom and independence come at the cost of an increasing sense of anxiety and uncertainty that makes this second moment the dialectical opposite of the first, as *the highest degree of freedom causes the degree of perceived safety to become lower and lower.*

At this juncture, a third moment takes shape as an attempt at a regression to the comfort and safety of the primary connections with nature. This, however, is an unsuccessful attempt, as regression, in this case, can never be complete and the lost unity can never be fully restored. The human being tries

> to give up her freedom and [...] overcome her aloneness by eliminating the gap that has arisen between her individual self and the world. This [...] course [, however,] never reunites her with the world in the way she was related to it

before she emerged as an "individual," for the fact of her separateness cannot be reversed. (ibid: 140)[4]

The three moments analyzed thus far outline a circular path that can be schematized through the conceptual triad of "subjection–liberation–new subjection." However, two points must be considered in this scheme:

a) The delineated circle is not perfect, as the third phase can never fully coincide with the first and the loss of certainty is, to some extent, irreversible.
b) The last transition – from feeling the discomfort of freedom to seeking refuge in a new submission – is not necessary, and an alternative is possible that can break the circle and open a new way. This is supposed to lead to a new dimension that maintains freedom without falling into the anguish of uncertainty.

Different terms are used for this new dimension, which, thanks to its ability to interrupt the dialectical process, could be seen as a fourth anti-dialectical moment: "spontaneity," "productive work," "freedom to," or "love," for example, are some of the terminological choices made in the works considered here.

The dialectical scheme is then employed in Fromm's socio-psychological approach and applied to two levels that he considers parallel: the fields of *individual development* and *social dynamics*. Against the opposite extremes of Freud's and Durkheim's views,[5] Fromm assumes a continuous exchange between individual drives and social forces, explicitly stating that

the human being is not only made by history – history is made by the human being. The resolution of this seeming contradiction constitutes the field of social psychology. Its task is to show not only how passions, desires, anxieties change and develop as a *result* of the social process, but also how human en-

---

4 The same remark is then repeated in other passages of the text, for example: "[The human being] is driven into new bondage. This bondage is different from the primary bonds, from which, though dominated by authorities or the social group, she was not entirely separated. The escape does not restore her lost security" (Fromm 1941: 257).

5 Freud and Durkheim are here presented as two opposite one-sided positions: while Freud tends to reduce the sociological dimension to purely psychological dynamics, Durkheim seems to aim at eradicating psychological aspects from sociology (cf. Fromm 1941: 14).

ergies thus shaped into specific forms in their turn become *productive forces, molding the social process.* (ibid: 13–14)[6]

The *trait d'union* between these two levels is recognized in the process of individualization that, for Fromm, characterizes both. Chapter II, "The Emergence of the Individual and the Ambiguity of Freedom" (ibid: 24–39), is entirely devoted to elaborating on a parallel between "the social history of humankind" and "the life history of an individual" (ibid: 24), showing that both levels have the same dialectical character. They may be as different as *micro* and *macro*, but in spite of this, they share the same inner dynamics. In conducting his comparative analysis, Fromm starts by correlating the individual change from fetal into human existence with its counterpart in the history of humankind; that is, the emergence of the human being from a prehuman stage in which she is a piece of nature, completely controlled by instinctive and reflex action mechanism.

Once separated from the mother's body by the cutting of the umbilical cord, the child starts to experience a world outside itself and forms a vague intuition of "otherness." The child begins to perceive itself as a separate independent entity, and this perception is the *one* cause that – dialectically – gives rise to *two* contradictory trends (ibid: 104): on the one hand, the process of individuation implies a growth in physical, emotional, and mental strength, but on the other, it has the negative side effect of a growing feeling of aloneness. The more freedom and independence are acquired through individuation, the more aloneness, powerlessness, and consequent anxiety are produced as side effects. As a result of this double process, the individual develops an impulse to reject individuality as the main source of her anxiety. She is led to reverse the process and let go of the acquired freedom in order to shun the disadvantages it entails.

This new impulse lies at the roots of the second dialectical moment, but before we take this latter into account, it is worth noting that a path that is analogous to the first movement – the acquisition of freedom and its repercussions – can be recognized at a more general level in the evolution of humankind.

---

6   In some passages, Fromm seems to think that the difference between psychological and social levels is just a matter of scale. For example, he says: "Any group consists of individuals and nothing but individuals, and psychological mechanisms which we find operating in a group can therefore only be mechanisms that operate in individuals. In studying individual psychology as a basis for the understanding of social psychology, we do something which might be compared with studying an object under the microscope. This enables us to discover the very details of psychological mechanism which we find operating on a large scale in the social process" (Fromm 1941: 137).

Just as a single individual acquires freedom by losing maternal protection, humankind emerges from a prehuman stage by leaving instinctual existence behind. Fromm considers a primordial phase in which the boundary between the animal and the human being is not neatly defined and all activities are still governed by instincts. The overcoming of instinctive drives and the opening of possibilities beyond the coercion of natural determination is what, in Fromm's view, characterizes freedom, and this marks the beginning of a lifeform that can be legitimately called "human." In other words, human existence begins as an act of liberation from natural necessity.

The acquisition of freedom, be it by way of separation from the maternal body or through emancipation from natural necessity, leads in both cases to a sense of aloneness that prompts a process of compensation and a tendency to find reassurance in new forms of submission. More precisely, the single individual, the child, tries to cope with the uncertainty of freedom by bowing to an adult authority (cf. ibid: 29–30). A similar reaction, though developed at a broader level, can be found in humankind and their search for safety through authoritarianism and conformism.[7] Despite their evident differences in scale, both processes have a common denominator in an attempt to reject individuation as a source of unease and find refuge in some form of authority that covers and suppresses individuality.

It is clear, however, that this kind of regression is tantamount to falling into a vicious circle, in which the goal of reestablishing the lost, reassuring pre-individual ties may be pursued but never fully reached, as the severed ties can never be completely restored. Nonetheless, as stated before, this continuous alternation of the acquisition and loss of freedom is not the only possible path: another way can be followed "that connects the individual with the world without eliminating her individuality" (ibid: 30). Obviously, the question arises as to how such apparently opposite features as "individuation" and "connection" can possibly be combined. Fromm's answer is very simple and extremely cryptic at the same time: "spontaneity" is the notion he introduces to indicate that new dimension that is supposed to break the dialectical process and lead out of its vicious circle, also adding that it consists in nothing else than the full realization of the human being, that is, in her "being herself."

---

7   For Fromm, authoritarianism and conformism represent the two main forms of escape from freedom: "The principal social avenues of escape in our time are the submission to a leader, as has happened in Fascist countries, and the compulsive conforming as is prevalent in our own democracy" (Fromm 1941: 134).

A first step toward delineating *spontaneous* activity is taken by contrasting it to its opposite – to *compulsive* activity. The conceptual pair "external–internal" can be useful to clarify this point. Thus, compulsive activity can be said to be "external" because it is based on a pattern coming from the outside as something given, imposed, uncritically accepted, and, broadly speaking, something to be aligned to. In contrast, spontaneous activity can be considered "internal" in the sense that it has its origin only in itself, without resorting to any pre-established model to follow.

However, the nature of "spontaneity" emerges far more easily from some concrete examples taken from the realm of human activity than it does from an abstract, theoretical definition. In this regard, Fromm concentrates on two main fields: love and creative work. These have a paradigmatic value, as "what holds true of love and work holds true of all spontaneous action" (ibid: 261), and both are able to forge connections without dissolving individuality. Love presupposes and maintains the polarity of the individual self and otherness, without one of the two poles being reduced to the other. Creative work shows the same polarity, but between the individual and the world in which she lives. The creative human being affirms herself in activity, but, by connecting the creator to the focus of her creative power, she affirms the otherness of nature at the same time. This peculiar capability of love, creativity, and spontaneity allows Fromm to conclude that "the birth of individuality and the pain of aloneness is dissolved on a higher plane by human spontaneous action" (ibid: 261).

The following notions appear to be particularly clarifying when summarizing Fromm's view of the dialectical circle of freedom and its anti-dialectical breaking. The first notion is "unaware submission," from which "negative freedom" is then achieved. This latter represents a decisive turning point from which two opposite ways can be followed: on the one hand, "negative freedom" can lead back to a new form of submission; on the other, there is also a chance that the negative will be converted into the positive, the reactive into the active. Thus, the level of "positive freedom" can finally be reached, and with it the full realization of the human being.

The Dialectic of Freedom, with a Jewish Inflection

About 20 years after Fromm's reflections on the dialectical nature of freedom, he revived and employed these notions in his "radical interpretation of the Old Testament" – which he makes no bones about calling "a revolutionary book"

(Fromm 1966: 7). The dynamics that Fromm analyzes in relation to freedom find close correspondence in the steps that constitute the history of the Jewish people. And this correspondence is corroborated by the fact that for Fromm, the Old Testament too has no other goal than liberation in the broadest sense of the term: "freedom for the individual, the nation, and for all of humankind" (ibid: 7). In this view, then, the history of the Jewish people can be seen as a progressive acquisition of freedom, which, as such, is subject to falling into pitfalls that are analogous to those delineated for freedom in general.

More precisely, the three dialectical moments of freedom, along with the fourth anti-dialectical way out of the vicious circle of liberation and submission, correlate with some of the most salient events in Jewish history: the slavery in Egypt, for example, represents the first dialectical moment, the starting phase of submission from which the process of liberation begins; the exodus of the Jewish people from Egypt represents the first – and thus also naïve – movement of liberation: "freedom from," in Fromm's terminology, which bears within itself a sense of uncertainty and the constant risk of falling into other forms of subjection. The risk then becomes reality in the biblical episode of the golden calf, which Fromm – along with many other interpreters[8] – sees as a relapse into a submissive *forma mentis*.

Following the same reasoning as for freedom in general, however, the liberation from Egypt does not necessarily lead back to the idolatry of the golden calf. Relapse into idolatry, in other words, is not unavoidable. According to the dynamics explained above, an evolutionary path toward positive freedom, "freedom to," spontaneity, is also possible – and, in the biblical context, this would lead to what can be called "godlikeness." This refers to a condition in which the human being can and must become *like* God; she has the task of acquiring and practicing "the main qualities that characterize God: justice and love" (ibid: 65).

After the liberation from Egypt – that is, negative freedom, "freedom from" – it was as if the Jewish people had come to a crossroads: on the one hand, the relapse into subjection, represented through the idolatry of the golden calf; on the other, the achievement of positive freedom, freedom to, in the form of the full development of human nature, up until the achievement of godlikeness. Thus conceived, idolatry turns out to be one of the major forms of escape from

---

8   The biblical episode of the golden calf has been the object of several studies. Without any claim to completeness, some of the most recent and relevant are Bori 1990, Mosès 1985, Freedberg 1989, Assmann 2000, and Freudenthal 2012.

freedom – to the point that it can even act as a paradigm for any other form. But if idolatry has a paradigmatic value for other moves away from freedom, then these can be considered "idolatrous" in a metaphorical sense of the term – as Fromm himself suggests by distinguishing between primitive (i.e., literal) and modern (i.e., metaphorical) idols:[9] "The history of humankind up to the present time is primarily the history of idol worship, from the primitive idols of clay and wood to the modern idols of the state, the leader, production and consumption" (ibid: 43).

The use of the same notion of "idolatry" to describe phenomena that can be very different from one another can be justified based on their being characterized by the same dynamics, which, in this case, consist in a two-phase process: a combination of "alienation" and "projection." The human being tries to separate herself from – that is, she tries to *alienate* – the freedom that has become unbearable and ascribes it to – or, in other words, *projects* it onto – something external, which, invested with new powers, ascends to the status of "idol." Essentially, Fromm describes a process of displacement:

> The human being transfers her own passions and qualities to the idol. The more she impoverishes herself, the greater and stronger becomes the idol. The idol is the alienated form of the human self-experience. In worshipping the idol, the human being worships herself. (ibid: 43–44)

An idol is a thing, a repository of those qualities – freedom, in particular – that the human being perceives as difficult and oppressive. Projecting them onto something external, something non-human, may have a relieving effect, but the alienated qualities cannot be completely severed from the human being, who constantly feels the need to keep in touch with them: "If the idol is the alienated manifestation of human powers, and if the way to be in touch with these powers is a submissive attachment to the idol, it follows that idolatry is necessarily incompatible with freedom and independence." (ibid: 46)[10] In this view, then, idolatry is a form of escape from the unbearable uncertainty of

---

9   The problem of distinguishing the literal and metaphorical use of the term "idolatry" has been dealt with by Fackenheim (1973) and Fortis (2023b).

10   An explanation of these dynamics can be found in Nietzsche's reflections on the origin of religious cults: "One will think first of that mildest kind of constraint, that constraint one exercises when one has gained the affection of someone. It is thus also possible to exercise a constraint on the powers ·of nature through prayers and pleadings, through submission, through engaging regularly to give presents and offerings, through flat-

freedom toward the reassuring and comforting submission to a force or entity whose freedom can be influenced. In other words, the direct responsibility of freedom, which generates anxiety, is exchanged for the possibility of indirectly affecting, and possibly controlling, a free force.

The anxiety of freedom, and the consequent attempt to cope with it by creating and worshipping an idol, is expressed in narrative form in the biblical episode of the golden calf. The conditions are well-known: Moses has been lingering for too long on Mount Sinai and the Israelites begin to mourn the loss of their intermediary with God.[11]

> God knew how much the Hebrews longed for visible symbols; it was no longer enough for them to be led by a God who had no name, who was not represented visibly. [...]. The people felt relatively secure as long as he [Moses], the powerful leader, the miracle worker, the feared authority, was present. Once he is absent, even for only a few days, they are gripped again with the fear of freedom. They long for another reassuring symbol. (ibid: 111)

From this passage, two points may be deduced that can be summarized under the conceptual label of "graduality." The human evolution from submission to freedom is not a direct one, in Fromm's view, but a gradual transition that needs to go through an intermediate phase of *partial* detachment from slavery before reaching *complete* freedom. More precisely, this middle position manifests itself in the *obedience* that the Israelites still need to render to God as well as in the *visual symbol* that they cannot give up yet. Both obedience and visual symbols show the advantages and disadvantages of intermediate elements, which can certainly ease the progression from the starting point to the end of a process, but make a relapse into the initial submissive condition all the more likely.

Fromm writes: "Against our thesis that the Jewish aim for the human being is independence and freedom, the objection may be raised that the Bible [...]

---

tering glorifications, inasmuch as by doing so one obtains their affection: love binds and is bound" (Nietzsche 1986: § 111, 64).

11 The passage from the Torah reads: "When the people saw that Moses was so long in coming down from the mountain, the people gathered against Aaron and said to him, 'Come, make us a god who shall go before us, for that fellow Moses – the man who brought us from the land of Egypt – we do not know what has happened to him'" (Ex. 32:1).

requires obedience" (ibid: 72). However, the objection can be overruled by remarking that obedience, though not the final goal, is nonetheless an essential step toward reaching it: "Obedience to rational authority is the path that facilitates the breaking up of [...] fixation to pre-individual archaic forces" (ibid: 73). Since it is impossible to go directly from submission to complete freedom,[12] the path of liberation must be divided into at least two segments: a first segment leads from a condition of slavery[13] to obedience to God, while a second is supposed to overcome obedience completely, leading to fully mature freedom.

As to the human need for visible symbols, Fromm does not go into much detail, but in the history of thought, it is not uncommon to acknowledge a close connection between a tentative definition of the human being and the notion of "symbol."[14] In these views, the human experience in the world is always mediated, and the mediation takes place through the creation and employment of symbols. For example, by applying the notion of "symbolizing being" to the episode of the golden calf, Stéphane Mosès (1985) describes the absence of the biblical Moses as a traumatizing experience that left the Israelites in the agony of living without the sense that had been guaranteed by Moses' visibility and mediation up to that point. The senselessness caused by such an unexpected loss of orientation in the world is then the trigger for idolatry. Without Moses, the Israelites feel the urge to find a replacement and think that they can find it in the golden statue of a calf.

From a more general perspective, obedience to authority and visual reference contribute to keeping contact with an idolatrous way of thinking, in order to make it easier and less traumatic to overcome. But in so doing, they do not sever the link with the previous mentality and thus expose themselves to the constant risk of relapsing into it. The episode of the golden calf testifies precisely to the actualization of this risk, as the core of its sinful meaning, the

---

12 Fromm explicitly says that "revolution [toward freedom] can succeed only in steps in time. [And] since there is no miraculous change of heart, each generation can take only one step" (Fromm 1966: 113).

13 In this context, "slavery" can be considered both the condition of captivity that the Jewish people suffered in the land of Egypt and the submissive attitude toward idols represented by Egyptian religion and culture.

14 The anthropological value of symbolization has been emphasized by several thinkers in the 20th century. Two particularly telling examples are Ernst Cassirer's conception of the human being as *animal symbolicum* (Cassirer 1944) and Hans Jonas' attempt to define the human being through the notion of *homo pictor* (Jonas 1962).

roots of its idolatrous essence, can be found in the persistence of a submissive *forma mentis* and the visual symbols this still requires.

The relapse into idolatry represented in the biblical episode of the golden calf is thus due to the process of the liberation of humankind being incomplete. For Fromm, obedience to God only partially emancipates humankind from its original condition, but the fact that the authority of God is a *rational* one – as opposed to the *irrational* ties to natural forces – can still be considered an advancement along the path of liberation. Similarly, Moses' role as a visual symbol testifies to a still-incomplete separation from the visual nature of idolatry, but despite this incompleteness, it must be remarked that Moses, in providing mediation between God and the Jewish people, is a *living* visual symbol. And this is certainly an improvement compared to the false mediation of an idol, whose essence, Fromm says, consists in being something *dead* (cf. ibid: 44–46).

If read through the prism of the dialectic of freedom, the conditions allowing a regression to idolatry correspond to the second dialectical moment; that is, to what Fromm calls "freedom *from*." But whereas the partial, negative "freedom *from*" can trigger a backward movement, it is equally true that this idolatrous regression is not necessary: it is just one among other potential outcomes, and alternative developments are possible. In fact, "freedom *from* may eventually lead to freedom *to* a new life without idolatry" (ibid: 113), or, to put it differently, negative freedom can also act as an intermediate step to reach positive freedom – which in the biblical context takes shape in terms of *godlikeness*.

In various passages, Fromm reaffirms the same concept: for example, he says that the main human task consists in emulating divine features (cf. ibid: 65), also adding that "the human being is not God, but if she acquires God's qualities, she is not beneath God, but walks *with* him" (ibid: 66) and concluding that "the human being can become *like* God, but she cannot become God" (ibid: 68). Fromm's conception of godlikeness, as the main task assigned to humankind, has its theoretical foundations in three main points, each of which is substantiated by the textual analysis of some Torah verses. The conception of the human being as *tselem Elohim* (אֱלֹהִים צֶלֶם, *image of God*), for example, is the basis of the human-divine analogy.[15] The notion of "openness," as Fromm's key to his reading of Genesis, lays the foundation for his idea of the human being as something that is still incomplete and aiming to become *like* God. Finally, the primacy of action over theory, which Fromm upholds by referring to Hermann

---

15   On the notion of God's image, cf. Lorberbaum 2015.

76   Philosophy and Jewish Thought

Cohen,[16] provides an insight into the *way* through which the human being can come closer to the divine ideal.

Gn. 1: 26–27 establishes the deepest analogy between God and the human being, which is described as *tselem Elohim* (צֶלֶם אֱלֹהִים, *image of God*). Following the biblical narration, then, Fromm also notes that after eating from the tree of knowledge (Gn. 3: 22–23), the divine-human affinity becomes even more accentuated, to the extent that "only mortality distinguishes [the human being] from God" (Fromm 1966: 64). In this view, the human being comes to be conceived as a sort of still *immature* form of the divine, entrusted with the task of reaching *maturity* and becoming *like* God. The human being is potentially and temporally what God is in a fully accomplished form and outside of time. But beyond this enormous difference, the viability of the human path toward the divine is guaranteed by the affinity implied in the expression *tselem Elohim* (צֶלֶם אֱלֹהִים, *image of God*).

A second aspect of the biblical conception of human nature may also be inferred from a philological remark. Referring to an unspecified Hasidic master, Fromm points out that "God does not say that 'it was good' after creating the human being" (ibid: 70). It is well known that the phrase "and God saw that this was good" (Gn. 1: 10, 12, 18, 25) can be found as a refrain concluding the various steps of creation, but the fact that the creation of the human being is an exception to this trend is, for Fromm, an argument in favor of the incomplete nature of humankind: "This indicates that while the cattle and everything else was finished after being created, the human being was not finished." (Fromm 1966: 70) From a theoretical point of view, it is worth noting that incompleteness is the main prerequisite for freedom. It is precisely because she is *incomplete* – that is, open to a development whose limits are not established in her nature once and for all – that the human being can be said to be *authentically free*.[17]

The third remark provides an answer as to *how* the human being can pursue the ideal of godlikeness. The Torah passages of relevance here are Ex. 34: 6[18] and Lv. 11: 44,[19] which Fromm considers through the mediation of Hermann

---

16   The central role of praxis in Judaism is investigated in Hermann Cohen's *Religion of Reason* (1995), especially in chapters VI and VII.

17   The same conception is then repeated in chapter VI of Fromm's book (Fromm 1966: 180).

18   "A God compassionate and gracious, slow to anger, abounding in kindness and faithfulness" (Ex. 34: 6).

19   "You shall sanctify yourselves and be holy, for I am holy" (Lv. 11: 44).

Cohen's interpretation.[20] For both Cohen and Fromm, it is not so much about *being* like God as it is about *acting* like him. By elucidating his understanding of *holiness* – which can be considered the Cohenian counterpart of Fromm's god-likeness – Cohen accounts for its divine and human inflections by resorting to the notions of "being" and "doing" respectively: "Holiness thus means a task for the human being, whereas for God it designates being" (Cohen 1995: 96). The same notion – that is, holiness – has an ontological meaning when referring to God, as it characterizes his essential traits, but acquires a practical connotation when referring to the human being, who has to *do* something to *achieve* the state in which God simply *is*. And, more precisely, what the human being has to do in order to come closer to Cohen's "holiness" or Fromm's "godlikeness" is to practice the divine precepts, following the law of God.[21]

These three aspects can thus be summarized as follows: 1) The human being's possibility of becoming like God is rooted in the notion of *tselem Elohim* (צֶלֶם אֱלֹהִים, *image of God*), which stands for an essential affinity between the human and the divine; 2) The incompleteness that characterizes the human being, moreover, allows her existence to take shape as the task of striving toward godlikeness, as being incomplete, without a predetermined form, is precisely what opens the space for human freedom; 3) Finally, the specific way through which the goal of godlikeness can be pursued is a practical one, which is dependent on interpretation and observance of the precepts. To illustrate the connection between the three main aspects of godlikeness as an alternative to idolatry, Fromm cites a famous episode narrated in the Talmud. This provides an example of what Fromm means by "being like God," while the anti-authoritative message that emerges from the text attests to its anti-idolatrous significance.

---

20   According to Cohen, the features listed in the first verse (Ex. 34: 6) "are not so much characteristics of God, but rather conceptually determined models for the action of the human being" (Cohen 1995: 95). As to the second verse (Lv. 11: 44), Cohen says: "Human beings fulfill their striving for holiness in the acceptance of the archetypal holiness of God, in imitation of which they sanctify themselves" (ibid: 103).

21   Another Torah verse that is usually adduced in support of Judaism being based on praxis is Ex. 24: 7: "We will do and we will listen to all that God has declared." The way this verse is formulated suggests that the practical moment ("we will do") precedes the theoretical one ("we will listen to"). This lends itself to being interpreted as the affirmation of a primacy of praxis over theory. A prominent supporter of this reading is, for example, Martin Buber, who writes: "First doing and then hearing […]. Not truth as idea nor truth as shape or form but truth as deed is Judaism's task" (Buber 1967: 113).

The episode discusses a halachic dispute between a group of rabbis, on one side, and Rabbi Eliezer, on the other. The specific topic is actually irrelevant, as the focus is on how the argumentation progresses. After failing to convince the rabbis with logical arguments, Rabbi Eliezer resorts to various forms of authority to back up his view. He invokes the authority of such natural elements as a tree and a stream, artificial constructions like the walls of the study hall, and goes on in a sort of crescendo, whose climax is a divine intervention: "A Divine Voice emerged from Heaven and said: Why are you differing with Rabbi Eliezer, as the halakha is in accordance with his opinion in every place that he expresses an opinion?" (TB, *Bava Metzia*: 59b). However, none of Rabbi Eliezer's attempts is successful. The rabbis are not convinced, as they do not acknowledge authority itself as a valid argumentative tool. Even divine authority, in this context, is no exception: "We do not regard a Divine Voice – say the Rabbis – as You [i.e., God] already wrote at Mount Sinai, in the Torah: 'After a majority to incline'" (ibid: 59b).

Beyond its strong anti-authoritative message, however, another decisive point that makes this episode particularly meaningful is God's reaction to the rabbis' claim to autonomy. Contrary to what one might believe, the rabbis do not provoke God's wrath, but are rather praised for their capability for critical and independent thinking: "The Holy One, Blessed be He, smiled and said: My children have triumphed over Me; My children have triumphed over Me" (ibid: 59b). In other words, God does not see the rabbis' behavior as a form of insubordination to be punished. Their sticking to the majority rule is instead the clearest proof that they have acquired and embraced the true spirit of the divine law, which is one of comment, interpretation, discussion, and critical thinking; it certainly does not require blind obedience, and even refuses it.

The Talmudic story is a valuable representation, in narrative form, of Fromm's understanding of godlikeness. Once she has reached an adequate level of maturity, says Fromm, the human being is able to "deal with God on terms of equality" (Fromm 1966: 77), as if they were equal partners. But the factor that more than any other allows the human being to emancipate herself up to the level of godlikeness is her adherence to the divine law, whose main teachings are probably suspicion and contempt toward any form of authority, even if divine in nature, and a questioning attitude that looks at the majority for always temporary and revisable answers.

The satisfaction that God derives from his "children" achieving autonomy, moreover, confirms Fromm's theory of graduality: obedience to God, in this view, is not the final goal, but just an intermediate, necessary step toward authentic freedom. Starting from the *submission to idolatry*, the Jewish human being transitions to an intermediate state of *obedience to God*, only to leave it behind when she becomes mature enough to bear the burden of freedom and reach *godlikeness*. The first transition, from idolatry to obedience to God, is necessary because of human constitutive weakness: "The human being is feeble and weak [...]. She needs to be obedient to God so that she can break her fixation to the primary ties [read: idolatry]" (ibid: 77). The second transition can be considered complete when the human being acquires that "spirit of independence from, and even challenge to, God" (ibid: 79) that is epitomized in the Talmudic story.

It is easy to see how the categories that Fromm elaborates in his 1941 book correspond to those expounded in his 1966 work. In fact, in the dynamics of freedom, *four* categories can be determined: 1) a primordial condition of *submission* to natural necessity and 2) the *negative freedom from* that submission. From here, then, two paths diverge: on the one hand, 3) a *relapse* into submission and, on the other, 4) the *positive freedom to*. However, each category can be paired with its theological counterpart: in this view, 1) submission corresponds to the human proneness to *idol worship*, represented by the Jewish slavery in Egypt; 2) the philosophical notion of *freedom from* coincides with the intermediate phase of *obedience to God* that the Israelites have to experience after their liberation from Egypt.[22] Finally, 3) a *regression* to the old idolatrous mentality, as in the episode of the golden calf, or 4) an evolution toward *godlikeness*, as in the Talmudic episode from *Bava Metzia*, represent the two potential paths – backward and forward, respectively – that can develop from a still-incomplete liberation such as that indicated at point 2.

Conclusion

It has been shown that along the path that leads to godlikeness as the human being's final goal, it is necessary to go through the intermediate stage of obedience to God. This appears to be the case because despite still being a form of submission, bowing to God's authority is an effective way to avoid other human or worldly – and therefore idolatrous – authorities. At the same time, however, it is crucial that the obedient attitude toward God remains just a transitional

---

22 Fromm defines the liberation from Egypt as "the central event in the Jewish tradition" (Fromm 1966: 187).

phase, destined to be overcome, as the risk subsists that God himself, in the long run, will come to be considered and treated as an idol.[23]

The following evolution of the human being – from obedience to God to godlikeness – is accompanied by a shift in emphasis from God himself to the law he provided, and this meets precisely that anti-idolatrous claim that the phase of obedience to God, intermediate as it is, cannot satisfy completely. The primacy of the law, which characterizes godlikeness as a condition of full freedom and independence, leads to an employment of critical thinking that is profoundly anti-authoritarian in nature. As the episode in *Bava Metzia* illustrates, through critical thinking, argumentation, and the democratic principle of majority rule, the human being can argue with God as an equal interlocutor; she can challenge and even contradict him. The God-given law is thus an emancipatory instrument in this view, which allows the human being to make the final evolutionary step and eventually "become like God," in Fromm's own words.

However, an objection can be raised that the risk of idolization implied in the obedience to God could very well apply to his law as well: If making an idol out of God is a real risk to be avoided through compliance with the law, what prevents the law itself from being idolized? It must be noted that Erich Fromm does not even pose this problem. However, going beyond his work, a possible answer can be found by looking at the *nature* of the divine law, at those essential traits that make it somehow immune to idolization.

One of the main traits that can be recognized in the Torah[24] is the constitutive openness of its verses, sometimes even verging on ambiguity, which puts them in constant need of *interpretation*. In her *Lire la Torah*, for example, Catherine Chalier insists on the importance of interpretation in Judaism by directly connecting it to the Jewish loathing for idolatry: "The need to interpret imposes itself on every reader because, unless we confuse it with an idol, no verse imposes a fixed and definitive meaning that it would suffice to receive" (Chalier 2014: 89, trans. BF). Arguably, if interpretation is a sort of alternative to idolatry – as Chalier presents it – then the fact that the Torah essentially requires an interpretive approach contributes to making it inherently impervious to any form of idolization.

For Chalier, a verse can be either interpreted or idolized, but on closer inspection, it is impossible to make an idol out of something that can never be

---

23   This risk is taken into account by such thinkers as Max Scheler (1960: 246–270) and Martin Buber (1970: 153–154). On this topic, cf. also Fortis 2023a.

24   The translation of the word "Torah" is "teaching," "law".

fully grasped. In fact, not even the literal sense of a verse can be considered clarified once and for all, and it will always require further interpretive efforts: "Such a sense [the literal one] cannot become a 'dogma' without turning into an imposture, so it must always remain open to hermeneutic plurality in order to avoid this drift" (ibid: 90, trans. BF). Stopping the process of interpretation to establish a single meaning is explicitly called "an imposture;"[25] it is tantamount to distorting what is supposed to be revealed.

Another major exponent of Jewish hermeneutics, Michael Fishbane, lays stress on the Scripture as something *living* and therefore in constant need of being accounted for through new interpretations. By distinguishing between *explicatio* and *interpretatio* as the two main modes of interpretation, Fishbane writes: "*Explicatio* is principally intent upon circumscribing the text within a specific historical horizon, whereas for *interpretatio* the horizon of the text is not temporally fixed, and it is read as a living document" (Fishbane 2009: 353).[26] Both *explicatio* and *interpretatio* are necessary components of a culture which, like Judaism, is based on texts but nonetheless a certain primacy has to be granted to *interpretatio*, as it is the main means through which a textual culture can adapt to different times and thus survive through the ages. Moreover, the transformations at the level of *interpretatio* quite frequently affect and mold the level of *explicatio*,[27] thus confirming the order of priority between them.

Fishbane describes *interpretatio* in Jewish hermeneutics as a two-pole activity. Only the first pole is fixed, in his view, while the second is movable and changes over time: "The eternity and centrality of the divine word [encounters] the necessary mutability of its reception and filtering. [...] The divine voice, while unique and authoritative, is always an unstable and changing voice filtered diversely in the human community." (ibid: 358) The mutability of *interpretatio* is thus a constitutive factor in the Jewish approach to the divine law,

---

25 "Meanings are therefore plural, and they do not cancel each other out" (Chalier 2014: 90, trans. BF).

26 Fishbane also adds: "In brief, the process of *explicatio* tends to lock a text into one historical period. [...] In contrast, *interpretatio* delivers the text from its original historical context, treating its linguistic content as powerfully multivalent and so, in principle, resistant to reductive or final readings – while treating its own work of interpretation as a fundamental moment in the creative life of the text" (Fishbane 2009: 354).

27 "It can be said that text-cultures are such primarily because of the *interpretatio* that animates them and which, aside from the meanest paraphrase or linguistic annotation, quickly conquers *explicatio* and transforms it into its own image. This is true especially of religious text-cultures and of Judaism in particular" (Fishbane 2009: 353).

which, despite its divine and immutable origin, needs continuous recontextualization on the side of its human reception. However, the main point here is that a variable reception of the law acts in an anti-idolatrous way, as it nips in the bud any possible idolization of the Torah.

The continuous activity of interpreting, with its always new nuances of meaning and its various layers,[28] keeps the law in a state of unfixedness that undermines the very condition of idolatry. In fact, in order to indulge the human need for certainty – that is, the main reason why the human being resorts to idol worship – the idol must be something stable. More than any other feature, an idol must display stability, fixity, for the human being to be able to grasp it – be it with her gaze or with her thought.[29] But this very determinateness and consequent graspability cannot be ascribed to a law whose meaning is constantly put into question, discussed, challenged, and reshaped in the ongoing process of interpretation it essentially requires. Bearing an irreducible core of indeterminateness that makes interpretation necessary and inexhaustible, the Jewish law resists any idolizing tendency. In this sense, it can be rightly considered the way out of the burden of idolatry and toward the goal of "being like God."

Finally, with Fromm, but now even beyond him, it is possible to conclude that the creativity[30] of an endless interpretation and the exercise of critical thinking that this demands pave the way toward the positive freedom that characterizes godlikeness. This represents the highest realization of the human being: a state of full maturity that is definitively beyond any need for idolatry – be it in literal or metaphorical form.

---

28 In chapter 3, Chalier refers to the four traditional hermeneutic approaches, that is: 1) *peshat* (פְּשַׁט), which indicates the literal and direct meaning; 2) *remez* (רֶמֶז), which stands for the deep meaning beyond the literal sense; 3) *derash* (דְּרַשׁ), the comparative meaning obtained through similar occurrences; and finally 4) *sod* (סוֹד), the level of secret meaning that can be reached through inspiration or revelation. Cf. Chalier 2014: 89–90.

29 Differences and relationships between material, visual idols, and idols of thought is dealt with in Fortis 2023b.

30 "The traditional hermeneutics of Jewish *interpretatio* [...] is the creative retrieval of meaningfulness in terms of, and, indeed, in the terms of, its sources" (Fishbane 2009: 357).

Bibliography

Assmann, Jan (2000): "Du sollst dir keine Bilder machen. Bedeutung und Kontext des Zweiten Gebots." In: Christian Scheib/Sabine Sanio (eds.), Bilder-Verbot und Verlangen in Kunst und Musik, Saarbrücken: PFAU, pp. 13–26.

Bori, Pier Cesare (1990 [1983]): The Golden Calf and the Origins of the Anti-Jewish Controversy, Atlanta: Scholars Press.

Buber, Martin (1967 [1919]): "The Holy Way: A Word to the Jews and to the Nations." In: Nahum N. Glazer (ed.), On Judaism, New York: Schocken, pp. 108–148.

Buber, Martin (1970 [1923]): I and Thou, New York: Charles Scribner's Sons.

Cassirer, Ernst (1944): An Essay on Man. An Introduction to the Philosophy of Human Culture, New Haven, CT: Yale University Press.

Chalier, Catherine (2014): Lire la Torah, Paris: Édition du Seuil.

Cohen, Hermann (1995 [1919]): Religion of Reason out of the Sources of Judaism, Atlanta: Scholars Press.

Fackenheim, Emil L. (1973): "Idolatry as a Modern Possibility." In: id. (ed.), Encounters between Judaism and Modern Philosophy, Philadelphia: Jewish Publication Society of America, pp. 173–198.

Fishbane, Michael (2009): "Hermeneutics." In: Arthur A. Cohen/Paul Mendes-Flohr (eds.), 20th Century Jewish Religious Thought, Philadelphia: JPS, pp. 353–361.

Fortis, Beniamino (2023a): "Idolatry and Relation. Martin Buber's View." In: European Judaism 56/2, pp. 8–19.

Fortis, Beniamino (2023b): "The 'Idolatry' Paradigm. Between Literal Meaning and Figurative Extension." In: Nuovo Giornale di Filosofia della Religione 3, pp. 166–186.

Freedberg, David (1989): The Power of Images. Studies in the History and Theory of Response. Chicago: University of Chicago Press.

Freudenthal, Gideon (2012): No Religion without Idolatry: Mendelssohn's Jewish Enlightenment, Notre Dame: University of Notre Dame Press.

Fromm, Erich (1941): Escape from Freedom, New York/Toronto: Rinehart & Company, Inc.

Fromm, Erich (1966): You Shall Be as Gods. A Radical Interpretation of the Old Testament and Its Tradition, New York/Chicago/San Francisco: Holt, Rinehart and Winston.

Jonas, Hans (1962 [1961]): "*Homo Pictor* and the *Differentia* of Men." In: Social Research 29/2, pp. 201–220.

Lorberbaum, Yair (2015): In God's Image. Myth, Theology, and Law in Classical Judaism, New York: Cambridge University Press.

Mosès, Stéphane (1985): "Le Pointe d'Énoch. L'art et l'idole selon les sources juives." In: Jean Halpérin/Georges Lévitte (eds.), Idoles. Données et Débats, Paris: denöel, pp. 133–144.

Nietzsche, Friedrich (1986 [1878]): Human, All Too Human, Cambridge: Cambridge University Press.

Scheler, Max (1960 [1954]): On the Eternal in Man, London/New York: Routledge.

Scholem, Gershom (1980 [1977]): From Berlin to Jerusalem. Memories of My Youth, New York: Schocken Books.

Standstill in Utopia: Walter Benjamin's Philosophy of History and the Ban on Images

Lars Tittmar

Benjamin's paradoxical and mysterious-sounding formulation of dialectics at a standstill is inextricably linked to his conception of dialectical images. These ideas permeate his late work and lead to the center of Benjamin's philosophy of history. In this, utopia and theology intertwine in a fruitful way: This occurs against the backdrop of Benjamin's thought seeking to undermine the linear conception of history. Finally, it becomes apparent that a certain understanding of the ban on images[1] is also present and effective in his late philosophy of history. This article discusses the connection between a certain understanding of the ban on images in Benjamin's late work and his conception of history. It starts with a brief description of what dialectical images are and how their mode of construction operates. The following two sections examine the elements that confront and come together in dialectical images: The destructiveness and suffering, which is subsumed (*aufgehoben*) in history but invisible, buried under the idea of progress, and the other side that is connected to the

---

1   This term refers to the second commandment, which was directed against the practice of idolatry: "Thou shalt not make unto thee any graven image, or any likeness of any thing that is in heaven above, or that is in the earth beneath, or that is in the water under the earth. Thou shalt not bow down thyself to them nor serve them" (Exodus 20: 4–6). If the German term "Bilderverbot" is translated here as "ban on images," it is because this is also the translation of the term in a passage from Adorno's "Negative Dialetics." Here, the connection between "Bilderverbot," which is transferred from its religious context into materialist thinking, and utopia becomes apparent: "The materialist longing to grasp the thing aims at the opposite: it is only in the absence of images that the full object could be conceived. Such absence concurs with the theological ban on images. Materialism brought that ban into secular form by not permitting Utopia to be positively pictured; this is the substance of its negativity. At its most materialistic, materialism comes to agree with theology" (Adorno 2004: 207).

idea of a messianic time, which is present but hidden. The conclusion shows that the confrontation of those elements causes a standstill, which leads to the appearance of a utopian force. The central role of theology in general and the ban on images in particular in the concept of dialectics at a standstill will be presented, which also points to the topicality of Benjamin's philosophy of history.

On the Construction of Dialectical Images

It is hard to give a clear definition of Benjamin's idea of a dialectical image. Its composition and the elements from which it is constructed are as complex as what it is supposed to express. Benjamin's dialectical images emerge in a specific situation characterized by upheaval: the time of the industrial revolution of so-called high capitalism, characterized by an enormous increase in production possibilities and also an attempt at radical upheaval on a political level. The contradictions between the economic and political possibilities and their actual development gives room for the construction of a dialectical image. This is particularly evident in the structure of Benjamin's Arcade Project: using the development of Paris in the 19th century, Benjamin makes generalizations about capitalist development. Against the backdrop of urban development under Baron Haussmann and the emergence of the arcades, the city seems to condense into an image of the time. The luxury goods in the arcades appear to be within reach, while at the same time the city itself is permeated by the contradictions of struggle, misery, splendor, and decay. This is condensed in the significance of the commodity and its character as something that makes a statement about the nature of the whole. In this sense, the dialectical image replaces allegorical observation, which previously had a similar function for Benjamin: "The commodity has taken the place of the allegorical mode of apprehension." (Benjamin 2006: 165) Where allegory, as Benjamin shows in *The Origin of German Tragic Drama* in an attempt to rehabilitate it, says something about the world as a whole as a monad in a kind of miniature, the commodity becomes the representative of capitalism. Its basic features and contradictions – that social mediation functions via value, that an excess of goods is produced while misery continues to exist – all of this is subsumed in the commodity. The commodity thus exemplifies the dream-filled sleep[2] into which the people of the highly industrialized and capitalized Europe of the middle and late 19th century have fallen. In dreams of luxury, truth and lies are inextricably linked.[3] This reveals a dialectical image of the present.[4]

Central to the construction of dialectical images is that, for Benjamin, the past is not understood as something completed in the process of history, which is constantly moving forward. A philosophy of history as he represents it is opposed to such a linear understanding of time and history. The potential that exists in the past to break open the seemingly unstoppable, unalterable course of history should be ignited in the present. This is the connection between past and present practice. In Benjamin's time, this course was not only the commodity-producing capitalism that had spread throughout the world and, in alliance with the nationalist elites, had caused the mass slaughter of the first World War twenty years earlier. He also refers to the rise of fascism, especially its specific German variant, National Socialism.

It is in this context that Benjamin writes in his reflections on the concept of history: "To articulate the past historically does not mean to recognize it 'the way it really was' (Ranke). It means to seize hold of a memory as it flashes up at a moment of danger." (Benjamin 2007: 255) This is not only a criticism of historicism and its positivist historiography, which believes that the truth about history is contained in a series of objective facts. In this passage, Benjamin rather proposes a view of history that does not accept the blurring of the traces of violence and that they also become invisible. The actualization of memory in the moment of danger is described by Benjamin as an empowerment in the face of that danger. It establishes a connection to those who were exposed to this danger, which is still understood as an acute threat. The interweaving of

---

2   Benjamin refers with that term to the connection between capitalism as something historically created and its appearance as something like nature, something that has always been there: "Capitalism was a natural phenomenon with which a new dream-filled sleep came over Europe, and, through it, a reactivation of mythic forces" (Benjamin 1999: 391).

3   As is also crystallized in the concept of phantasmagoria: "The metaphor of phantasmagoria makes it possible to focus on tensions and contradictions without using modern critical topoi" (Blättler 2021: 106, trans. LT).

4   For Benjamin, Baudelaire becomes an exemplary witness of this time: "If it can be said that for Baudelaire modern life is the reservoir of dialectical images, this implies that he stood in the same relation to modern life as the seventeenth century did to antiquity" (Benjamin 2006: 134).

these initially seemingly divergent elements ultimately converges in the formulation of dialectics at a standstill: "It's not that what is past casts its light on what is present, or what is present its light on what is past; rather, image is that wherein what has been comes together in a flash with the now to form a constellation. In other words, image is dialectics at a standstill." (Benjamin 1999: 462)

In this context, Benjamin defines images as something that is meant to be read, rather than viewed. This legibility is bound to a certain time, not only the time to which they belong, but also the time in which they first become truly legible. Benjamin describes this as the "historical index of the images" (ibid: 462). The legibility is linked to a "movement at their interior" (ibid: 462). This movement is rooted in the constellated character of such images, which do not address a static object but processes. It is precisely this movement that leads to the coming together of the past and the present. This is not only a specific element of cognition, but also the formulation of dialectics at a standstill: The past stands in a dialectical relationship to the present, which is why it communicates something to the latter in its images. Thus, through this dialectical movement, in the very moment of realization that such a connection exists, the dialectical element creates this connection and in it a brief moment of interruption of the present. Dialectical images are the conception which might allow such a constellation and only in this way can the past and present be related to each other and intertwined. This would not be possible in a static image.

Elsewhere, Benjamin specifies the relationship between such an image and the question of time: "All in all, the temporal momentum (*das Zeitmoment*) in the dialectical image can be determined only through confrontation with another concept. This concept is the »now of recognizability« (*Jetzt der Erkennbarkeit*)." (ibid: 867) This formulation suggests that for Benjamin there is a distinction between the present, i.e. the now, and the now of recognizability, which is then not a mere temporal moment in a linear sequence, where the present is precisely that which is located between the past and the future. The now of recognizability does not mean the actual present. Rather, it is the connection between the past and now-time, which makes it possible to recognize the past, but which is only possible in this very now. Thus, the now of recognizability is the coming together of past and present as a constellation. Something from and in the past becomes recognizable in the present and thus all these elements together become the now of recognizability. For Benjamin, this is the reason for the disruptive effect of a dialectical-materialistic view of history – in contrast to a linear one, as in historicism, for example. That is why he says:

"The dialectical penetration and actualization of former contexts puts the truth of all present action to the test." (ibid: 857) The dialectical standstill of events opens the continuity of the presence through a practice oriented in this way, which then actually points beyond the apparent immutability of the present and the apparent closure of the past. This is made possible by the fact that, according to Benjamin, the materialist theorist refers to the apparent harmonization of contradictions in the present. On the other hand, he also looks at the contradictions in the past that have become invisible, thereby drawing attention to the possibility of a different course of history. These contradictions became invisible because the history written by the victors was able to present itself retrospectively as the only possible course. Benjamin describes his process accordingly: "Here, this occurs through the ambiguity peculiar to the social relations and products of this epoch. Ambiguity is the manifest imaging of dialectic, the law of dialectics at a standstill. This standstill is utopia and the dialectical image, therefore, dream image." (ibid: 10) It is noteworthy at this point that Benjamin does not conceive of utopia as lying in the future, i.e. a goal that is moved forward in time in action. Instead, the place of and for the utopian is opened at a standstill. On the one hand, this refers to the utopian aspect of the idea of stopping and thus halting the events of the present, which are seen as destructive. On the other hand, it also recalls the utopian content of the past, which can be found in the interstices, contradictions, and ambiguities. Instead of shifting utopias into the future, Benjamin points to the necessity of understanding the past as the scene of lost battles for this future, as well as a place where unfulfilled promises await redemption. This points to the great importance of theological thinking, especially for Benjamin in the 1930s, who was committed to materialism.

Suffering and Catastrophe

In his dissertation, Benjamin already speaks of an "ideology of progress" (Benjamin 1996b: 168), referring to Schlegel's early critique of Romanticism, according to which this concept had lost its meaning at the beginning of the 19th century and had thus become empty. The increasing questioning of the rule of the nobility on a political level corresponded to the spirit of the Enlightenment in philosophy, the climax of which was reached in Hegel's philosophy, which also placed the concept of progress at its center. According to Benjamin, the climax is also the beginning of the decline. With the rise to power of the bourgeoisie and the hypostatization of progress, it became an empty concept rather than a critical one: "The concept of progress had to run counter to the critical theory of history from the moment it ceased to be applied as a criterion to specific historical developments and instead was required to measure the span between a legendary inception and a legendary end of history." (Benjamin 1999: 478) Everything was characterized by progress, which primarily meant technical achievements, but not social conditions. There is therefore a close connection between the concept of progress and its supposed negative: "Overcoming the concept of 'progress' and overcoming the concept of 'period of decline' are two sides of one and the same thing." (ibid: 460) If Benjamin parallels these concepts, it is because neither has room for the countless victims of history: these do not decide on a characterization of time as one of progress or decay. They are merely extras.

Benjamin puts this in the following context in a famous formulation: "The concept of progress must be grounded in the idea of catastrophe. That things are 'status quo' is the catastrophe. It is not an ever-present possibility but what in each case is given." (Benjamin 2006: 161) Decay and eternal progress are two expressions of the same point of view because they are based on the same destructive principle: that there is something higher than the human individual and that the majority of those individuals are only significant as cogs in a process that serves that higher purpose. Such a view of history knows no individual victim, but only the sacrifice made by the individual in the service of the greater good. The idea of being in league with history and the most drastic demonstration of the narcotic effect of "how it actually was" is made fatally clear by the attitude of the German working class in the Weimar Republic, which was oriented towards social democracy: "Nothing has corrupted the German working class so much as the notion that it was moving with the current." (Benjamin 2007: 258) Benjamin also has a concept of progress in mind here, which he describes in the same passage as "vulgar-Marxist" (ibid: 259). Basically, he is attacking the evolutionary socialists, i.e. the social democracy of the Second International, as well as Stalinism, which believes it must walk over dead bodies in the name of supposed progress. What they have in common is that, for different reasons, they devalue the individual in the process in favor of an idea of progress that takes on the traits of idolization. Progress is stylized into a force whose content does not need to be proven by anything but is on the right side for itself and as the quality of being progress.

Against this backdrop, the victims become invisible and with them the immense suffering in the past: this has no place in the story of progress, either because it clouds this narrative or because it is no longer perceived at all. Instead, it appears to be so self-evident that it takes on the status of a natural order. The extras of history bring their share so that progress can shine in the guise of the rulers. Benjamin, on the other hand, demands a different view of what we call history: "The tradition of the oppressed teaches us that the 'state of emergency' in which we live is not the exception but the rule. We must attain to a conception of history that is in keeping with this insight." (ibid: 257) At this point, Benjamin refers to Paul Klee's well-known painting *Angelus Novus*, whose fame is linked to Benjamin's use of it. In the angel of history that Benjamin recognizes in it, the contours of a concept of history that he calls for converge, which corresponds to the state of exception in which the oppressed have always lived:

> Where we perceive a chain of events, he sees one single catastrophe which keeps piling wreckage upon wreckage and hurls it in front of his feet. The angel would like to stay, awaken the dead, and make whole what has been smashed. But a storm is blowing from Paradise; it has got caught in his wings with such violence that the angel can no longer close them. This storm irresistibly propels him into the future to which his back is turned, while the pile of debris before him grows skyward. This storm is what we call progress. (ibid: 257–258)

The talk of paradise here connects Benjamin's early essay on language, where the loss of the paradise is a strong motif, with his last text *On the Concept of History*: Out of the lost paradise comes the storm, for as long as the problem is not solved, of which the expulsion from paradise is the remembrance, the storm will rage. And it will rage more violently, unstoppably into a future from which nothing can be expected. Rolf Tiedemann interpreted the angel's averted gaze as "the ban on images in theology and its transformation into profanity: Marx's refusal to paint the communist society in detail" (Tiedemann 1983: 104, trans. LT).

Marx's[5] refusal to draw a concrete picture of communist society was based on the viewpoint that the development of society was fundamentally heading

---

5   This refers to a sentence in the epilogue to the second edition of the first volume of *Das Kapital*. There, Marx takes up the accusation that he would limit himself to "the critical analysis of the actual facts, instead of writing recipes (Comtist ones?) for the cook-shops of the future" (Marx 1982: 99).

in the direction of such a future. Benjamin's angel, on the other hand, is confronted with the ruins that the actual course of history has produced. He turns his gaze away, out of horror, but also to focus it on something else. Instead of a linear conception of time, the reference to an element of the ban on images also stands for the warning and reminder that this course of history was not the only conceivable one. There is a passage in the notes to *On the Concept of History* that explicates and illuminates this connection: "The existence of the classless society cannot be thought at the same time that the struggle for it is thought. But the concept of the present, in its binding sense for the historian, is necessarily defined by these two temporal orders." (Benjamin 2003: 407) The ban on images thus also stands for a critical movement as an intrusion into an idea of history that only knows a linear course. Benjamin vehemently criticizes this view and the angel's refusal to look into such a future is also an attempt not to lose sight of something else. Benjamin concludes his criticism of such a view of history together with its corrective. In doing so, he creates a dialectical image in which utopia is also given a place, as Susann Buck-Morss explains following a note from Konvolute N:[6] "Today's bomb-dropping airplanes are the dialectical antitheses of Da Vinci's utopian anticipation. When the philosophical gaze scrutinizes the juxtaposition of these images, utopian and real, it is compelled not only to recognize technical nature's original state of innocence, but to study empirical history for the reasons why technology nonetheless came to terrorize humanity." (Buck-Morss 1989: 245)

Benjamin's view of history should be understood as an attempt to focus on precisely this: to look at the actual course of events from the point of view that it was not only a destructive one, but also to raise the question of why. At the same time, the possibility of a different course that the development could have taken (but did not for reasons that need to be explained) must be present in the background. Benjamin is therefore not only concerned with questioning the myth of eternal progress, but also with questioning the mythological narrative of a natural progression of human development towards a capitalist society without alternative: "That, of course, can happen only through the awakening of a not-yet-conscious knowledge of what has been." (Benjamin 1999: 458) In this borrowing from Ernst Bloch,[7] he aims to relate his approach of releasing

---

6   Buck-Morss takes up a quote from Pierre-Maxime Schuhl, which Benjamin included in his notes (cf. Benjamin 1999: 486).

7   In distinction to Sigmund Freud's Unconscious, which is connected to the past, the Not-Yet-Conscious in Bloch's works is one of the foundations of utopian thinking,

the potentials of utopia to the past in this double movement of real destruction and possible utopian anticipation. At this point, the ban on images stands in the way of an escape into the future, but this does not mean merely opposing the present with a different image of the future:

> We know that the Jews were prohibited from investigating the future. The Torah and the prayers instruct them in remembrance, however. This stripped the future of its magic, to which all those succumb who turn to the soothsayers for enlightenment. This does not imply, however, that for the Jews the future turned into homogeneous, empty time. For every second of time was the strait gate through which the Messiah might enter. (Benjamin 2007: 264)

Benjamin draws on the idea of the dawning of messianic time, which is not simply in the future, but signifies a different idea of time, in which different temporal levels and elements intertwine.

Messianism and Remembrance

Benjamin's reference to a paradise before the beginning of time, as echoed in his talk of a classless primordial society,[8] is not only related to theology due to its Old Testament origins: a kind of prehistory tells of an original unity between humans and nature that was lost.[9] Jewish messianism, as Benjamin claims it,

---

linked to something which is not, but could be: "For only in the discovery of the Not-Yet-Conscious does expectation, above all positive expectation, attain its proper status: the status of a utopian function, in emotions as well as in ideas and in thoughts" (Bloch 1986: 113).

8   He wrote in the draft to the Arcades Project of 1935: "In the dream in which each epoch entertains images of its successor, the latter appears wedded to elements of primal history 'Urgeschichte' that is, to elements of a classless society" (Benjamin 1999: 4).

9   This is also the approach taken in Benjamin's early text "On Language as Such and on the Language of Man." The Genesis narrative of paradise lost is the starting point for a reflection on language. This falls apart from the one language of the name into a multitude of languages: "There is, in the relation of human languages to that of things, something that can be approximately described as 'overnaming' – the deepest linguistic reason for all melancholy and (from the point of View of the thing) for all deliberate muteness." (Benjamin 1996a: 73) This sadness is therefore also a reaction to the loss of the paradise.

is basically a way of thinking between the religious and the profane, in that it takes up the prehistoric-religious narrative of paradise but relates it to events in the empirically profane world. Benjamin's thinking is strongly influenced by the understanding of rabbinical messianism, which, according to Gershom Scholem, is characterized by the fact that it contains both a restorative and a utopian element:

> There is a common ground of Messianic hope. The utopianism which presents the Jew of that epoch with the vision of an ideal as he would like to see it realized, itself falls naturally into two categories. It can take on the radical form of the vision of a new content which is to be realized in a future that will in fact be nothing other than the restoration of what is ancient, bringing back that which had been lost; the ideal content of the past at the same time delivers the basis for the vision of the future. However, knowingly or unknowingly, certain elements creep into such a restoratively oriented utopianism which are not in the least restorative and which derive from the vision of a completely new state of the Messianic world. The completely new order has elements of the completely old, but even this old order does not consist of the actual past; rather, it is a past transformed and transfigured in a dream brightened by the rays of utopianism. (Scholem 1971: 4)

Benjamin starts from a kind of prehistoric idea that refers to something like utopia. But not because he actually considers the Genesis narrative to be true history that really happened, but because it represents a counternarrative that is as old as the development of human history itself. Michael Löwy describes the connection between messianism and utopia as follows: "The elective affinity between the two was also based on their common restorative/utopian structure: that of the redeemed future as a restoration of paradise lost (Tikkun)." (Löwy 2022: 184, trans. LT) The restitutionist[10] aspect of this is the approach of understanding such thinking not as having suddenly emerged, but as having

---

10   The extent to which Benjamin's early language essay represents this utopian core can be seen in the drafts of the history text, where he sees the universal language rising again in the messianic age: "The messianic world is the world of universal and integral actuality. Only in the messianic realm does a universal history exist. Not as written history, but as festively enacted history. This festival is purified of all celebration. There are no festive songs. Its language is liberated prose-prose which has burst the fetters of script [Schrift] and is understood by all people (as the language of birds is understood by Sunday's children)" (Benjamin 2003: 405–406).

always been present. Also the *Tikkun Olam*, the kabbalistic idea of repairing of the broken vessels, is more a utopian idea in the sense that it is more about changing the current state of the world than restoring a lost one:

> The world of *tikkun*, the re-establishment of the harmonious condition of the world, which in the Lurianic Kabbalah is the Messianic world, still contains a strictly utopian impulse. That harmony which it reconstitutes does not at all correspond to any condition of things that has ever existed even in Paradise, but at most to a plan contained in the divine idea of Creation. (Scholem 1971: 13)

By drawing on such motifs, Benjamin is able to counter the universal history of the victors, the lack of alternatives of how-it-really-has-been, with a different principle:

> Historicism rightly culminates in universal history. Materialistic historiography differs from it as to method more clearly than from any other kind. Universal history has no theoretical armature. Its method is additive; it musters a mass of data to fill the homogeneous, empty time. Materialistic historiography, on the other hand, is based on a constructive principle. (Benjamin 2007: 262)

The irruption of the theological figure of messianism is this constructive principle, or more specifically the irruption of messianic time.

The fact that Benjamin is not concerned with the intervention of a real Messiah and thus the fulfillment of a religious promise of salvation can be seen in his reference to Marx in connection with messianic thinking: "In the idea of classless society, Marx secularized the idea of messianic time. And that was a good thing." (Benjamin 2003: 401) The idea of liberation, of transforming the possibility of an end to destruction, oppression, and suffering from its religious-theological connotation into a real task in the here and now is central to this: a different state no longer lies in the hereafter or a lost past but seems possible in the present. Buck-Morss has expressed impressively and vividly what actualization means here:

> The Messianic Age as "actual," that is, as potentially present, is the temporal dimension that charges images in the collective unconscious with explosive power in the political sense. Plotting the events of empirical history in relation to this time register provides the third axis in the coordinate structure

of dialectical images – the crucial axis for both the political *and* the philosophical power of the project. (Buck-Morss 1989: 243–244)

The other two axes she names are transcendence, which is represented by theology, and empirical history, which is represented by Marxism (cf. Buck-Morss 1989: 304). Messianic time is therefore not something that waits in the future (or even the past), but something that is present. The confrontation of the empirical and transcendental axes results in the point at which the dialectical images in turn unfold their effect or even condense and crystallize. What emerges and refers to the concepts of remembrance and redemption is "the idea of a solidarity of humanity across time (between generations) and not merely across spatial boundaries (in one's own time)." (Kompridis 2013: 32, trans. LT) This idea is related to the weak messianic power that also points to the past. This conception of dialectical images that subvert linear time for the initially paradoxical-sounding movement of dialectics at a standstill expresses the historical-philosophical explosive force of Benjamin's thinking, which is characterized in particular by its reference to theological motifs.

The importance of theology for materialism is already emphasized in Benjamin's first thesis on the concept of history in the famous image of the chess automaton. There, Benjamin postulates a connection between theology and materialism, as otherwise the latter threatens to succumb to destructive forces (here Benjamin has fascism in particular in mind) in the struggle for the liberation of humanity. Benjamin describes his method of stillness with explicit reference to the category of the messianic:

> Where thinking suddenly stops in a configuration pregnant with tensions, it gives that configuration a shock, by which it crystallizes into a monad. A historical materialist approaches a historical subject only where he encounters it as a monad. In this structure he recognizes the sign of a Messianic cessation of happening, or, put differently, a revolutionary chance in the fight for the oppressed past. (Benjamin 2007: 262–263)

Here, cessation must be explicitly understood as a countermovement to forgetting. He sees this as being rooted in the fact that the victors write history and, accordingly, the defeated become invisible and forgotten. In the face of this destructive violence, which passes over all those who stand in the way, Benjamin calls for a messianic halt: messianic because something awakens in it, and something is to be redeemed. In the destruction, Benjamin thus discovers something that points to the presence of something different, something better. The shok as a blast; the blasting out of an element from the supposedly linear universal history of progress is then the constructive principle – constructive not only because it arranges the elements as a constellation, but also constructive in contrast to destructive, because it wants to point to something better.

Particularly relevant, also for the question of the ban on images, is Benjamin's interweaving of memory as a practice of mourning and his attempt to create a constructive way of thinking history. Here, his rejection of the narrative of history as a series of facts, the "how it really was," combines a Marxist-inspired critique of ideology with a theologically tinged practice of memory, which is always also an expression of mourning. Remembrance here is the recognition of what was lost in the course of history: the invisible, forgotten victims of this history. It is mourning for these as well as for the loss of what could have been.

In an early draft for the Arcades Project, Benjamin talks about a special form of remembering that would not necessarily be associated with it at first glance. There he says: "[A]wakening is the great exemplar of memory." (Benjamin 1999: 883) While memory is perceived as something directed backwards, into the past, awakening appears to be an act directed towards or related to the present. Waking up from a dream, for example, ends the state of sleep. One can awaken from a memory by locating oneself in the present again, by returning from wallowing in the past. For Benjamin, however, awakening has a dialectical character, and he links this to a far-reaching assumption: "Dialectical structure of awakening: remembering and awaking are most intimately related. Awakening is namely the dialectical, Copernican turn of remembrance 'Eingedenken.'" (Benjamin 1999: 884)

In Benjamin's thinking, the influence of the Jewish tradition is combined with the materialist critique of ideology, particularly in the concept of remembrance (Eingedenken) itself. Burkhard Schmidt writes about dialectics at a standstill that "its ambiguity cannot be due to anything other than the intertwining of utopia and ideology." (Schmidt 1988: 92, trans. LT) Schmidt's point is that the dialectical image shows the false world of reification and the deceptive glitter of commodities on the one hand, but also the flip side, the possible realization of utopia. This is an appearance of ambiguity in the image. However, the question of catastrophe, of the oppressed, the forgotten, the defeated, the victims of history is not just a question of ideology or utopia. Depending on the understanding of what ideology means, this history of violence cannot be subsumed under this term without further ado and, above all, completely. This is why the dialectical image is not only the coming together of these two elements, but also raises a central question that does not simply settle in the middle, the contradiction between ideology and utopia: How can there be a moment of awakening in the mourning of loss, in the remembrance of the victims, in the unraveling of history, in the opening to the messianic?

Dialectics at a Standstill: The Moment of Awakening

The aforementioned sentence about the connection between awakening and memory is explicated by Benjamin in that he also takes up another of Bloch's motifs, but instead of focusing on the dimension of the future as Bloch does, Benjamin's gaze is directed towards the past: "[W]hat Bloch recognizes as the darkness of the lived moment, is nothing other than what here is secured on the level of the historical, and collectively. There is a not-yet-conscious knowledge of *what has been*: its advancement has the structure of awakening." (Benjamin 1999: 883)

The not-yet-unconscious knowledge of what has been is the practice of memory as mourning as well as the practice of recognizing what is lost and could have been. It is an awakening because it is a realization of the present as a false state – and thus the awakening from a nightmare, a subjugation to a seemingly natural state and thus the opposite of conscious action. Remembering as a form of this practice connects these moments. It is the "enslaved ancestors" (Benjamin 2007: 260) who are mourned on the one hand in order not to abandon them to oblivion, but in the mourning lies a power that points to the necessity and determination for liberation. This is why Benjamin brings this into play as a motivation, as a driving force of liberation, and not the "image [...] of liberated grandchildren" (Benjamin 2007: 260). The remembrance refers directly to a second motif of Judaism or, without it, is virtually powerless in Benjamin's reflection: messianism, especially in the form of a weak messianic power.

The following formulation can be found in the drafts of *On the Concept of History*: "The dialectical image can be defined as the involuntary memory of redeemed humanity." (Benjamin 2003: 403) Such a memory is involuntary because what has happened is not presented to it as a mere sequence, but as an image: "The involuntary memory – this is what distinguishes it from the arbitrary memory – is never presented with a course but only with an image."

(Benjamin 2010: 129, trans. LT) That is why it is also a standstill, but a dialectic that stands still and thus the opposite of something static. Such a thing would be the mere stringing together of events, which then present themselves as a progression with a necessary end point in the present. Thus, the task formulated here by Benjamin in view of the dialectical image focuses on those things that seem forgotten but refer to the demand for redemption and detaches them from the supposedly homogeneous course of linear time. The task is to "take up the broken dialectic of past testimonies of history and culture in a new way, in other words to 'redeem' those moments of history." (Hillach 2011: 223, trans. LT) By using such a procedure, Benjamin suddenly gives the past an actuality by pointing to the necessary redemption, a connection is created between the people of the past and those of the present. This is the "secret agreement between past generations and the present one. Our coming was expected on earth. Like every generation that preceded us, we have been endowed with a *weak* Messianic power, a power to which the past has a claim." (Benjamin 2007: 254)

The past has a claim to this power because what has happened cannot simply be allowed to pass, to lie in the distant past, to be irrelevant to the present and ultimately forgotten. This is the secret agreement of which the present generation can, or rather must, become aware and which can develop the explosive force that is capable of blowing up the continuum of history. Stefan Gandler also refers to this connection in *Materialismus und Messianismus* when he emphasizes "that the past is present in the present in a completely different way than we generally assume: 'We [have] been expected on earth' by the preceding generations" (Gandler 2008: 12, trans. LT). At the moment of defeat, they hope those who follow will not simply resign themselves to this defeat, but keep alive the hope that the last word in the development of humanity has not yet been spoken. This last word has so far been destructiveness, suffering, violence. In the first thesis, Benjamin therefore refers directly to the role, or rather importance, of theologians for materialism. Gandler expresses this lesson from theology as follows and also refers to the context in which Benjamin's reflections arose:

> What visibly exists today is not the totality, is not the last word of history, there is something outside this destructive force that is almost omnipresent in Benjamin's present. It is the hopelessness that, according to many testimonies, prevailed among non-fascists and non-National Socialists in this epoch, against which Benjamin takes up the old theological idea of hope

100   Philosophy and Jewish Thought

again, even if he forbids himself to do so with the immediacy of Bloch. (Gandler 2008: 18–19, trans. LT)

This outside is not to be understood as outside this world, but as outside the seemingly unchangeable course of the world and our entanglement in it. The weak but nonetheless existing power to be drawn from this creates a political messianism that never thinks of liberation in such a way that every sacrifice must be accepted for it, but which draws its justification from the remembrance of the victims of the past. Benjamin's messianism is thus a backward-looking one, but not in a reactionary sense. Rather in the sense that he does not make a promise about a redeemed future but demands the fulfillment of a promise to the past in the present. So, what is the connection with the ban on images?

The world is damaged, incomplete, and in need of redemption. Therefore, any complete image of the world would be a false one or would promote the false which already exists. This idea is based on a philosophy of history that does not believe in the end of history, in which destructive tendencies have triumphed. Rather, the hope for change is necessary and in force as long as the world has not changed for the better. Benjamin insists on this with his theses. That is why he points out the state of the world and, instead of looking ahead, focuses on the suffering and victims behind us. They must not be consigned to oblivion; the weak messianic power can then be perceived in connection with them. "Only for the sake of the hopeless ones have we been given hope" (Benjamin 1996c: 356) is the last sentence from his essay "Goethe's Elective Affinities." He insists that hope can only ever be cherished for someone else, never for oneself. A source of hope thus lies in the act of remembering, here explicitly understood as part of the dialectical image. Not by showing something that is not, but that there is a force that does not cease to demand this possible other by not being prepared to forget and at least accept the victims in the name of a logic of progress. If the present only becomes recognizable when it becomes the past and a secret, invisible connection exists between the people of the past and those of the present, then the angel of history must also look back. He then stands for the reference to the ban on images and it is not without reason that Benjamin's reference to the prohibition on investigating the future, which stems from Jewish monotheism, is accompanied by the complementary commandment of remembrance.

The ban on images thus points to the past: or rather, it is the grief over the suffering of the past and the catastrophe of the present that reminds us not to look only to the future (which is why this problem cannot simply be countered with utopian thinking), especially since the past, together with its unfulfilled promises, is, in Benjamin's words, awaiting redemption. The angel also looks towards the past because only by overcoming the past, by settling the unfinished business from there, does a future seem possible that is not catastrophic and therefore deserves its name. The weak messianic power in the present also exists because the past has a claim on it. Therein lies the interplay between materialism and theology. This then also forms the third point alongside ideology and utopia, which, when they come together, allow the dialectical image to emerge.

An image should show something, and it should express something. But above all, it also should not be a false image.[11] The ban on images stands for this movement, especially when it is not understood as a prohibition of pictorial representation in general, but as an intrusion into the images themselves. Benjamin named this movement in concrete terms, the flash and disappearance that characterizes the true image: "The true picture of the past flits by. The past can be seized only as an image which flashes up at the instant when it can be recognized and is never seen again." (Benjamin 2007: 255) What is the true image of the past? It is the brief flash of the possibility of a different course, of a development towards the messianic era or, in other words, towards the realization of the utopia of a liberated society. It always also consists of looking at something from the past that has already been suppressed, defeated, or even destroyed in the real development of time and now is in danger of being wiped out by the historical narrative: those victims of history, the enslaved, the starving, the murdered – whether the history of progress passed over them or they were buried under the ruins of history in an attempt to give development a different direction.

But why does this image disappear the moment it flashes up? For one thing, it is already in the process of disappearing, as the course of history continues to bury it. On the other hand, the reason why such an image hides is nested in

---

11   So Max Horkheimer and Theodor W. Adorno in *Dialectic of Enlightenment* state: "The Jewish religion brooks no word which might bring solace to the despair of all mortality. It places all hope in the prohibition on invoking falsity as God, the finite as the infinite, the lie as truth. [...] The self-satisfaction of knowing in advance, and the transfiguration of negativity as redemption, are untrue forms of the resistance to deception. The right of the image is rescued in the faithful observance of its prohibition" (Horkheimer/Adorno 2002: 17–18).

the interstices of history, persistently but secretly. Hence the suggestion that "[t]he past carries with it a temporal index by which it is referred to redemption" (Benjamin 2007: 254). The fleeting nature of the true image of the past also points to the danger of mistaking a false image of the past for a true one. Instead, in the constellation of dialectical images, a brief flash of such a true image of the past can occur precisely because it is not a static image: the moment it is recognizable, it is also already gone.

Benjamin's last text is characterized in a particularly impressive way by the tension between theology and materialism, which, according to their basic conception, should be mutually exclusive. The movement which lies in the theses on history between these two poles does not reveal any priority of one over the other, even if the first thesis with the image of the chess automaton might suggest this.[12] At the same time, however, this is precisely where the necessary intertwining of the two seemingly opposing currents becomes apparent: they need each other if they want to achieve their common goal. Theology is a corrective for materialistic thinking. The second entry in Konvolut N reads: "What for others are deviations are, for me, the data which determine my course. On the differentials of time (which, for others, disturb the main lines of the inquiry), I base my reckoning." (Benjamin 1999: 456)

Where the present is not readily recognizable, the past paints a false picture and the future appears as a catastrophe against this background, for Benjamin it is only dialectics at a standstill that is able to break open the continuum of history. This is what he aims for when he writes: "To be sure, only a redeemed mankind receives the fullness of its past – which is to say, only for a redeemed mankind has its past become citable in all its moments." (Benjamin 2007: 254) Elsewhere he explains:

> The historical materialist who investigates the structure of history performs, in his way, a sort of spectrum analysis. Just as a physicist determines the presence of ultraviolet light in the solar spectrum, so the historical materialist determines the presence of a messianic force in history. Whoever wishes

---

12   "The puppet called 'historical materialism' is to win all the time. It can easily be a match for anyone if it enlists the services of theology, which today, as we know, is wizened and has to keep out of sight." (Benjamin 2007: 253) This can be understood as the late revenge of philosophy, which for centuries, from the early Middle Ages to the Renaissance, had to play the role of handmaiden to theology. Or that, in truth, theology is more powerful in secret. However, no hierarchy of the two poles is recognizable in Benjamin's thinking or can be intrinsically justified in it.

to know what the situation of a "redeemed humanity" might actually be, what conditions are required for the development of such a situation, and when this development can be expected to occur, poses questions to which there are no answers. He might just as well seek to know the color of ultraviolet rays. (Benjamin 1996c: 402)

Only "redeemed humanity" as Benjman formulates it, aiming at the realization of humane conditions liberated from domination and violence, would be able to draw a complete picture of this humanity, as only it can truly understand.[13] Within that what is, the view of this existing is clouded. This is why Benjamin calls for looking back instead of forward. This is precisely the connection between messianism and the ban on images, which calls for looking back instead of looking towards the future as a part of turning our backs on the horrors of the present, to be able to think of a possible other, as something that has not yet been realized. History thus becomes "a negative index of some utterly inconceivable transcendence waiting patiently in the wings" (Eagleton 1990: 326). The weak messianic power is similar, in that it refers to something that is not visible but exists (just not in the sense of the existence of a God). This reference to Jewish motifs – the ban on graven images and messianism – is intended to show that what is, is not everything. As Gandler points out, the confrontation between materialism and theology "leads to a new form of historical materialism that does not yet have a name" (Gandler 2008: 45, trans. LT). Therein lies the explosive power of Benjamin's philosophy of history, because it does not draw hope from the uncertain possibility of a potential future, but from what has already happened and what therein points to an incompleteness. It is sometimes argued that the ban on images in relation to utopia prevents political action from being motivated. Another point of critique connected to this is that those who are to be motivated are denied a view of what is to be gained. But one could counter with Benjamin that looking back is enough to recognize that this world cannot and must not remain as it is and was.

---

13   This is a direct parallel or correspondence to what Adorno (2005: 247) called the standpoint of redemption.

Bibliography

Adorno, Theodor W. (2004 [1966]): Negative Dialectics, London/New York: Routledge.

Adorno, Theodor W. (2005 [1951]): Minima Moralia. Reflections on a Damaged Life, London/New York: Verso.

Benjamin, Walter (1996a): "On Language as Such and on the Language of Man." In: Marcus Bullock/Michale W. Jennings (eds.), Walter Benjamin. Selected Writings Vol. 1. 1913–1926, Cambridge, MA/London: The Belknap Press of Harvard University Press, pp. 62–74.

Benjamin, Walter (1996b [1920]): "The Concept of Criticism in German Romanticism." In: Marcus Bullock/Michale W. Jennings (eds.), Walter Benjamin. Selected Writings Vol. 1. 1913–1926, Cambridge, MA/London: The Belknap Press of Harvard University Press, pp. 116–200.

Benjamin, Walter (1996c [1924/1925]): "Goethe's Elective Affinities." In: Marcus Bullock/Michael W. Jennings (eds.), Walter Benjamin. Selected Writings Vol. 1. 1913–1926, Cambridge, MA/London: The Belknap Press of Harvard University Press, pp. 297–360.

Benjamin, Walter (1999 [1982]): The Arcades Project, Cambridge, MA/London: The Belknap Press of Harvard University Press.

Benjamin, Walter (2003 [1972]): "Parapilomena to 'On the Concept of History.'" In: Howard Eiland/Michael W. Jennings (eds.), Walter Benjamin. Selected Writings Vol. 4. 1938–1940, Cambridge, MA: Harvard University Press, pp. 401–411.

Benjamin, Walter (2006 [1974]): "Central Park." In: Walter Benjamin: The Writer of Modern Life. Essays on Charles Baudelaire, Cambridge, MA/London: The Belknap Press of Harvard University Press, pp. 134–210.

Benjamin, Walter (2007 [1955]): "Theses on the Philosophy of History." In: Walter Benjamin: Illuminations, New York: Schocken, pp. 253–264.

Benjamin, Walter (2010): Über den Begriff der Geschichte. Werke und Nachlass. Kritische Gesamtausgabe Band 19, Berlin: Suhrkamp.

Bloch, Ernst (1986 [1959]): The Principle of Hope, Cambridge, MA: MIT Press.

Blättler, Christine (2021): Benjamins Phantasmagorie. Wahrnehmung am Leitfaden der Technik, Berlin: Dejavu Theorie.

Buck-Morss, Susan (1989): The Dialectics of Seeing. Walter Benjamin and the Arcades Project, Cambridge, MA/London: MIT Press.

Eagleton, Terry (1990): The Ideology of the Aesthetic, Malden/Oxford/Carlton: Blackwell.

Gandler, Stefan (2008): Materialismus und Messianismus. Zu Walter Benjamins Thesen "Über den Begriff der Geschichte," Bielefeld: Aisthesis.

Hillach, Ansgar (2011): "Dialektisches Bild." In: Michael Opitz/Erdmut Wizisla (eds.), Benjamins Begriffe. Erster Band, Frankfurt a.M.: Suhrkamp, pp. 186–229.

Horkheimer, Max/Adorno, Theodor W. (2002 [1944]): Dialectic of Enlightenment. Philosophical Fragments, Stanford, CA: Stanford University Press.

Kompridis, Nikolas (2013): "Kritik, Zeit, Geschichte." In: Christian Schmidt (ed.), Können wir der Geschichte entkommen? Geschichtsphilosophie am Beginn des 21. Jahrhunderts, Berlin/New York: Campus, pp. 21–41.

Löwy, Michael (2022): Erlösung und Utopie. Jüdischer Messianismus und libertäres Denken. Eine Wahlverwandtschaft, Hamburg: Europäische Verlagsanstalt.

Marx, Karl (1982 [1867]): Capital. Critique of Political Economy. Volume One, Middlesex/London/New York: Penguin/New Left Review.

Schmidt, Burghart (1988): Kritik der reinen Utopie. Eine sozialphilosophische Untersuchung, Stuttgart: Metzler.

Scholem, Gershom (1971): The Messianic Idea in Judaism and Other Essays on Jewish Spirituality, New York: Schocken.

Tiedemann, Rolf (1983): "Historischer Materialismus oder politischer Messianismus?" In: Rolf Tiedemann: Dialektik im Stillstand. Versuche zum Spätwerk Walter Benjamins, Frankfurt a.M.: Suhrkamp, pp. 99–142.

The Approach of an Inverse Theology: A Commentary on the Aesthetic Dimension of the Jewish Prohibition of Idolatry, particularly in Adorno's and Benjamin's Philosophical Thinking

Mario Cosimo Schmidt

"[D]ialectic discloses each image as script" (Adorno/Horkheimer 2002:18): This sentence from the *Dialectic of Enlightenment* can be found in a passage where Theodor Wiesengrund Adorno and Max Horkheimer try nothing less than to adapt the Jewish prohibition of idolatry to their own philosophy. They associate the Jewish prohibition of idolatry with Hegel's notion of the "determinate negation" (*bestimmte Negation*) (ibid:18). This association is, of course, not based on historical-philological grounds. Hegel did not remotely refer to the Jewish prohibition of idolatry when he spoke of "determinate negation" within the dialectical movement of the "*Geist*." Nevertheless, Adorno and Horkheimer discern a philosophical closeness. Obviously, this adaptation takes place in a context where the authors explore the epistemological dimension of the process of enlightenment, tracing this process throughout the history of humankind. Therein, they assign a particular value to the Jewish religion:

> In the Jewish religion, in which the idea of the patriarchy is heightened to the point of annihilating myth, the link between name and essence is still acknowledged in the prohibition on uttering the name of God. The disenchanted world of Judaism propitiate magic by negating it in the idea of God. (ibid: 17)

In the Jewish religion they see a sort of enlightenment that frees the world from mythical thinking, from the belief that all life is bound to fate and death, which disenchants the world without reducing what the world is to "what the world is" – a tautological epistemology, as Adorno and Horkheimer recognized in the process of enlightenment since its inception in the sources of ancient Greek philosophy: the modern notion of truth, linked with an approach to nature which only seeks to master it, and finally the philosophical positivism, which expresses this tautology without any decorative metaphysics, but also without any doubt or reflection on its own history. However, such a reflection on itself is desperately needed, as Adorno and Horkheimer argue:

> Enlightenment is more than enlightenment, it is nature made audible in its estrangement [*Entfremdung*]. In mind's self-recognition [*Selbsterkenntnis des Geistes*] as nature divided from itself, nature, as in prehistory, is calling to itself [...]. Through this remembrance of nature within the subject, a remembrance which contains the unrecognized truth of all culture, enlightenment is opposed in principle to power [*Herrschaft*]. (ibid: 31–32).

In the Jewish religion the prohibition of idolatry – the prohibition on using the name of God, the prohibition on making an image of God – ensures this kind of self-recognition and provides the remembrance of nature within the subject. At least Adorno and Horkheimer present this interpretation of the Jewish religion in their text.[1]

But their adaptation of this commandment of the Jewish religion not only has an epistemological but also an aesthetic dimension, which does not condemn the image as such, as the historical process of enlightenment did, but instead saves the image as an epistemological form:

> The right of the image is rescued in the faithful observance of its prohibition. Such observance, "determinate negation," is not exempted from the enticements of intuition by the sovereignty of the abstract concept, as is skepticism, for which falsehood and truth are equally void. Unlike rigorism, determinate negation does not simply reject imperfect representations of the absolute, idols, by confronting them with the idea they are unable to match. Rather, dialectic discloses each image as script. It teaches us to read from its features the admission of falseness which cancels its power and hands it over to truth. (ibid: 18)

At first glance it seems strange that the dialectic method could and should be able to provide this rescue of the image. Adorno and Horkheimer do not say

---

1   I have given a much more detailed account of Adorno's and Horkheimer's epistemological adaptation elsewhere: Schmidt 2022.

much more about how this method should be employed. One reason for this is that we see it in action throughout the text and it is not possible to describe the dialectical method without employing it at the same time. Another reason is that this method is not like a finished tool, but rather changes depending on what it approaches. Finally, the description that "dialectic discloses each image as script" is itself an image that requires some kind of reading. To understand this image, it might help us to explore its origins, which leads us to the relationship between Adorno and Benjamin. An intellectual relationship with rich and complex exchanges of thoughts and critical interventions, which make it difficult to reconstruct an exact authorship of a thought – a question that, anyhow, isn't important for our philosophical interests here, but shows the fruitfulness of their dialogue. That dialogue came to a sudden end when Benjamin died while attempting to escape the mostly Nazi-occupied European continent in 1940.

In 1934, a decade after Franz Kafka's death, Walter Benjamin dedicated an essay to him. The essay provides a unique interpretation of Kafka's writings. When Adorno received a copy of Benjamin's unpublished essay he reacted with great excitement:

> Do not take it for immodesty if I begin by confessing that our agreement in philosophical fundamentals has never impressed itself upon my mind more perfectly than it does here. Let me only mention my own earliest attempt to interpret Kafka, nine years ago now – I claimed he represents a photograph of our earthly life from the perspective of a redeemed life, one which merely reveals the latter as an edge of black cloth, whereas the terrifyingly distanced optics of the photographic image is none other than that of the obliquely angled camera itself [...]. (Adorno/Benjamin 1999: 66)

In other words, Adorno sees Benjamin's essay as describing the relationship between the earthly life and a redeemed life similar to the relationship he sketched by his own image. Adorno's reaction is based not only on a similar interpretation of Kafka but also on a similar approach to thinking, which he recognizes in the method Benjamin used in his essay. Adorno calls this approach "'inverse' theology" (ibid: 67), juggling with his metaphor that Kafka's perspective is like that of an angled camera. Adorno characterizes this approach as opposing both a "natural" and a "supernatural" interpretation of Kafka, which takes up Benjamin's own words that it is only possible to miss the core of Kafka's writings by one of two divergent paths of interpretation.[2] Fortunately, it is possible to confirm Adorno's impression that in this point indeed lies the principal approach of Benjamin's interpretation. Benjamin himself wrote, in a letter to Gershom Scholem, an insightful explanation of why he thinks the essay is methodologically so challenging: "The image of the arc suggests why: I am dealing with two ends at once: the political and the mystical." (Benjamin 1978: 624, trans. MCS) Benjamin's image of an arc or bow (*Bogen*) may remind us of the rainbow as the symbol of the covenant between God and humankind. Especially in Judaism this covenant represents the relation between God and all humans, not only the special relation between God and the Jewish people. It is possible that this image is actually meant as a hint to Scholem. However, Benjamin refuses both a mere political or materialistic and a mere theological interpretation of Kafka. The tensions between a materialistic and theological point of view in Benjamin's Kafka essay were even increasing in his later thinking and appear to be unresolvable in Benjamin's thoughts *Über den Begriff der Geschichte* ("about the concept of history"), where the dialectical materialism, derived from a Marxist understanding of history, look to be superimposed on a messianic conception of history, soaked up by elements of the Jewish tradition, or – if you will – vice versa.

In the Kafka essay, it seems as if there is a closer or at least more mediated relationship between politics and mysticism, between a natural and a supernatural reading of Kafka's stories. Adorno describes what this approach of an inverse theology means from his perspective, where he is influenced by his studies of Søren Kierkegaard. In his habilitation thesis about Kierkegaard, titled *Die Konstruktion des Ästhetischen* ("The Construction of the Aesthetical"), Adorno, mentored by the theologian Paul Tillich, makes many critical and dismissive remarks concerning Kierkegaard's philosophy. However, Adorno does emphasize one particular aspect of Kierkegaard's approach, which could be seen as the model of inverse theology. Due to a Christian understanding of the self, Kierkegaard has a sense of the alienated subject and its broken relationship to the modern world. Adorno repeatedly draws attention to this sensibility. One could argue that the metaphor of a divine light, which Adorno uses to characterize the idea of an inverse theology in his letter to

---

2   In his essay on Kafka, Benjamin enumerates some authors from both "ends": On one side he names Hellmuth Kaiser, who interpreted Kafka's writing from a psychoanalytical perspective, and on the other side Hans-Joachim Shoeps, Bernhard Rang, Groethuysen, and Willy Haas.

Benjamin, is directly derived from Kierkegaard's Christian philosophy. It lies in the dissonance between the Christian notion of the human being, conceived as a creature of God and especially for the Christian understanding as a – dialectically speaking – mediation between the divine and the earthly sphere, and an alienated world where this mediation proves to be impossible.[3] If this were the case, it would be right to criticize Adorno's philosophical negativity as an critique of the current world which needs an anchor in a positive theology acting as a kind of countermodel, even if it is not made explicit by Adorno. But the idea of an inverse theology is not about this content: Christian doctrine versus an alienated world. Adorno is concerned with the approach to thinking in Kierkegaard's writings. Unlike Hegel, who views truth as the result of a continuous mediation between subject and object, Kierkegaard's philosophy involves a leap from the world of phenomena to the world of intelligibility. For this reason, Adorno comments on a passage from Kierkegaard's *Practice in Christianity* where Kierkegaard, thinking of purchasing an object, describes how the recognition of an object must lead to a loss of subjectivity, to a reification of the relationship between subject and object, which is at the same time a loss of truth. For Kierkegaard, Christianity salvages this situation. Adorno translates this idea into his own terminology: "Truth is not thing-like. It is the divine gaze which, acting as *intellectus archetypus*, looks at alienated things and redeems them from their enchantment." (Adorno 1979: 60, trans. MCS) Kierkegaard's doctrine rests in an idealistic comfort that truth may not lies in the real world but in the world of the spirit (*der Welt des Geistes*), a conception that Adorno strongly refuses (ibid: 61). For Adorno, the force of Kierkegaard's philosophy lies in its principal form. Kierkegaard does not find the objects of his philosophy in a Christian catechism or in a scholastic discussion or in the great artworks but in ordinary phenomena. "What the pathos of total subjectivity has conjured up in vain rests poor, discarded, but unlosable in the excreted sediment of the aesthetic." (ibid: 183, trans. MCS) Kierkegaard found truth in all the fragmented phenomena that he describes: for example, in his *Diapsalmata*. Adorno insists on Kierkegaard's manner of thinking.

> If the history of culpable nature is that of the disintegration of its unity, then it moves towards reconciliation as it disintegrates, and its fragments bear tears of disintegration as promising ciphers. This is why Kierkegaard's opinion that through sin man stands higher than before proves itself; hence his

---

3   Maximilian Krämer argues in such a direction (Krämer 2023: 65).

doctrine of the ambivalence of fear, of sickness unto death as a cure. With his negative philosophy of history as the expression of "existence," a positive-eschatological one offers itself in inversion to the mourning gaze of the idealist without his involvement. (ibid: 198, trans. MCS)

The mourning gaze of the idealistic philosophy – and here we might bear in mind not only Kierkegaard's but also Hegel's conception of the *"unglückliches Bewußtsein"* (Cf. ibid: 248) – cannot be the last anchor for the human mind. At this point the idea of an inversion occurs but combined with a very important notion for Adorno's thinking, namely the need to read the fragments as "promising ciphers." In this approach Adorno recognizes the relationship between Kafka and Kierkegaard. In his letter to Benjamin, he insists on this relationship by formulating a similar thought:

This relationship is to be found rather precisely with respect to the position of 'scripture' [*die Stelle der 'Schrift'*], and here you claim so decisively that what Kafka regarded as a relic of scripture can be understood much better, namely in social terms, as the prolegomenon of scripture. And this is indeed the secret coded character of our theology, no more, and indeed without loss of a single iota, no less. (Adorno/Benjamin 1999: 67)

This remark closely references Benjamin's essay. In the third section, entitled *Das bucklicht Männlein* (The little Hunchback), script ("Schrift") becomes a central motif for describing the constellation of guilt and justice, or, as we might say, a mythical and a redeemed life. When Kafka tells the story of the *Penal Colony*, where a machine engraves letters onto the backs of the delinquents, Benjamin interprets this as: "the back of the guilty man becomes clairvoyant and is able to decipher the script from which he must derive the nature of his unknown guilt." (Benjamin 2002: 811) The back has to endure this guilt. The little hunchback becomes a figure, an image, of the human being, loaded with an unknown guilt. In the last section – titled after Kafka's *Sancho Pansa* – this image is juxtaposed to the figure of the student, which occurs several times in Kafka's stories:

The gate to justice is study. Yet Kafka doesn't dare attach to this study the promises which tradition has attached to the study of the Torah. His assistants are sextons who have lost their house of prayer; his students are pupils who have lost the Holy Writ [*Schrift*]. (ibid: 815)

Both times when script appears as a motif in Benjamin's essay it describes a bow with two ends: a political and a religious one. But this is not the end of how Benjamin brings Kafka's writings into this constellation. He also includes Kafka as a writer himself:

> [...] he divests human gesture of its traditional supports, and then has a subject for reflection without end. Strangely enough, these reflections are endless even when their point of departure is one of Kafka's philosophical tales. Take, for example, the parable 'Vor dem Gesetz' [Before the Law]. The reader who read it in *Ein Landarzt* [A Country Doctor] may have been struck by the cloudy spot at its interior. But would it have led him to the neverending series of reflections traceable to this parable at the spot where Kafka undertakes to interpret it? This is done by the priest in *Der Prozess*, and at such a significant moment that it looks as if the novel were nothing but the unfolding of the parable. The word 'unfolding' has a double meaning. A bud unfolds into a blossom, but the boat which one teaches children to make by folding paper unfolds into a flat sheet of paper. This second kind of 'unfolding' is really appropriate to parable; the reader takes pleasure in smoothing it out so that he has the meaning on the palm of his hand. Kafka's parables, however, unfold in the first sense, the way a bud turns into a blossom. That is why their effect is literary. This does not mean that his prose pieces belong entirely in the tradition of Western prose forms; they have, rather, a relationship to religious teachings similar to the one Haggadah has to Halachah. They are not parables, yet they do not want to be taken at their face value; they lend themselves to quotation and can be recounted for purposes of clarification. (ibid: 802–803)

Benjamin refers to two essential forms of the Jewish tradition of writing. The Halacha is seen as a category of texts that provides legal advice on the commandments of the Torah or the teachings of the Talmud, while the Haggadah offers moral or ethical advice by telling a meaningful story – it is not directly concerned with the commandments. Kafka's stories are like a Haggadah unfolding a law, which is unknown. This is the interpretation, the reading of Kafka by Benjamin. It points in two directions or to two sorts of laws: the mythical fate and the law of justice, which in a Jewish understanding would be the Torah itself. But Benjamin's reading of Kafka's writing does not stop here. He makes a final turn, taking into account that Kafka considered his own writings as having failed, necessarily failed, and therefore demanded their destruction, which ultimately did not take place. Kafka's documented will,

> which no one interested in Kafka can disregard, says that the writings did not satisfy their author, that he regarded his efforts as failures, that he counted himself among those who were bound to fail. He did fail in his grandiose attempt to convert poetry into teachings, to turn it into a parable and restore to it that stability and unpretentiousness which, in the face of reason, seemed to him the only appropriate thing for it. No other writer has obeyed the commandment 'Thou shalt not make unto thee a graven image' so faithfully. (ibid: 808)

Benjamin does not interpret Kafka's order as an expression of personal dissatisfaction. Rather, Kafka demanded that his writings should not become a part of a literary tradition which gives advice to someone. He feels about his stories that they should provide advice, but in fact they could not. For Benjamin this respect for the prohibition of idolatry – the *Bilderverbot* – is inherent as a genuine quality of Kafka's writing. The unfolding process of the parabolic storytelling does not come to an end because the end would mean you would hold the right and final answer in your hands. Kafka's texts respect the *Bilderverbot* by not offering some kind of divine truth or divine revelation. They need to be interpreted but could not be solved. Therefore, the structure of Kafka's writing itself, or as Benjamin calls it his "gesture" (ibid: 806), points to redemption as something that is missing. Kafka's texts don't need the image of a redeemed life to come this point. They turn the whole (modern) world into writing which demands to be deciphered, as a world that is awaiting its redemption.

In his letter to Benjamin, Adorno gives his interpretation of Kafka through an image that also describes the approach of an inverse theology. Even there, Adorno says that this image was already ten years old. However, it was several more years until 1953 before he himself would compile his thoughts on Kafka in a detailed essay: *Notes on Kafka* (*Aufzeichnungen zu Kafka*). One reason for this long period lies in the inferno, which had become a historical reality. The essay responds to this and attempts to deal with it. In several instances this essay echoes Adorno's own remarks about an inverse theology from his letter. At in one particular point it merges all the motifs we have encountered:

> Kafka's artistic alienation, the means by which objective estrangement is made visible, receives its legitimation from the work's inner substance. His writing feigns a standpoint from which the creation appears as lacerated and mutilated as it itself conceives hell to be. In the middle ages, Jews were tortured and executed [...] inversely [*verkehrt*]; as early as Tacitus, their religion was branded as perverse [*verkehrt*] in a famous passage. Offenders

were hung head down. Kafka, the land-surveyor, photographs the earth's surface just as it must have appeared to these victims during the endless hours of their dying. It is for nothing less than such unmitigated torture that the perspective of redemption presents itself to him. The light-source which shows the world's crevices to be infernal is the optimal one. (Adorno 1997: 268)

Adorno resumes the image, but couples it with a much more brutal scenario. This may remind us of the machine in the *Penal Colony* that Benjamin spoke of earlier. Here, the deadly penalty is associated with an anti-Jewish or even early antisemitic characterization of Tacitus. A terrifying association, if we bear in mind that Adorno thought of this in a moment when the persecution and extermination of the European Jews was taking place and brought antisemitism to a horrifying and unbelievable new reality. But in a way, Adorno inverts the characterization of Tacitus. Kafka's perspective shows a damaged creation, a damaged life – as Adorno subtitles his book *Minima Moralia* (Cp. Adorno 2005). The inverted perspective gives more justice to the damaged life than another one which contrasts the earthly light with a celestial one. Therefore, the approach of an inverse theology is not the same as the notion of a dialectical or, I would say, even a negative theology, when the absence of God and the negativity act as an *eschaton*, as the last thing where the mind can find its rest and comfort:

> But what for dialectical theology is light and shadow is reversed. The absolute does not turn its absurd side to the finite creature – a doctrine which already in Kierkegaard leads to things much more vexing than mere paradox and which in Kafka would have amounted to the enthroning of madness. Rather, the world is revealed to be as absurd as it would be for the *intellectus archetypus*. The middle realm of the finite and the contingent becomes infernal to the eye of the artificial angel. (Adorno 1997: 269)

Undoubtedly, this passage can be seen as a self-commentary on Adorno's characterization of Kierkegaard's philosophical approach. Even when Adorno speaks here about a divine perspective, the perspective of the *intellectus archetypus*, it remains only an assumption, an "as-if." Kafka's writing, with its ambivalent form of his parabolic tales, converts the reality into a place where the search for the divine turns into an endless vortex.

In Adorno's and Benjamin's interpretation of Kafka the inner link between the approach of an inverse theology and the commandment that prohibits idolatry appears. To read each image as script, it is not necessary to have in mind a positive notion of redemption. On the contrary, a concrete notion of redemption obstructs or even makes it impossible to decipher the damaged life as such. Inverse theology does not presuppose an image or a notion of the absolute. It requires a sensibility to the damaged life, a capacity to recognize it in its fragmented, seemingly irrelevant phenomena like Kierkegaard's *Diapsalmata* or abandoned things, which Benjamin sees embodied in the figure of Kafka's Odradek. It does not require the whole picture to identify a fragment as such. Of course, all these expressions are metaphors that encircle the approach of an inverse theology.

However, this approach cannot be directly transferred into a method. There are in fact several models for this approach which can be found in the thinking of Adorno and Benjamin. One of these is what Benjamin called the "dialectical image," important for so many of Benjamin's writings and especially for his project about the arcades of Paris. The dialectical image brings the movement of thinking to a standstill, but without resolving the movement to a viewpoint where it can rest. As Benjamin himself describes it, when he speaks about the conception of a materialistic approach to writing history:

> Thinking involves not only the movement of thoughts, but their arrest [*Stillstellung*] as well. Where thinking suddenly comes to a stop in a constellation saturated with tensions, it gives that constellation a shock, by which thinking is crystallized as a monad. (Benjamin 2003: 396)

Benjamin does not understand a thought as a monad that rests in itself. The movement of the spirit does not come to rest in the dialectical image or in the monad for the historical materialist. But it is interrupted. He emphasizes the leap that is displayed in the dialectical image. This is where the anti-idealistic trait of Benjamin's dialectic of standstill lies, which cannot be reconciled with the dialectic of Hegelian provenance.

Benjamin's idea of a dialectic in a standstill (*Dialektik im Stillstand*) is similar to the dialectic that Adorno and Horkheimer had in mind when they spoke of the implementation of the prohibition of idolatry. Similar to Benjamin's conception, Adorno and Horkheimer are also concerned with the image not just in the sense of a mere illustration, but as appearance in which the conceptual and sensual are intertwined: "[D]ialectic discloses each image as script." (Adorno/Horkheimer 2002: 18) This sentence could be regarded not only as the epistemological program of the *Dialectic of Enlightenment*, but also as an epistemological principle of Walter Benjamin's philosophy. At the very least, the deciphering of images or an entire imagery is a central method in many of Benjamin's and Adorno's studies.

In the motif of inverse theology, Adorno saw a convergence between his and Benjamin's philosophy. A convergence that was, of course, already recognizable in other motifs and that Adorno was also aware of. One example of this would be the idea of a natural history, which Adorno developed in his lecture *On the Concept of Natural History* in 1932 (Cp. Adorno 1990b: 383), in which he references Benjamin's philosophy, and in particular his study on *The Origin of German Tragic Drama* (Cf. Adorno 1990a: 357). However, anyone who continues to follow the correspondence between Adorno and Benjamin will also notice the divergences in their thinking, and indeed the controversies that arose between the two. One of these controversies also concerns the understanding of the "dialectical image." Susan Buck-Morrs has not only reconstructed this debate in her study on the origins of negative dialectic, but also analyzed it in detail. She characterizes Adorno's intellectual efforts around Benjamin as follows: "During all of their disagreements Adorno's goal was to rescue Benjamin from what he considered the Scylla of Brechtian materialism on the one hand and the Charybdis of Judaic theology on the other." (Buck-Morss 1979: 141)

The tension between materialism and theology in Benjamin's thinking finds (as mentioned) a degree of intensity in the theses on the concept of history that seems to tear apart the unity of Benjamin's thinking. On the other hand, Adorno himself envisioned a kind of salvation of theology through materialism, as he wrote to Benjamin in his letter of August 4 and 5, 1935: "A restoration of theology, or better still, a radicalization of dialectic introduced into the glowing heart of theology, would simultaneously require the utmost intensification of the social-dialectical, and indeed economic, motifs." (Adorno/Benjamin 1999: 108) In this letter, Adorno does not bring dialectics – certainly in its Hegelian variety – into play as a countermodel, but rather to correct a dangerous understanding of the dialectical image, which he spots in Benjamin's approach, an understanding of the dialectical image that, following Adorno's argumentation, we can call a surrealist understanding.

In this surrealist understanding, Adorno primarily perceives the problem that the dialectical image is understood as an archetype of a collective unconscious that needs to be deciphered, but is only a sheathed archetype, and that, so to speak, a dialectical movement does not come to a halt, but rather the movement of thought proves to be only a pseudo-movement. Adorno's methodological criticism refers to Benjamin's attempt in his exposé of the passage to analyze the commodity as a dialectical image. In principle, Adorno considers this approach to be right; indeed, he encourages Benjamin to uncover a decisive point, a point of convergence, in the relationship between theology and materialism in modernity:

> It is through commodities, and not directly in relation to human beings, that we receive the promise of immortality; and develop the relationship which you have rightly established between the Arcades project and the book of the Baroque, we could regard fetish as a final faithless image for the nineteenth century, one comparable only to a death's-head. It seems to me that this is where the basic epistemological character of Kafka is to be identified, particularly in Odradek, as a commodity that has survived to no purpose. Perhaps surrealism finds its fulfilment in this fairy-tale of Kafka's as much as a baroque drama found its fulfilment in Hamlet [*in diesem Märchen mag der Surealismus sein Ende haben wie das Trauerspiel im Hamlet*]. (ibid: 107–108)

Adorno considers the surrealist understanding of the dialectical image to be insufficient and regards Benjamin's own reflections from the *Trauerspielbuch* as contrary to this understanding.

This passage shows how convinced Adorno was of the convergence of his and Benjamin's thinking. Even through his sharp criticism, Adorno shows his devotion to Benjamin's thought – at least to what Adorno called an inverse theology as a shared intention. The constellation of commodity, fetish, and image was to lead Adorno in his *Aesthetic Theory* to a theory of art in modernity. The work of art seems to take the place of theology. However, it is probably more reasonable to say that Adorno conceives works of art more as a surrogate for the theological than as objects of a theology. One can read Adorno's remarks as a late explication of his critique of Benjamin and as his own attempt to read the commodity or the work of art as a dialectical image. A conflict, or rather perhaps the constellation of theology and materialism, is also present here in Adorno's aesthetics, in which he develops the dialectic of commodity and artwork.

Adorno's description of an inverse theology is itself a dialectical image. Adorno himself allowed it some variation over time, as we could see. If we want to understand the dialectical image in the same sense as the phrase from the *Dialectic of Enlightenment* mentioned before – that dialectic discloses each image as script – then we would also have to regard, or rather read, the image of an inverse theology not as an illustration of a method of thinking, but as a momentary glimpse of thinking in motion.

This thinking also moves in a dynamic between theology and materialism. Adorno's image may bring this movement to a halt, but it only does so for a moment. The tension, which is also captured in Adorno's image of photography, may clarify something, but it also leaves as much open; indeed, it virtually demands an explanation. In this respect, it is a dialectical image, an image that already sets out to be read as such. The art of this required dialectic would be to read an image not as an immediate appearance, but rather, like characters that refer to something that they themselves are not, as an appearance of something else.

Bibliography

Adorno, Theodor W. (1979): "Kierkegaard: Konstruktion des Ästhetischen." In: Theodor W. Adorno: Gesammelte Schriften: Band 2, Frankfurt am Main: Suhrkamp, pp. 7–213.

Adorno, Theodor W. (1997): "Notes in Kafka." In: Theodor W. Adorno: Prisms, Cambridge, MA: MIT Press, pp. 243–271.

Adorno, Theodor W./Benjamin, Walter (1999): The Complete Correspondence: 1928–1940, Cambridge, MA: Harvard University Press.

Adorno, Theodor W./Max Horkheimer (2002 [1944]): Dialectic of Enlightenment: Philosophical Fragments, Stanford, CA: Stanford University Press.

Adorno, Theodor W. (1990a): „Die Idee der Naturgeschichte.", in: Theodor W. Adorno: Gesammelte Schriften: Band 1, Frankfurt am Main: Suhrkamp, pp. 345–365.

Adorno, Theodor W. (1990b): „Editorische Nachbemerkung.", in: Theodor W. Adorno: Gesammelte Schriften: Band 1, Frankfurt am Main: Suhrkamp, pp. 379–384.

Adorno, Theodor W. (2005 [1951]): Minima Moralia. Reflections on a Damaged Life, London/New York: Verso.

Benjamin, Walter (1978): Briefe Band II, Frankfurt am Main: Suhrkamp.

Benjamin, Walter (2002): "Franz Kafka, On the Tenth Anniversary of His Death." In: Walter Benjamin: Selected Writings. Volume 2 1931–1934, Cambridge, MA: Harvard University Press, pp. 794–818.

Benjamin, Walter (2003) [1940]): "On the Concept of History." In: Walter Benjamin: Selected Writings: Volume 4 1938–1940, Cambridge, MA: Harvard University Press, pp. 389–411.

Buck-Morss, Susan (1979): Origin of Negative Dialectics, New York: Simon and Schuster.

Krämer, Maximilian (2023): Idealismus und Entfremdung: Adornos Auseinandersetzung mit Kierkegaard, Berlin/Boston: De Gruyter.

Schmidt, Mario Cosimo (2022): "Die Adaption des jüdischen Bilderverbots in der Dialektik der Aufklärung: Zum Verhältnis von Sprache, Aufklärung und Offenbarung." In: Beniamino Fortis (ed.), Bild und Idol, Frankfurt am Main: Peter Lang, pp. 103–134.

"A Singular Dossier of the Undiscovered": Intersections between Hans Blumenberg and Aby Warburg

Ellen Rinner

Introduction

In his speech "In Memory of Ernst Cassirer" on receiving the Kuno-Fischer Prize in 1974, the laureate Hans Blumenberg (1920–1996) made one of his rare references to the Kulturwissenschaftliche Bibliothek Warburg (KBW), praising the private book collection-turned research institute as a "singular dossier of the undiscovered" (Blumenberg 2022: 217). Aby Warburg's (1866–1929) library was "singular" indeed: It served not only as the centerpiece, laboratory, and vehicle of his new critical method of cultural science[1] but also as a meeting place and training ground for "the next generation that would carry the torch of German-Jewish intellectuality"[2] (Warburg 2007: 263), as Warburg put it in the library's diary on May 30, 1928.[3] The KBW also owed its uniqueness to its interdisciplinary collection, encompassing history of art, cultural and religious history, astrology, ethnology, psychology, and philology among others. Funded

---

1 The term *Kulturwissenschaft* is notoriously difficult to translate as it falls somewhere between cultural study and cultural science but also refers to Warburg's specific method of psycho-historical research and enquiry. This unique oscillation between theory, practice, and diagnostic tool links Warburg's cultural science to his contemporary Sigmund Freud, who also conceived his Psychoanalysis as a mode of cultural critique, a method of treatment and a theory of psychodynamics.

2 "[…] Vertreter der nächsten Generation würde[n] die Fackel deutsch-jüdischer Geistigkeit weiter tragen." All translations of Warburg's quotes in the text are my own, unless otherwise stated.

3 Examples of recent publications that focus on Warburg's relationship to Judaism include: Treml/Meyer 2005; Levine 2015; Pollock 2016; Rinner 2022.

by his family's banking business, it grew out of Warburg's private library and expanded in line with his changing research interests to comprise some 60,000 volumes by the time of his death in 1929 (cf. Diers 1995). As such, it represented the spatial externalization of Warburg's cultural science.

The KBW offered "practical help in the fight against chaos through systematic book guidance for everyone"[4] (Warburg 1928), equipped with the latest technology and implementing a unique classification system he called the "law of the good neighbor"[5] (quoted in: Saxl 1970: 327), meaning that "the book of which one knew was in most cases not the book which one needed" (ibid: 333), as his assistant and successor as institute director Fritz Saxl explained. Books were not arranged chronologically or along strict disciplinary boundaries but instead around questions and problems. Publications on alchemy neighbored works on chemistry, volumes on astrology shared shelves with books on mathematics. Thus, by using the library to trace the development of natural science from magical thinking, the readers were also inadvertently trained in Warburg's method. The aim was not to find answers to predetermined questions, but to practice open and unbiased, self-critical thinking and interdisciplinary research in order to sharpen one's awareness of problems and develop what Warburg called "antennas" for cultural symptoms of psycho-historical crises. As an "arsenal" (cf. Johnson/Wedepohl 2012), the KBW provided the necessary weapons to "seek out our ignorance and fight it wherever we find it"[6] (Warburg 1905–1970: fol. 21), as he put it. At Heilwigstraße 116 in Hamburg, everything revolved around the problem of the afterlife of antiquity, i.e. the continuing influence and impact of paganism, superstition, and irrationality in a self-proclaimed enlightened and rational modern Europe.

Unfortunately, we can only speculate about the fruitful exchange that might have developed between Warburg's "problem library" (Saxl 2023: 44) and the young Blumenberg during his student days in Hamburg. In December 1933, only four years after Warburg's death, the KBW and its staff were forced to emigrate to London – just in time before the Nazi authorities shut down this option for good. Under the direction of Warburg's most important colleagues, Fritz Saxl and Gertrud Bing, the library developed into one of the most significant research institutes for art and cultural studies in Great Britain and –

---

4   "Praktische Hilfeleistung im Kampfe wider das Chaos durch systematische Buchweisung für Jedermann."

5   "Gesetz der guten Nachbarschaft" (Saxl 1996: 337).

6   "Wir suchen unsere Ignoranz auf und schlagen sie, wo wir sie finden."

thanks to personalities such as Erwin Panofsky and Raymond Klibansky – also in America and Canada.

While Warburg came from an orthodox, or rather orthoprax (Warburg Spinelli 1990: 43), family home and was deeply shaped by the history and traditions of Judaism – although he himself wasn't religious and vehemently rejected orthodoxy since his student days –, Blumenberg grew up in a Catholic household. His mother was Jewish but had converted and his Jewish heritage didn't seem to have played a role in his upbringing. Following the Nuremberg racial laws passed by the National Socialist regime in 1935, Blumenberg was barred from continuing his studies of Catholic theology. He lost his library in the Allied bombing of Lübeck in 1942 and was assigned as a compulsory worker first to an airplane manufacturer, then to a large-scale producer of gasmasks. In February 1945, he was sent to a Nationalist Socialist work camp but was later released. He survived the last month of the war in hiding in the attic of his future wife's family home in Lübeck (cf. Nicholls 2015: 11–13). Incidentally it was Warburg's nephew, Eric M. Warburg, who had worked to ensure that Lübeck was spared further bombing raids, a feat he is still remembered for in local newspapers to this day (cf. Bahnsen 2012; Kabel 2017). When Blumenberg picked up his studies in philosophy, German and classical philology at the University of Hamburg in 1945, the KBW, now called the Warburg Institute, had already been permanently incorporated into the University of London for a year. It is not clear exactly when and how Blumenberg encountered Warburg's work – most likely he was introduced to it through the cultural philosophy of Ernst Cassirer. The latter had not only written his *Philosophy of Symbolic Forms* (Cassirer 1923–1929) largely at the KBW, but had also been a close friend and academic colleague of Warburg's since Cassirer's appointment to the University of Hamburg in 1920 (cf. Levine 2013).

Warburg and Blumenberg as "Good Neighbors"

It remains unclear whether Blumenberg's praise was intended to highlight the KBW's unique methodological orientation towards the yet "undiscovered," or whether the philosopher was primarily drawing attention to the almost nonexistent research on Warburg at the time. Comprehensive research on Warburg and the work of the KBW only began in the 1970s, after Ernst Gombrich's influential but controversial *Aby Warburg: An Intellectual Biography*, which was not published in German until 1980 (Gombrich 1970). What also seems to have remained largely "undiscovered" to this day, however, are the thematic and methodological similarities between Warburg and Blumenberg – not least because there a few direct references to Warburg in Blumenberg's work. Taking the title of this volume as a starting point, I would like to present some points of intersection between Blumenberg's philosophical anthropology and Warburg's anthropological cultural science. One reason for this comparison is the observation that Blumenberg's philosophy is generally not seen from a Jewish perspective, although the significance for his work of Jewish thinkers such as Warburg (and Cassirer), whose philosophical concepts and cultural-historical questions are rooted in the history, culture, and tradition of Judaism, is beyond question. Additionally, such a comparative perspective also serves to highlight the philosophical aspirations and foundations of Warburg's method, of which he himself was well aware: "When I look back on my development it becomes clear that it was based primarily on my will to philosophy, and that I arrived at the visual element secondarily, as a substrate of this thinking."[7] (Warburg 1928) Finally, with the emigration of the KBW and the expulsion of its staff, the tradition of German-Jewish cultural science in Germany was broken off for decades. In view of this caesura, the essay aims to show that a transdisciplinary perspective can reveal hitherto undiscovered forms of afterlife, to use Warburg's expression, of Jewish thought.

I will begin by pointing out some "family resemblances" – to borrow Wittgenstein's term – that are apparent even at a cursory glance. Then I will track down specific traces of Warburg in Blumenberg's work and offer some reflections on common methodological and ethical aspects, before concluding with an actual Blumenbergian take on Aby Warburg. This essay is only a first attempt towards a comparative perspective, which, in true Warburgian manner, proceeds associatively rather than systematically. It doesn't seek to hide the differences between Warburg's cultural-scientific "psycho-history" (Warburg 2007: 429) and Blumenberg's phenomenology of history, but does aim to highlight the multitude of aspects connecting them, thereby opening up new perspectives on the relationship and continuities between the two thinkers.

---

7   "Wenn ich einen Blick auf meine Entwicklung werfe, so ist es klar, dass sie primär ge-
      tragen wird vom Willen zur Philosophie und sekundär als Substrat des Denkens auf
      das bildliche Element gekommen ist."

Family Resemblances

Given the scarcity of Blumenberg's direct references to Warburg, it is all the more surprising how many similarities can be found between the two in anthropological, methodological, and thematic terms. Both defined fear of the indifference of the cosmos and powerlessness in the face of the forces of nature as the fundamental human condition. For both, the existential need for meaning and consolation stands at the beginning of any human relationship to the world. "The conscious creation of distance between oneself and the external world can probably be designated as the founding act of human civilization"[8] (Warburg 2017: A1), Warburg wrote programmatically in the introduction to the *Bilderaltas Mnemosyne*, his unfinished magnum opus, a visual map of European cultural memory comprising images from over three millennia (cf. Warburg 2012; Johnson 2012).

For him, the fear of disorientation in the cosmos was the fundamental traumatic experience that drove human beings in their struggle for self-location and self-assurance, and to which they gave expression in myths, metaphors, symbols, and, above all, images, thereby removing its horror. Thus, Warburg described himself as a "image historian" (quoted after McEwan 2004: 12), not an art historian: As he was interested in images as an expression of psychological behavior towards the world and the memory of these attempts to gain orientation, he did not differentiate between everyday images and "masterpieces," but examined newspaper photographs, advertisements, stamps, and pamphlets with the same attention as works of supposedly "high art." Similarly, in his *Work on Myth*, Blumenberg (1985: 16) speaks of "the gaining of a distance, of a moderation of bitter earnestness" through myths and metaphors, through "*Kunstgriffe*" (Blumenberg 1979: 11, original emphasis), i.e. "through devices like that of the substitution of the familiar for the unfamiliar, of explanations for the inexplicable, of names for the unnameable" (Blumenberg 1985: 5).

The process of this struggle for relief from the "absolutism of reality" (ibid: 3) could thus be traced along works of art of all kinds, according to Blumenberg; for "to have a world is always the result of an art, even if it cannot be in any sense a 'universal artwork' [*Gesamtkunstwerk*]" (ibid: 7). Warburg also emphasized the importance of artistic expression and creation in the cultural-historical analysis of the changing forms these interpretations of reality took: "When this in-

---

8   "Bewusstes Distanzschaffen zwischen sich und der Außenwelt darf man wohl als Grundakt menschlicher Zivilisation bezeichnen" (Warburg 2012: 3).

terval [between oneself and the outside world] becomes the basis of artistic production, the conditions have been fulfilled for this consciousness of distance to achieve an enduring social function [...]."[9] (Warburg 2017: A1) Likewise, Blumenberg aimed to understand human reality through metaphors and involuntary expressions and also emphasized the importance of image creation, when he spoke of "*Homo Pictor* [man the painter] [as] the creature who covers up the lack of reliability of his world by projecting images" (Blumenberg 1985: 8, original emphasis).

As is well known, Blumenberg concentrated primarily on written or literary works, on rhetoric, while Warburg dealt with works of visual art, although finding the "word to the image"[10] (Warburg 1928) was always his motto. However, the category of "non-conceptuality" (*Unbegrifflichkeit*) could be taken as a unifying element that links the two. For Blumenberg, metaphors and myths, even though they are themselves results of conceptual thinking, remain examples of non-conceptuality because, unlike abstract concepts, they preserve the connection between human beings and the world by preserving their rootedness in the living world, thus offering the world in a "tangible" form, so to speak. An analogous position between magic and logic, between "grasping animal" (*Greiftier*) and "conceptual human" (*Begriffsmensch*) is what Warburg ascribes to the image.[11] "You live and do nothing to me"[12] (quoted in: Fehrenbach 2010: 124) was his formula to describe the specific mode in which humans refer to the world through images, a "harmless" liveliness, a balance between closeness and distance, in which physical experience and reflective rationality participate in equal measure. Thus, what Warburg emphasizes in the image and Blumenberg in myths and metaphors is a form of understanding and rationalizing the world that reflects "both the human thirst for knowledge, and the limits of human knowledge" (Ifergan 2023: 1240).

Both thinkers also shared the Renaissance and the Modern Age as their central research interests. For Warburg, the main task of the KBW was to explore and uncover the "afterlife of antiquity" and its imagery in European cultural

---

9   "[...] wird dieser Zwischenraum das Substrat künstlerischer Gestaltung, so sind die Vorbedingungen erfüllt, daß dieses Distanzbewußtsein zu einer sozialen Dauerfunktion werden kann" (Warburg 2012: 3).

10 "[...] die allgemeine Bedeutung des von mir seit den Anfängen meiner Tätigkeit vertretenen Grundsatzes 'das Wort zum Bild'."

11 In German, the relationship between "greifen" (to grasp for sth) and "begreifen" (to grasp sth in the sense of understanding sth) is much more direct.

12 "Du lebst und thust mit nichts."

history; Blumenberg's specific form of "work on myth" also revolved around the phenomenon of the enduring attractiveness and historical impact of Greek mythology and its figures such as Prometheus or Orpheus, its zodiac signs, and planetary gods.[13]

Pendulum vs. Progress

It seems, however, that Warburg also remained a "dossier of the undiscovered" for Blumenberg himself, as his statement in the above-mentioned speech seems to indicate, namely that "the library's theory, if one may say so, and later that of the eponymous institute, was Cassirer's three-volume *Philosophy of Symbolic Forms*" (Blumenberg 2022: 217). However, a systematic examination quickly brings to light the subtle but decisive differences between Warburg's method of cultural science and Cassirer's philosophy of culture. Blumenberg criticizes Cassirer's concept for clinging to the hope that it should be possible to compile a complete and conclusive list of all symbolic forms, analogous to Kant's table of categories:

> In spite of all the affirmations of the autonomous quality of this symbolic system of forms [i.e. myth], it remains, for Cassirer, something that has been overcome [...] My opinion, in contrast to this, is that in order to perceive myth's genuine quality as an accomplishment one would have to describe it from the point of view of its *terminus a quo* [limit away from which the process is directed]. (Blumenberg 1985: 168, original emphasis)

Therefore, according to Blumenberg, Cassirer's "ideas of the kind that seek to promote 'the Education of [Humankind]'[14] defend the meaning of history at

---

13   For a comprehensive discussion of Blumenberg's theory of myth, cf. Nicholls 2015; Ifergan 2016; Ifergan 2023. Likewise, one of Warburg's main research interests was ancient astrology and its afterlife in the age of the Reformation and the Peasants' Wars through to the war superstitions of the First World War, cf. McEwan 2006; Newman 2008.

14   The 2022 translation of Blumenberg's speech uses the expression "Human Race" instead.

the expense of those born too early already to be 'well-brought-up'" (Blumenberg 2022: 220).[15]

The importance of Cassirer for Warburg and vice versa is beyond question and will not be discussed here. However, Blumenberg's hasty conflation of the projects of the cultural philosopher and the cultural scientist is surprising, not only in view of the differences between their anthropological and cultural-historical approaches, but also in view of the similarities that exist between Warburg and Blumenberg himself.

In fact, for Warburg, myth was by no means a system of thought that could be overcome or brought to an end, as shown by one of his amusing and self-reflexive bon mots, which is preserved in a posthumous collection of proverbs entitled *Warburgisms*: "Give me this day my daily illusion!"[16] (Warburg 1905–1970: 10) Already here it becomes clear that Warburg was just as aware of the necessity to clarify the historical and psychological conditions of the emergence of mythical interpretations of the world as he was of the impossibility of dispensing with mythical thinking if one was to succeed in gaining intellectual distance. Warburg coined the neologism *"Denkraumschöpfung"* (quoted in: Wedepohl 2014: 47) for this, which could be translated as "creation of the conceptual space" or "thinking space."

The impossibility of having the world as a whole, so to speak, was captured by Warburg in the figure of the pendulum of consciousness, always swinging back and forth between the poles of myth and logos, "oscillating between the religious and the mathematical world view"[17] (Warburg 2017: A2). The phobic energies could only ever be reconciled temporarily; reason, rationality, and contemplation had to be fought for again and again – a program that is closely related to Blumenberg's concept of the "work on myth" as an "endless task" (Blumenberg 1985: 164) that could never be brought to an end: "The boundary line between myth and logos is imaginary and does not obviate the need to inquire about the logos of myth in the process of working free of the absolutism of reality. Math in itself is a piece of high-carat 'work of logos.'" (ibid: 12)

---

15   The question of the validity of Blumenberg's verdict in view of Cassirer's later writings such as "Judaism and the Modern Political Myths" (1944) or *The Myth of the State* (1946) cannot be pursued here.

16   "Meine tägliche Illusion gib mir heute!"

17   "[...] zwischen religiöser und mathematischer Weltanschauung schwankend" (Warburg 2012: 3).

The two thinkers share the diagnosis that the paradoxical relationship between myth and logos cannot be rationalized as a linear history of progress or decay; rather, it is necessary to focus on the different interpretations of the world humans construct and transmit in order to make plausible and legitimize their own systems of belief and knowledge. It should be pointed out here that for Warburg, antisemitism – the irrational and hostile exclusion of Jews and Judaism as something alien to European or German culture – was a clear and incriminating symptom that there could be no talk of steady progress towards reason and rationality in the process of European civilization (cf. Schoell-Glass 2008). Thus, Warburg deliberately spoke of the "attempt at self-education of European humankind"[18] (quoted in: Bauerle-Willert 1988: 4), a creative endeavor that had to be taken up again and again and was always in danger of failing.

Metaphor and Pathos Formula

Blumenberg's use of Warburgian concepts, such as that of "afterlife," which he refers to in "Wirklichkeitsbegriff und Wirkungspotential des Mythos" to characterize the "secularization of Christianity," as well as his reference to the "afterlife of ancient mythology" (Blumenberg 1971: 27), shows that he was certainly aware of Warburg's work. This becomes even clearer in *Lebenszeit und Weltzeit* when he uses Warburg's concept of the "pathos formula" (*Pathosformel*) to describe specific forms of "absolute metaphors" – in this case the metaphor of the "infinite task" (Blumenberg 1986: 359).

In the context of his metaphorological work, Blumenberg uses the term to describe affect-laden special cases of concepts of totality, problematic ideas or figures of thought, such as "change of consciousness" (*Bewusstseinswandel*), "life," or "zeitgeist." On the latter, he says in *Begriffe in Geschichten*:

Zeitgeist research should not investigate what zeitgeists contain and demand to receive, not to say: infiltrate or impose; it should describe *how* zeitgeist-ness (*Zeitgeistigkeit*) exercises its dominance, through which transmission channels it induces itself, how it achieves devotion and frowns upon

---

18 "Selbsterziehungsversuch des europäischen Menschengeschlechts." Like Blumenberg and Cassirer, Warburg also refers to Gotthold Ephraim Lessing's *Die Erziehung des Menschengeschlechts* (1780).

aversions. The gestures and gesticulations of submission, the rituals and ceremonies of the profession of irresistibility, the "pathos formulae" of their conformities would be the subject of research.[19] (Blumenberg 1998: 248, original emphasis)

Anyone who is even superficially familiar with Warburg will immediately recognize here the familiar vocabulary: In Warburg's sense, "pathos formulae" are "ancient superlatives of the language of gestures," i.e. manifestations of the greatest sufferings and passions, of extreme physical or psychological experiences, which have been both imprinted and expressed in images. As artistic expressions, they have a calming potential, because they capture the overwhelming emotions in images; at the same time, they possess a tremendous inciting potency, because as "formulae" they can be revived and semantically recast in different constellations and for different purposes at any given time, which is particularly dangerous if the historical transformation processes that these images have already undergone remain unknown or unconscious. In Warburg's words: "Only contact with time causes polarization," i.e. the "incitement" to violence or a calming of the emotions. "This can lead to the radical reversal (inversion) of the true ancient sense."[20] (quoted in Raulff 2003: 136)

The prime example of this "inversion" is Warburg's favorite pathos formula, the nymph or Ninfa, who appeared in antiquity as a raging, bloodthirsty maenad and was recast since the Renaissance as a mourning Mary Magdalene under the cross, a dancing muse, or as an allegory of Fortuna, always keeping the same gestures and physical expressions but with radically transformed meaning (cf. Baert 2014).

Another of Warburg's examples that illustrates the threatening potential of such preconceived image formulae is the political instrumentalization of ancient Roman symbols of power, the *fasces*, as party insignia of Mussolini's Na-

---

19 "Zeitgeistforschung sollte nicht untersuchen, was Zeitgeister enthalten und zu rezipieren aufgeben, um nicht zu sagen: infiltrieren oder oktroyieren; sie sollte beschreiben, *wie* Zeitgeistigkeit ihre Dominanz ausübt, auf welchen Übertragungswegen sie sich induziert, wie sie Zuwendungen bewirkt und Abwendungen verpönt. Die Gebärden und Gesten der Unterwerfung, die Rituale und Zeremonien der Bekundung von Unwiderstehlichkeit, die 'Pathosformeln ihrer Konformitäten wären das Thema der Erforschung" (transl. ER).

20 "Erst der Kontakt mit der Zeit bewirkt Polarisation. Diese kann zur radikalen Umkehr (Inversion) des echten antiken Sinns führen."

tional Fascist Party. On this, Warburg's diary entry of December 31, 1926 reads: "It can be seen how the sovereign insignia's sublime antique style is replaced by the emblem of the inner dynamic of market value. Antiquity as a brand (*fasces*) leads to the revelation of the schizophrenic power mania in Italy."[21] (Warburg 2007: 39)

Warburg understood "pathos formulae", with their uncanny emotional charge and their readoption for different expressive needs, as symptoms of instances of unresolved psychological crisis, as windows into the "souterrain of psychic life"[22] (Warburg 1964/65: fol. 25). He traced their wanderings and transformations in the process of European civilization in order to expose the problematic, irrational parts of the conceptualization of national identity and history up to his own time. In this way, his agenda comes remarkably close to Blumenberg's call to question the "how" of their dominance and transmission:

> Metaphors can first of all be *leftover elements*, rudiments of the path *from mythos to logos*. [...] Even absolute metaphors therefore have a *history*. They have history in a more radical sense than concepts, for the historical transformation of metaphor brings to light the metakinetics of the historical horizon of meaning and ways of seeing within which concepts undergo their modifications. [...] [M]etaphorology seeks to burrow down to the substructure of thought, the underground, the nutrient solution of systematic crystallizations, but it also aims to show with what "courage" the mind preempts itself in its images and how its history is projected in the courage of its conjectures. (Blumenberg 2020: 173; 176)

Metaphorology and Mnemosyne

Similarities between the two can also be found in their methodological approaches. For example, there are parallels in the way Blumenberg traces the changing meanings of the metaphor of the shipwreck in different contexts, epochs, and genres, while retaining its fundamental structure in *Shipwreck with Spectator* (Blumenberg 1996), and Warburg's *Bilderatlas Mnemosyne* (Warburg 2012), which showcases images from different artists and eras as variations on

---

21   "Es läßt sich zeigen, wie der erhabene antike Stil des Hoheitszeichens ersetzt wird durch das Sinnbild der Eigendynamik des Verkehrswerthes. Die Antike als Marke (fasces) führt in Italien zur Offenbarung des schizophrenen Machtfimmels."

22   "[...] das Souterrain des Seelenlebens [...]."

specific pathos formulae. Warburg constantly rearranged his material from different artists, countries, and genres on large canvases in order to sharpen the eye for the deviating details and the transformations that the images had undergone on their wanderings.

Both approaches could be described as montages, as constellations that are based on a nonconceptual logic of similarity. Transformations and continuities across epochs are revealed but without abstracting from the concrete individual case or turning it into a mere intermediate step in a teleological narrative. Thus, both projects – Blumenberg's metaphorology and Warburg's Mnemosyne – remain necessarily and programmatically unfinished:[23]

> Common to all affinities to myth is the fact that they do not make one believe or even allow one to believe that anything could have been definitely "come through" in the history of mankind, however often people believed they had put it behind them. [...] we have learned to regard "overcomings" of this and that with mistrust, especially since the conjecture, or the suspicion, of latencies has arisen. We are acquainted with regressions to early states, with primitivisms, barbarisms, brutalisms, atavisms. (Blumenberg 1985: 52)

Thus, the awareness of the limits of conceptuality, of the irrational parts of all human histories of the world and the recognition that the assumption of the possibility of a purely rational explanation of the world is itself mythological, can help to protect against ideologization and totalitarian systems of thought. In his speech on Cassirer, Blumenberg emphasizes the provisional nature of all history:

> This ethos, so proper to the historian, denies that any present state might ever be something like the goal of history or the preferred means by which such a goal might be approached [...]. And we are better off for it, for there being no goal to history preserves us from remaining in 'anticipation' of such a goal, of being a means subservient to its fulfilment. (Blumenberg 2022: 220)

With this clear rejection of a teleology of history and its focus on a purely chronological sequence, Blumenberg not only pleads for an appreciation of the remote and the marginal, but also repeats the credo of Warburg's cultural science: an emphatic commitment to a principle of the provisional, and thus

---

23 On Blumenberg's metaphorology, cf. Ifergan 2015; Moyn 2000.

a mode of interpretation that does not seek the original text or the archetype, but understands each individual phenomenon as a symptom of a processing that has already taken place. Instead of linear historiography, Warburg considered the work of the cultural historian to be essentially one of continuous commentary, the telling of symptom histories. Thus, on antiquity and its persisting influence, he said: "This history should be told fairytale-like, a ghost story for fully grown-ups."[24] (Warburg 1925–1929: fol. 3)

Memoria and Afterlife

History invokes another field where Blumenberg and Warburg meet, that of memory. Mnemosyne, the patron goddess of memory and mother of the Muses, was not only the title of Warburg's *Bilderatlas* and the motto of his library, but also lay at the heart of the ethical orientation of his method of cultural science. In his words: "In the KBW, 'Mnemosyne' and 'Sophrosyne' should find the cult of silent readers."[25] (Warburg 1926) Self-cognition, contemplation, and prudence could only be achieved by remembering one's own prehistory, by preserving the memory of the painful attempts at orientation of previous generations and by locating oneself in the process of cultural history. Only through such a continuous work of remembrance could "the treasure trove of humanity's suffering become a humane possession"[26] (quoted in: Warnke 1980: 113), i.e. the experience of suffering in human history be understood in its humane dimension and retain "ethical and practical value for those who come after us"[27] (Warburg 1915). This ethical agenda was rooted in the historical experience of Judaism, not only in its rich culture and traditions developed in the millennia-long struggle for orientation in the cosmos and the world, but also in the continuing experience of discrimination and violent expulsion and the challenge of coming to terms with it culturally and psychologically, or, as Warburg put it: "We have been patients of world history for 2000 years longer."[28] (quoted in Bing 1992: 464)

---

24 "Vom Einfluss der Antike. Diese Geschichte ist märchenhaft to vertellen, Gespenster-geschichte für ganz Erwachsene."
25 "'Mnemosyne' und 'Sophrosyne' sollen in der K.B.W. [...] den Kult stiller Leser finden."
26 "Der Leidschatz der Menschheit wird humaner Besitz."
27 "[...] für die Nachfolger ethischen und praktischen Wert behält."
28 "Wir sind eben schon 2000 Jahre länger Patienten der Weltgeschichte gewesen."

In the context of the "humanity of myth" (Blumenberg 1971: 33), Blumenberg also refers to "memoria" as a remembering reinterpretation and speaks of memory itself as work on myth, as an ongoing reception and transformation of great mythical narratives in specific historical-cultural contexts. Myths can provide orientation and comfort by fulfilling time- and situation-specific plausibility functions through their mutability. At the same time, for both Blumenberg and Warburg, they are grounded in the basic anthropological disposition, which accounts for their enormous power of attraction and connectivity for the specific contexts, as Blumenberg explains in *Work on Myth*:

> The fundamental patterns of myths are simply so sharply defined [*prägnant*], so valid, so binding, so gripping in every sense, that they convince again and again and still present themselves as the most useful material for any search for how matters stand, on a basic level, with human existence. (Blumenberg 1985: 150, original emphasis)

Warburg points to the same basic structure of mythical world-reference, which has its roots in the "torturing questions on the why and wherefore of things"[29] (Warburg 1938/1939: 291) that impose themselves on every individual, every generation everywhere, plunging people time and again into the "tragic struggle between imagination and logic"[30] (quoted in: Bauerle-Willert 2001: 249). Warburg's anthropological concept is echoed in Blumenberg's statement that "absolute metaphors 'answer' the supposedly naïve, in principle unanswerable questions whose relevance lies quite simply in the fact that they cannot be brushed aside, since we do not *pose* them ourselves but find them already *posed* in the ground of our existence" (Blumenberg 2010: 14, original emphasis).

In the face of existential questions, images and metaphors function as a source of consolation because they provide orientation and self-assertion. For Warburg, the prime example of this was Dürer's *Melencolia I*, because the engraving gives expression to the state of indecision between the modern claim to self-reliant subjectivity and the unbroken power of magic and superstition, thereby having a consoling effect: "The truly creative act – that which gives [it] its consoling, humanistic message of liberation from the fear of Saturn – can be

---

29   "Die quälende Frage nach dem Warum der Dinge" (Warburg 2018: 91).
30   "Der tragische Kampf zwischen Phantasie und Logik."

understood only if we recognize that the artist has taken a magical and mythical logic and made it spiritual and intellectual."[31] (Warburg 1999a: 644)

Thus, every age has its myths and remains dependent on them. In order to escape the rigidity of ideologization and dogmatization – this would be, in Blumenberg's words, "the work of myth" (*Arbeit des Mythos*) – their stories would have to be constantly rewritten and retold. For Warburg, this involves an element of personal responsibility towards tradition: How the ancient heritage is received and used does not depend on any fixed meaning of the "pathos formulae," but "on the subjective character of those who live after"[32] (Warburg 2016: 101). In this respect, as Warburg writes somewhat aphoristically: "Every age has the Renaissance of antiquity that it deserves."[33] (ibid: 101)

The agenda of his critical cultural studies was to counter the remythicizations of his time, which he registered with horror, with a different understanding of antiquity, its heritage, and its afterlife. Warburg wanted to counteract the nationalist myths and the irrational racist and antisemitic outbreaks of violence that went hand in hand with them by programmatically enlightening the transmission history of the ideologically used and unconsciously handed down image formulae, since only insight into one's own prehistory could "help them gain clarity about the mental place, in which they find themselves"[34] (Warburg 1929). For this specific mode of historical consciousness, Warburg coined the expression afterlife (*Nachleben*): the memory of the history of suffering of previous generations and its commemoration in the collective memory and in art as an "organ of social memory"[35] (Warburg 1999b: 715). For all their differences, in this Warburg echoes Blumenberg's call to make "a claim to the respect of those who are yet to come – by extending that respect to those who preceded us" (Blumenberg 2022: 222).

---

31 "Der recht eigentlich schöpferische Akt, der Dürer's 'Melencolia I' zum humanistischen Trostblatt wider Saturnfürchtigkeit macht, kann erst begriffen werden, wenn man diese magische Mythologik als eigentliches Objekt der künstlerisch-vergeistigenden Umformung erkennt" (Warburg 1998a: 528).

32 "[...] der subjektive Charakter der Nachlebenden [...]."

33 "Jede Zeit hat die Renaissance der Antike, die sie verdient."

34 "[...] dass historisches Bewusstsein [...] ihnen zur Klarheit über den seelischen Ort verhelfen kann, an dem sie sich befinden [...]."

35 "[...] als soziales Erinnerungsorgan [...]" (Warburg 1998b: 586).

Conclusion

I will conclude with Blumenberg's only explicit engagement with Warburg that I know of, the miniature "Geschmacksurteil" ("Judgment of taste"), which first appeared in the *Frankfurter Allgemeine Zeitung* in March 1990 and was later published in *Begriffe in Geschichten*.[36] In his critique of the judgment of taste, this at first glance meaningless nobilization of subjective pleasure, Blumenberg comes to speak of the postage stamp and states: "Those who are sure of their taste rarely get excited when it comes to the most widely used object of trivial art. The 'recipients' silent adhesion has a discouraging effect." (Blumenberg 1998: 69)

As a "lone example of what is also possible," he cites Aby Warburg and his keen sensitivity to the impact of trivial everyday images. Warburg recognized the postage stamp, this "image vehicle"[37] (Warburg 2017: D6), as the first truly global image medium, as an act of world appropriation in miniature format, whose visual language and symbolism involuntarily provided a direct insight into the intentions and self-imaginations of its creator. "Precisely at the turn of the century, the mythological figure of Germania appeared serially on the stamps of the German Empire," Blumenberg says, and was thus sent out all over the world as an emblem of German sovereignty. Aby Warburg's reaction to the stamp was drastic; his indignant statement that this Germania looked like a costumed cook, is, in Blumenberg's view "a demonstration of utmost secureness in matters of taste" (Blumenberg 1998: 69).

The fact that the lady who posed for the stamp was not a cook, but an actress, does not detract from Warburg's intuition. His eye unmasked the theatrical pose aiming to establish itself as a symbol of national identity and the equally bland and pompous nationalistic self-dramatization revealed in it; elsewhere, Warburg also spoke of "German glory-exhibitionism under state protection"[38] (Warburg 1928). For Blumenberg, the anecdote not only confirmed Warburg's judgment of taste, but also the "triumph" of his method, which allowed him to recognize the stamp as a "metaphor of singular precision for an epoch that presents itself in a seemingly unspecific 'label'" (Blumenberg 1998: 69).

---

36   The following translations from "Geschmacksurteil" are my own.

37   "Bilderfahrzeug" (Warburg 2012: 5).

38   "[…] deutscher Herrlichkeits-Exhibitionismus unter staatlichem Schutz […]."

Perhaps Blumenberg's unerring grasp of the core of Warburg's cultural science is rooted in the fact that they were working on the same problem from different angles and at different times – and he therefore perceived the other's work as, in Warburg's words, "a knocking on the other side of the tunnel"[39] (Warburg 1926).

Archival Sources

The following sources are held in the *Warburg Institute Archive* (WIA), which also owns the copyright for the letters and notes quoted in this article.

Family Correspondence (FC)
General Correspondence (GC)
(Warburg 1915): WIA, FC, Aby Warburg an Max Warburg, 03.12.1915.
(Warburg 1926): WIA, GF, Aby Warburg an Johannes Geffcken, 16.01.1926.
(Warburg 1928): WIA, FC, Aby Warburg to Max Warburg, 13.06.1928.
(Warburg 1929): WIA, FC, Aby Warburg to Gisela Warburg vom 14.05.1929.
(Warburg 1905–1970): WIA.III.1.7.2.4.4., Max Adolph Warburg (1905–1970s), exercise book, "Warburgismen," 47 fols.
(Warburg 1925–1929): WIA.III.102.3.2. Mnemosyne Notes 1925–1929, Posthumes Typoskript von 102.3.1. Mnemosyne. Grundbegriffe I., 1929, 84 fols.
(Warburg 1964/65): WIA, III.1.7.2.4.3.2.2.3. Max Adolph Warburg, c. 1964–65, Notebook III, MS, 47 fols.

Bibliography

Baert, Barbara (2014): Nymph: Motif, Phantom, Affect, a Contribution to the Study of Aby Warburg 1866–1929 [Studies in Iconology, 1], Leuven: Peeters.
Bahnsen, Uwe (2012): "Der Mann, der Lübeck vor den Bomben bewahrte." In: Welt, March 25, 2012 (https://www.welt.de/regionales/hamburg/article119322471/Der-Mann-der-Luebeck-vor-den-Bomben-bewahrte.html).
Bauerle-Willert, Dorothée (1988): Gespenstergeschichten für ganz Erwachsene. Ein Kommentar zu Aby Warburgs Bilderatlas Mnemosyne [Kunstgeschichte: Form und Interesse, Bd. 15], Münster: Lit.

39　"[…] ich hörte ihn auf der anderen Seite des Tunnels klopfen." Warburg was referring to his friend and colleague, the historian of astrology and astronomy Franz Boll.

Bauerle-Willert, Dorothée (2001): "Aby Warburgs Daimonium. Die Kulturwissenschaftliche Bibliothek." In: Susanne Bieri/Walther Fuchs (eds.), Bibliotheken Bauen. Tradition und Vision, Basel/Boston/Berlin: Birkhäuser, pp. 237–269.

Bing, Gertrud (1992 [1958]): "Aby M. Warburg." In: Dieter Wuttke (ed.), Aby Warburg, Ausgewählte Schriften und Würdigungen [Saecula Spiritalia 1], Baden-Baden: Körner, pp. 455–464.

Blumenberg, Hans (1971): "Wirklichkeitsbegriff und Wirkungspotential des Mythos." In: Manfred Fuhrmann (ed.), Terror und Spiel. Probleme der Mythenrezeption [Poetik und Hermeneutik, 4], Munich: Fink, pp. 11–66.

Blumenberg, Hans (1979): Arbeit am Mythos, Frankfurt a.M.: Suhrkamp.

Blumenberg, Hans (1985 [1979]): Work on Myth, transl. by Robert M. Wallace, Cambridge, MA/London: MIT Press.

Blumenberg, Hans (1986): Lebenszeit und Weltzeit, Frankfurt a.M.: Suhrkamp.

Blumenberg, Hans (1996 [1979]): Shipwreck with Spectator. Paradigm of a Metaphor for Existence, transl. by Steven Rendall, Cambridge, MA/London: MIT Press.

Blumenberg, Hans (1998): Begriffe in Geschichten, Frankfurt a.M.: Suhrkamp.

Blumenberg, Hans (2010 [1960]): Paradigms for a Metaphorology, transl. by Robert Savage [signale: Modern German Letters, Cultures, and Thought], Ithaca, NY: Cornell University Press/Cornell University Library.

Blumenberg, Hans (2020 [1960]): "Introduction to Paradigms of a Metaphorology." In: Hannes Bajohr et al. (eds.), History, Metaphors, Fables. A Hans Blumenberg Reader, transl. by Hannes Bajohr/Florian Fuchs/Joe Paul Kroll, Ithaca, NY/London: Cornell University Press, pp. 170–176.

Blumenberg, Hans (2022 [1974]): "In memory of Ernst Cassirer: Speech Delivered in Acceptance of the Kuno Fischer Prize of the University of Heidelberg, 1974." In: New German Critique 145, 49/1, pp. 215–224.

Cassirer, Ernst (1923–1929): Philosophie der symbolischen Formen I-III, Berlin: Bruno Cassirer.

Cassirer, Ernst (1944): "Judaism and the Modern Political Myths." In: Contemporary Jewish Record 7, pp. 115–126.

Cassirer Ernst (1946): The Myth of the State, New Haven, CT: Yale University Press.

Diers, Michael (1995): "Warburg and the Warburgian Tradition of Cultural History." In: New German Critique 65 (Spring-Summer), pp. 59–73.

Fehrenbach, Frank (2010): "'Du lebst und thust mir nichts' Aby Warburg und die Lebendigkeit der Kunst." In: Hartmut Böhme/Johannes Endres (eds.), Der

Code der Leidenschaften. Fetischismus in den Künsten, Paderborn: Fink/Brill, pp. 124–145.

Gombrich, Ernst (1970): Aby Warburg: An Intellectual Biography, Chicago: University of Chicago Press.

Ifergan, Pini (2015): "Hans Blumenberg's Philosophical Project: Metaphorology as Anthropology." In: Continental Philosophy Review 48, pp. 359–77.

Ifergan, Pini (2016): "Reading Hans Blumenberg's Work on Myth." In: Iyyun: The Jerusalem Philosophical Quarterly 65, pp. 55–72.

Ifergan, Pini (2023): "Blumenberg: On Bringing Myth to an End." In: History of European Ideas 49/8, pp. 1236–1251.

Johnson, Christopher D. (2012): Memory, Metaphor, and Aby Warburg's Atlas of Images, Ithaca, NY: Cornell University Press.

Johnson, Christopher D./Wedepohl, Claudia (2012): "From Arsenal to the Laboratory." In: West 86th. A Journal of Decorative Design, History and Material Culture 19/1 (Spring-Summer), pp. 106–124.

Kabel, Hanno (2017): "Eine Tafel für den Retter Lübecks." In: Lübecker Nachrichten, June 16, 2017 (https://www.ln-online.de/lokales/luebeck/eine-tafel-fuer-den-retter-luebecks-CR4QMMWIYV4T4DIHIHF2UAS5AY.html).

Levine, Emily J. (2013): Dreamland of Humanists. Warburg, Cassirer, Panofsky, and the Hamburg School, Chicago/London: University of Chicago Press.

Levine, Emily J. (2015): "Aby Warburg and Weimar Jewish Culture: Navigating Normative Narratives, Counternarratives, and Historical Context." In: Steven Aschheim/Vivian Liska (eds.), The German-Jewish Experience Revisited, Berlin/Boston: De Gruyter, pp. 117–134.

McEwan, Dorothea (2004): Wanderstraßen der Kultur. Die Aby Warburg – Fritz Saxl Korrespondenz 1920–1929, Munich/Hamburg: Dölling und Galitz.

McEwan, Dorothea (2006): "Aby Warburg's (1866–1929) Dots and Lines. Mapping the Diffusion of Astrological Motifs in Art History." In: German Review 29, pp. 243–268.

Moyn, Samuel (2000): "Metaphorically Speaking: Hans Blumenberg, Giambattista Vico, and the Problem of Origins." In: Qui Parle 12, pp. 55–76.

Newman, Jane O. (2008): "Luther's Birthday. Aby Warburg, Albrecht Dürer, and Early Modern Media in the Age of Modern War." In: Daphnis 37, pp. 79–110.

Nicholls, Angus (2015): Myth and the Human Sciences. Hans Blumenberg's Theory of Myth [Theorists of Myth 16], New York/London: Routledge.

Pollock, Griselda (2016): "Aby Warburg (1866–1929): 'Thinking Jewish' in Modernity." In: Jacques Picard et al. (eds.), Makers of Jewish Modernity. Thinkers,

140 Philosophy and Jewish Thought

Artists, Leaders, and the Worlds They Made, Princeton, NJ/Oxford: Princeton University Press, pp. 108–125.

Raulff, Ulrich (2003): "Der Teufelsmut der Juden." In: id., Wilde Energien. Vier Versuche zu Aby Warburg, Göttingen: Wallstein, pp. 117–150.

Rinner, Ellen (2022): "'Von der kultisch erheischten Hingabe an das geschaffene Idolon'. Aby Warburgs Kulturwissenschaft als Idologiekritik." In: Benjamino Fortis (ed.), Bild und Idol. Perspektiven aus Philosophie und jüdischem Denken, Frankfurt a.M.: Peter Lang, pp. 75–102.

Saxl, Fritz (2023 [1923]): "Die Bibliothek Warburg und ihr Ziel." In: Ernst Müller/Barbara Picht (eds.), Vorträge der Bibliothek Warburg. Das intellektuelle Netzwerk der kulturwissenschaftlichen Bibliothek Warburg, Göttingen: Wallstein, pp. 33–45.

Saxl, Fritz (1996 [1943–1944]): "Die Geschichte der Bibliothek Aby Warburgs (1886–1944)." In: Aby Warburg, Ausgewählte Schriften und Würdigungen, ed. by Dieter Wuttke, Baden-Baden: Körner, pp. 331–334.

Saxl, Fritz (1970 [1943–1944]): "The History of Warburg's Library 1886–1994." In: Ernst Gombrich, Aby Warburg: An Intellectual Biography, Chicago: University of Chicago Press, pp. 325–338.

Schoell-Glass, Charlotte (2008 [1998]): Aby Warburg and Anti-Semitism. Political Perspectives on Images and Culture, Detroit: Wayne State University Press.

Treml, Martin/Meyer, Thomas (2006): "Kulturwissenschaft aus dem Geist des Judentums. Aby Warburgs Transformation der religiösen Tradition." In: Neue Zürcher Zeitung, December 10/11, 2005, pp. 67–68.

Warburg, Aby (1938/1939): "A Lecture on Serpent Ritual." In: Journal of the Warburg and Courtauld Institutes 2, pp. 277–292 (https://archiv.ub.uni-heidelberg.de/artdok/8387/1/Warburg_A_lecture_on_serpent_ritual_1938.pdf).

Warburg, Aby (1998a [1920]): "Heidnische-antike Weissagung in Wort und Bild zu Luthers Zeiten." In: id., Gesammelte Schriften, I.2: Die Erneuerung der heidnischen Antike. Kulturwissenschaftliche Beiträge zur Geschichte der europäischen Renaissance, ed. by Horst Bredekamp et al., Berlin: Akademie, pp. 487–558.

Warburg, Aby (1998b [1910]): "Die Wandbilder im Hamburgischen Rathaussaale." In: id., Gesammelte Schriften, I.2: Die Erneuerung der heidnischen Antike. Kulturwissenschaftliche Beiträge zur Geschichte der europäischen Renaissance, ed. by Horst Bredekamp et al., Berlin: Akademie, pp. 579–587.

Warburg, Aby (1999a [1920]), "Pagan-Antique Prophecy in Words and Images in the Age of Luther." In: id., The Renewal of Pagan Antiquity, transl. by David

Britt, Los Angeles: The Getty Research Institute for the History of Art and the Humanities, pp. 597–697.

Warburg, Aby (1999b [1910]): "The Mural Paintings in Hamburg City Hall." In: id., The Renewal of Pagan Antiquity, transl. by David Britt, Los Angeles: The Getty Research Institute for the History of Art and the Humanities, pp. 711–716.

Warburg, Aby (2007): Gesammelte Schriften, VII: Tagebuch der Kulturwissenschaftlichen Bibliothek, ed. by Karen Michels/Charlotte Schoell-Glass, Berlin: Akademie.

Warburg, Aby (2012): Gesammelte Schriften, II.1: Der Bilderatlas Mnemosyne, ed. by Martin Warnke et al., Berlin: Akademie.

Warburg, Aby (2016): "Italienische Antike im Zeitalter Rembrandts." In: id. Nachhall der Antike. Aby Warburg. Zwei Untersuchungen, vorgestellt von Pablo Schneider, Zürich: diaphanes, pp. 69–101.

Warburg, Aby (2017 [1929]): "Mnemosyne Altas. Introduction." In: Engramma, February 142, transl. by Matthew Rampley (http://www.engramma.it/eOS/index.php?id_articolo=3082).

Warburg, Aby (2018): "Bilder aus dem Gebiet der Pueblo-Indianer in Nord-Amerika, 1923." In: id.Gesammelte Werke, III.2: Bilder aus dem Gebiet der Pueblo-Indianer in Nord-Amerika. Vorträge und Fotographien, ed. by Uwe Fleckner, Berlin: Akademie, pp. 65–104.

Warburg Spinelli, Ingrid (1990): Die Dringlichkeit des Mitleids und die Einsamkeit, nein zu sagen, Hamburg: Dölling und Galitz.

Warnke, Martin (1980): "Der Leidschatz der Menschheit wird humaner Besitz." In: Werner Hofmann/Georg Syamken/Martin Warnke, Die Menschenrechte des Auges. Über Aby Warburg, Frankfurt a.M.: Europäische Verlagsanstalt, pp. 113–189.

Wedepohl, Claudia (2014): "Pathos – Polarität – Distanz – Denkraum." In: Martin Treml et al. (eds.), Warburgs Denkraum. Formen, Motive, Materialien [= Trajekte], München: Fink, pp. 17–51.

"One Ought to Pray, Day and Night, for the Thousands": Etty Hillesum's Approach to Prayer and Hasidic Thought

Silvia Richter

Etty (Esther) Hillesum's (1914–1943)[1] diaries, published in the Netherlands for the first time in 1981, have since been translated into 18 languages and received worldwide attention. Nevertheless, the academic study of her thought is still far from exhausted. In particular, the influence of Jewish thought on her work has been little studied. One reason for this is the fact that, apart from the Bible, she herself does not cite any explicitly Jewish sources, but rather Rilke, Augustine, and Dostoevsky, whose influence has been well studied (cf. Woodhouse 2017; Grimmelikhuizen 2016; Gérard 2007; Bercken 2010). In contrast to comparisons between her work and that of other Jewish thinkers – such as Martin Buber and Emmanuel Levinas (cf. Coetsier 2014) – this chapter, based on the quoted sources Rilke and Augustine, would like to direct special attention to Hasidic concepts that up to now have not been associated with Etty Hillesum's spirituality and her approach to prayer. This new theoretical approach reveals a hitherto undiscovered aspect between Jewish thought and Etty Hillesum's philosophical and spiritual quest.

Although at first glance prayer does not play a prominent role in her diaries – between the descriptions of everyday life under the occupation, her daily routine with its worries and hardships, her impressions of reading and reflections on her friends – it becomes more and more important over time. Through the pages of her diaries and letters, a great spiritual quest shines through, which finds expression both in her writing and in her life. However, it is obvious that Etty Hillesum is not a "Jewish thinker" in the classical sense. She came from an

---

1   I am indebted to Prof. Daniel Krochmalnik (School of Jewish Theology, University of Potsdam), who first introduced me to the life and work of Etty Hillesum, for his inspiring discussions and comments on this work at various stages.

assimilated household and grew up far from practicing Judaism, although her paternal grandfather played an active role in the Amsterdam Jewish community (Koelemeijer 2022: 48–49). At school, she also studied Hebrew and occasionally "attended the meetings of a Zionist young people's group in Deventer" (Smelik 2018: 25); a recently published study highlights her interests and involvement in communist circles as well (cf. Beuker 2020). And yet, driven by her own spiritual search and the circumstances of the time, she increasingly found her way to an individual approach to prayer and even to a personal dialog with God. Similar to Augustine in his "Confessions," who consistently addresses God in the second person singular ("Great art *Thou*, O Lord [...]," cf. Augustine, Book 1, I.1., emphasis added), Etty also addresses God directly. Furthermore, she sees herself inspired by Augustine not only in style, but also in his spiritual attitude, as she points out on October 9, 1942: "I am going to read Saint Augustine again. He is so austere and so fervent. And so full of simple devotion in his love letters to God. Truly those are the only love letters one ought to write: *love letters to God.*" (Hillesum 2014: 880, emphasis added)

In order to find access to God, however, she must first discover a way to access her inner herself and to find an inner peace. This is one of the reasons why Etty Hillesum started writing a diary in the first place: on March 9, 1941, most likely on the advice of her therapist – the German-Jewish emigrant Julius Spier (1887–1942), a psychoanalyst trained by C.G. Jung – Etty Hillesum took up the practice of writing a diary, which she would continue from then on (Pleshoyano 2010: 45). Her diaries start with a letter written in German to "Lieber Herr S.!" (Hillesum 2014: 1) – also in the following, Spier will only ever be addressed as "S." – and also become a space for dialog with herself. Family life was chaotic and destabilizing for her (Woodhouse 2009: 6–13). As she came from a dysfunctional family that did not allow her to grow into a stable young woman, she sought refuge in writing, to have a focal point for her feelings and thoughts. Her pen became a compass that led her further and further inside herself. She expressed this using a term from Rilke's poetry ("*Weltinnenraum*," inner universe) at various points in her diary: "A few lines from *Es winkt zu Fühlung fast aus allen Dingen*: Durch alle Wesen reicht der *eine* Raum: Weltinnenraum. Die Vögel fliegen still durch uns hindurch. O, der ich wachsen will, ich seh hinaus, und *in* mir wächst der Baum." (Hillesum 2014: 444; cf. Rilke 2004: 878; Schrijvers 2018: 319)

The feeling of inwardness and, at the same time, a deep connection with the whole environment, especially with nature, is reflected from very early on in her diary. After the first few months of writing, she notes her turn to what she calls a kind of "quiet hour." Every morning, she wants to withdraw from everything for a while to find her inner peace: "I think that I'll do it anyway: I'll 'turn inward' for half an hour each morning before work, and listen to my inner voice. Lose myself. You could also call it meditation. I am still a bit wary of that word. But anyway, why not? A quiet half-hour within yourself." (Hillesum 2014: 94) Nevertheless, she is aware that the desired calm does not come in the blink of an eye, as she points out: "It has to be learned. A lot of unimportant inner litter and bits and pieces have to be swept out first. Even a small head can be piled high inside with irrelevant distractions. [...] So let this be the aim of the meditation: to turn one's innermost being into a vast empty plain, with none of that treacherous undergrowth to impede the view. So that *something of 'God' can enter you*, just as if there is something of 'God' in Beethoven's Ninth. So that something of 'love' can enter you too." (ibid: 94, emphasis added)

This opening to transcendence and finding a conscious and intense focus for prayer is a central point of what is called *kavanah* in Jewish thought (cf. Enelow 1913; Krochmalnik 2023). To emphasize just a few nuances of this rich term, it can be translated, depending on the context, as "preparation, direction, intention, orientation, motivation, attention, concentration, meditation, introspection (inwardness)" (Krochmalnik 2023: 495). In fact, Maimonides is very strict regarding *kavanah* when it comes to prayer, as he points out: "Any prayer that is not [recited] with proper intention (*kavanah*) is not prayer." (Maimonides, Mishneh Torah, Hilchot Ahawa 4,15) It is therefore of great importance to prepare very carefully for prayer in order to make the body and mind receptive to it, as Louis Jacobs points out:

> Preparation (*hakhanah*, plural *hakhanot*, "preparations") for prayer occupies an important role in Hasidic life. Precisely because prayer had so important a role to play it should not be engaged in, taught the Hasidim, without eager anticipation beforehand. Prayer had to be preceded by a period of preparation during which the mind would be cleared of unworthy thoughts and the body cleansed of impurities. (Jacobs 1978: 46)

For Etty Hillesum, what is careful preparation for prayer in the Hasidic context was to find a gesture and attitude that made her *receptive* to prayer. One could say that for her the gesture was there even before the prayer: that is, first she found a form (kneeling) – and then the content (prayer). It is interesting to see that, coming from an assimilated household, she at first had no idea what it meant to pray: what happens when a person prays and how does it actually work? She did not hesitate to ask her mentor and therapist Julius Spier:

> [...] shameless and brazen as always, wanting to know everything there is to know, I asked, "What exactly do you say when you pray?" And he was suddenly overcome with embarrassment, this man who always has clear, glass-bright answers to all my most searching and intimate questions, and he said shyly: "That I cannot tell you. Not yet. Later." (Hillesum 2014: 294)

This did not, however, prevent Etty Hillesum from discovering her own personal approach to prayer. This happened, first, in finding a form that came suddenly, without her consciously looking for it. At the very beginning of her diary, on Sunday, March 16, 1941, we find a first reference to the gesture of kneeling and the feeling of peace that it gives her – a kind of unconscious, spontaneous healing from within: "As I sat there like that in the sun, I bowed my head unconsciously as if to take in even more of that new feeling for life. Suddenly I knew deep down how someone can sink impetuously to his knees and find peace there, his face hidden in his folded hands." (ibid: 42) At the end of the same year, on December 14, 1941, the gesture of kneeling is no longer just a random, spontaneous act, but becomes a regular habit and, moreover, something that she is forced to do, as she highlights:

> Last night, shortly before going to bed, I suddenly went down on my knees in the middle of this large room, between the steel chairs and the matting. Almost automatically. Forced to the ground *by something stronger than myself.* Some time ago I said to myself: "I am a kneeler in training." I was still embarrassed by this act, as intimate as gestures of love that cannot be put into words either, except by a poet. (ibid: 294, emphasis added)

It is interesting to mention in this context, that Simone Weil, only a few years earlier, had a very similar experience of being forced to kneel down, as she points out in a letter to her spiritual advisor Father Perrin:

> In 1937 I had two marvelous days at Assisi. There, alone in the little twelfth-century Romanesque chapel of Santa Maria degli Angeli, an incomparable marvel of purity where Saint Francis often used to pray, something stronger than I was compelled me for the first time in my life to go down on my knees. (Weil 2009: 26; cf. Bowie 1995)

For Etty Hillesum, however, the gesture of kneeling down is not something purely "spiritual," but it can rather be characterized as "bodily prayer" (*leibliches Beten*, cf. Bühler 2014), as she emphasizes on April 3, 1942: "It has become a gesture embedded in my body, needing to be expressed from time to time. And I remember: 'The girl who could not kneel,' and the rough coconut matting in the bathroom." (Hillesum 2014: 516) By "the girl who could not kneel," she actually means herself: she intended to give her inner experience and spiritual development a literary form (for example, a novel) when she had time for it one day and this was the intended title. This literary elaboration tragically did not come about due to her murder by the Nazis in November 1943 (cf. Clement 2019).

To come back to our question of what Etty Hillesum's act of kneeling has to do with Hasidic thought and why it is so important to emphasize this gesture: firstly, I believe it is the key to Etty Hillesum's personal approach to prayer, and secondly, it opens up two other aspects associated with Hasidic thought: the concept of *hitbodedut* (literally: seclusion, loneliness, isolation) of Rabbi Nachman of Bratzlav (1772–1810) and the individuality of personal belief that Hasidism emphasizes – an approach that has an echo in Etty Hillesum's spirituality. As she was well aware, kneeling is not particularly part of the Jewish religious tradition, and yet it gives her the strength she needs to get through difficult times, as she observes on October 10, 1942:

> I think that I can bear everything life and these times have in store for me. And when the turmoil becomes too great and I am completely at my wits' end, then I still have my folded hands and bended knee. A posture that is not handed down from generation to generation with us Jews. I have had to learn it the hard way. (Hillesum 2014: 880)

Kneeling in prayer provides her with a "safe space" to gather herself and build herself up. While the Jewish community in the Netherlands was exposed to increasing persecution and legal restrictions, Etty found refuge in her prayer. While the outer social space may increasingly disappear and dissolve, the inner space that prayer opens up for her becomes a wealth that no one can take away from her. She therefore compares prayer to a kind of portable "monastery cell" (*kloostercel*, cf. ibid: 583) into whose seclusion she can retreat when the outer world vanishes. With this in mind, she writes in her diary on May 18, 1942:

> The threat grows ever greater, and terror increases from day to day. I draw prayer round me like a dark protective wall, withdraw inside it as one might

into a convent cell and then step outside again, calmer and stronger and more collected again. Withdrawing into the closed cell of prayer is becoming an ever-greater reality for me as well as a necessity. That inner concentration erects high walls around me within which I can find my way back to myself, gather myself together into one whole, away from all distractions. I can imagine times to come when I shall stay on my knees for days on end waiting until the protective walls are strong enough to prevent my going to pieces altogether, my being lost and utterly devastated. (ibid: 584)

Although being alone and living in segregation is generally an ideal among mystics in various religious movements, the Bratzlaver Hasidim stress particularly the ideal of *hitbodedut*. This concept goes back to the work "Likkutei Moharan," written by the founder of the Bratzlav Hasidic movement, Rabbi Nachman (cf. Buber 1988), a great-grandson of the founder of Hasidic Judaism, the Baal Shem Tov (1698–1760). According to Rabbi Nachman,

> to be in solitude is a supreme advantage and the most important ideal. This means that a man sets aside at least an hour or more during which he is alone in a room or in the field so that he can converse with the Maker [one's Creator] in secret, entreating and pleading in many ways of grace and supplication, begging God to bring him near to His service in truth. (Jacobs 1976: 63)

One should address God in one's mother tongue and speak to him as we would to a friend. Thus, it is not an asymmetrical relationship, but rather one at eye level, just as Etty Hillesum addresses God in her diaries. It has been pointed out, however, that it is in a way a "very unsophisticated approach to prayer" (Jacobs 1976: 64). However, Rabbi Nachman is today considered one of the most influential Hasidic rabbis in history: "The interest in his works and the pilgrimages to his grave in Uman are only partial indicators of how influential he has become." (Leshem 2014: 59)

In my view, Rabbi Nachman's ideal of *hitbodedut* and the "meditative technique in which the Hasid engages in free dialogue with God in his own language" (Leshem 2014: 60; cf. Mark 2009: 131–147) shows clear parallels with Etty Hillesum's approach to God. The boundary that prayer erects around her as a shelter and refuge is, however, never a barrier to the outside world – on the contrary. Her isolation in prayer did not result in an existence in an ivory tower, but rather in a special turning towards others, something she described in her diaries using a particular term:

Hineinhorchen – I so wish I could find a Dutch equivalent for that German word. Truly, my life is one long hearkening unto myself and unto others, unto God. And if I say that I hearken, it is really God who hearkens inside me. The most essential and the deepest in me hearkening unto the most essential and deepest in the other. God to God. (Hillesum 2014: 830–832)

The inner dialog is thus not only expanded to the outer world, to nature and the fellow human being, but is actually acknowledging the *Shekhina* ("Divine Presence") in the world and in the relationship among men (Jacob 1978: 23; cf. Clement 2018).

Another aspect of Hasidism that I find strikingly echoed in Etty Hillesum's spirituality is that of the individuality of personal beliefs. Etty Hillesum did not care about religious authorities or how things were done according to the rules – she simply did them her way. It is precisely in this way that she remains so inspiring and groundbreaking for us today, as Patrick Woodhouse points out: "This makes her a woman for our time, when institutional religion is in decline and yet the hunger for authentic spirituality is more keenly felt than ever." (Woodhouse 2009: xiii) Regarding Hasidism, Martin Buber emphasized, especially in his work "The Way of Man According to the Teachings of Hasidism," the uniqueness of each individual human being, which results from the infinite richness of God's creation. This makes it impossible to prescribe a universally valid path to spirituality – everyone has to find their own way:

Rabbi Baer of Radoshitz once said to his teacher, the "Seer" of Lublin: "Show me one general way to the service of God." The zaddik replied: "It is impossible to tell men what way they should take. For one way to serve God is through learning, another through prayer, another through fasting, and still another through eating. Everyone should carefully observe what way his heart draws him to, and then choose this way with all his strength." (Buber 1967: 15)

In this sense, Etty Hillesum was aware that she had to find her own way and she called this her own "rhythm," as if there were a melody deep within us that is only drowned out by the noise of the outside world and that we have to find again in order to be able to live in harmony with it and with ourselves. On December 12, 1941 she wrote in her diary:

If only I listened to my own rhythm, and tried to live in accordance with it. Much of what I do is mere imitation, springs from a sense of duty or from preconceived notions of how people should behave. The only certainties about what is right and wrong are those that spring from sources deep inside oneself. (Hillesum 2014: 286)

In the same way that Buber highlights the uniqueness of spiritual beliefs, bound to every single human existence – "All men have access to God, but each man has a different access" (Buber 1967: 17) – Etty Hillesum sought and found her own personal prayer rhythm, her unique *nigun*, which, even in the transit camp Westerbork and in the face of death, tunes into the prayer of the whole world when one reads her dialog with God against the background of Hasidic spirituality: "Rabbi Nahman believes that every tree and every leaf and every blade of grass say their own prayers to God. Only the dead don't pray." (Wiesel 1996: 5)

The emphasis on Hasidic joie de vivre, not only when praying but in every little activity in everyday life (cf. Jacobs 1976: 62), is another parallel to Etty Hillesum's approach to spirituality. She was not only a deep thinker but also a life-affirming young woman, as evidenced by her numerous affairs with men, her intellectual open-mindedness, and her courage to go her own way even in difficult times. She felt connected to her environment and not only had a feeling for the *hitbodedut*, but also a strong sense of community (cf. Gur-Klein 2018).

Even in the Westerbork transit camp, where she was interned with her family, she did not lose her faith and did not blame God – on the contrary, she thanked him for the wealth and abundance he had given her. Even there, she was still able to pray, as she wrote in one of her last letters from Westerbork to her friend Henny Tideman on August 18, 1943, citing her own dialog with God:

You have made me so rich, oh God, please allow me to share out with full hands. My life has been transformed, in a continuous dialogue with you, my God, one great dialogue. Sometimes when I stand in some corner of the camp, my feet planted on your soil, my face turned toward your heaven, tears sometimes run down my face, tears of my emotion and inner gratitude looking for a way to express itself. At night, too, when I lie in my bed and rest in you, my God, tears of gratitude run down my face, and that is my prayer. [...] I am not challenging You, oh God; my life is one great dialogue with You. I may never become the great artist I would really like to be, but I am already secure in You, God. Sometimes I wish to write down few words of wisdom, and some short and fascinating stories, but I always end up straight to the same, and single word: "God." And that word contains everything, and I do not need to say anything else. (Hillesum 2014: 1050)

Her life had turned into one long, "existential prayer": "One ought to pray, day and night, for the thousands. One ought not to be without prayer for even a single minute." (ibid: 876)

Finally, I would like to address a messianic perspective, which for me is reflected in Etty Hillesum's life and work. In the last pages of her diary, her existence takes on an almost Eucharistic attitude when she writes, on October 13, 1942: "I have broken my body like bread and shared it out among men. And why not, they were hungry and had gone without for so long." (ibid: 886) This attitude reflects an ethical sovereignty that no longer needs words to pray, but praises God in silence (cf. Borgna 2024: 43–47). Even the bodily gesture of kneeling is no longer necessary, nor is the communication of words. She takes responsibility for everyone and courageously writes in her diary about the situation:

Of course, it is our complete destruction they want! But let us bear it with grace – [...] At night, as I lay in the camp on my plank bed, surrounded by women and girls gently snoring, dreaming aloud, quietly sobbing and tossing and turning, women and girls who often told me during the day, "We don't want to think, we don't want to feel, otherwise we are sure to go out of our minds," I was sometimes filled with an infinite tenderness, and lay awake for hours letting all the many, too many impressions of a much-too-long day wash over me, and I prayed, "Let me be the thinking heart of these barracks." And that is what I want to be again. The thinking heart of a whole concentration camp. (Hillesum 2014: 874)

In conclusion, going beyond the perspective of Hasidic thought, I would like to draw attention to Emmanuel Levinas' Talmudic readings in light of Etty Hillesum's aforementioned statement. In "Difficult Freedom," in his commentaries on the final chapter of *Tractate Sanhedrin*, Levinas points out:

Messianism is no more than this apogee in being, a centralizing, concentration or twisting back on itself of the Self [*Moi*]. And in concrete terms this means that each person acts as though he were the Messiah. Messianism is therefore not the certainty of the coming of a man who stops History. *It is my power to bear the suffering of all.* It is the moment when I recognize this power and my universal responsibility. (Levinas 1990: 90, emphasis added; cf. Krochmalnik 2022)

In fact, Levinas defines selfhood as "the fact of not escaping the burden imposed by the suffering of others"; being an I means "bearing all the responsibility of the world" (Levinas 1990: 89), similarly to Atlas, the figure in Greek mythology, who bears the whole world on his shoulders. In my opinion, Levinas' philosophical interpretation outlines a "messianic subjectivity," of which Etty Hillesum can give us an impressive example and lasting legacy in the extreme poverty and misery of the camp.

As Hetty Berg, Director of the Jewish Museum Berlin, points out, Etty Hillesum's writings remain up to today "one of the most important first-person documents on the deportation and internment of Jews from the Netherlands" (Berg 2023: 8). It is to be hoped that the complete translation of Etty Hillesum's work in German, which has only recently, in March 2023, been published, will provide new insights for research, also taking into account concepts from the field of Jewish thought that have received less attention to date but, as this essay has shown, can be fruitfully linked to her rich and innovative spirituality (cf. Hillesum 2023).

Bibliography

Augustine, The Confessions of Saint Augustine, transl. by E. B. Pusey (Edward Bouverie) (https://www.gutenberg.org/files/3296/3296-h/3296-h.htm).

Bercken, Wil van den (2010): "Etty Hillesum's Russian Vocation and Spiritual Relationship to Dostoevsky." In: Spirituality in the Writings of Etty Hillesum. Proceedings of the Etty Hillesum Conference at Ghent University, November 2008, Leiden/Boston: Brill, pp. 147–171.

Berg, Hetty (2023): "Vorwort." In: Etty Hillesum, Ich will die Chronistin dieser Zeit werden. Sämtliche Tagebücher und Briefe 1941–1943, ed. by Klaas A. D. Smelik/Pierre Bühler, transl. by Christina Siever/Simone Schroth, München: C. H. Beck.

Beuker, Chris (2020): Etty Hillesum, verwevenheid met het communisme, Soesterberg: Uitgeverij Aspekt BV.

Borgna, Eugenio (2024): In ascolto del silenzio, Turin: Einaudi editore.

Bowie, Fiona (1995): "Modern Women Mystics: Etty Hillesum and Simone Weil." In: New Blackfriars 76/892, pp. 175–187.

Buber, Martin (1988 [1906]): The Tales of Rabbi Nachman, transl. by Maurice Friedman, with a new introduction by Paul Mendes-Flohr and Ze'ev Gries, Atlantic Highlands, NJ: Humanities Press.

Buber, Martin (1967 [1948]): The Way of Man According to the Teaching of Hasidism, New York: Citadel Press.

Bühler, Pierre (2014): "Leibliches Beten bei Etty Hillesum." In: Hermeneutische Blätter 2, pp. 91–99.

Clement, Marja (2018): "*Hineinhorchen* and Writing. The Language Use of Etty Hillesum." In: Klaas Smelik/Gerrit Van Oord/Jurjen Wiersma (eds.), Reading Etty Hillesum in Context: Writings, Life, and Influence of a Visionary Author, Amsterdam: Amsterdam University Press, pp. 51–77.

Clement, Marja (2019): "The Girl Who Could Not Kneel. Etty Hillesum and the Turn Inward." In: Klaas Smelik (ed.), The Lasting Significance of Etty Hillesum's Writings. Proceedings of the Third International Etty Hillesum Conference at Middleburg, September 2018, Amsterdam: Amsterdam University Press, 2019, pp. 139–155.

Coetsier, Meins G. S. (2014): The Existential Philosophy of Etty Hillesum. An Analysis of Her Diaries and Letters, Leiden/Boston: Brill.

Enelow, Hayman Gerson (1913): "Kawwana. The Struggle for Inwardness in Judaism." In: David Philipson (ed.), Studies in Jewish Literature Issued in Honor of Professor Kaufmann Kohler on the Occasion of his Seventieth Birthday, Berlin: Georg Reimer, pp. 82–107 (https://sammlungen.ub.uni-frankfurt.de/freimann/content/pageview/804606).

Gérard, Rémy (2007): "Etty Hillesum et Saint Augustin: l'influence d'un maître spirituel?" In: Recherches de Science Religieuse, 95/2, pp. 253–280.

Grimmelikhuizen, Frits (2016): Etty Hillesum leest Rainer Maria Rilke: de invloed van Rainer Maria Rilke op het kunstenaarschap van Etty Hillesum, Deventer: Uitgeverij Oorsprong.

Gur-Klein, Thalia (2018): "From Separation to Communitas. Etty Hillesum, A Jewish Perspective." In: Klaas Smelik/Gerrit Van Oord/Jurjen Wiersma (eds.), Reading Etty Hillesum in Context: Writings, Life, and Influences of a Visionary Author, Amsterdam: Amsterdam University Press, pp. 333–360.

Hillesum, Etty (2014 [1986]): The Complete Works 1941–1943, Bilingual, Annotated and Unabridged, 2 vols., ed. by Klaas A. D. Smelik/Meins G. S. Coetsier, transl. by Arnold J. Pomerans, Maastricht: Shaker Publishing House.

Hillesum, Etty (2023 [1986]): Ich will die Chronistin dieser Zeit werden. Sämtliche Tagebücher und Briefe, 1941–1943, ed. by Klaas A. D. Smelik/

Pierre Bühler, with a foreword by Hetty Berg, transl. by Christina Siever/ Simone Schroth, Munich: C. H. Beck.

Jacobs, Louis (1976): Hasidic Thought, New York: Behrman House.

Jacobs, Louis (1978 [1972]): Hasidic Prayer, New York: Schocken Books.

Koelemeijer, Judith (2022): Etty Hillesum: Het verhaal van haar leven, Amsterdam: Uitgeverij Balans.

Krochmalnik, Daniel (2022): "Der Messias im rabbinischen Judentum." In: Walter Homolka/Juni Hoppe/Daniel Krochmalnik (eds.), Der Messias kommt nicht. Abschied vom jüdischen Erlöser, Freiburg i.Br.: Herder, pp. 73–167.

Krochmalnik, Daniel (2023): "Kawwana. Sieben Bemerkungen zu einem Zentralbegriff der jüdischen Religiosität." In: Barbara Schmitz/Thomas Hieke/ Matthias Ederer (eds.), Vor allen Dingen: Das Alte Testament – Festschrift für Christoph Dohmen, Freiburg i.Br.: Herder, pp. 495–504.

Leshem, Zvi (2014): "Pouring Out Your Heart: Rabbi Nachman's Hitbodedut and Its Piaseczner Reveberations." In: Tradition. A Journal of Orthodox Jewish Thought 47/3, pp. 57–65.

Levinas, Emmanuel (1990 [1963]): Difficult Freedom. Essays on Judaism, trans. by Seán Hand, London: Athlone Press.

Maimonides, Moses (1170–1180): Mishneh Torah, Hilchot Ahawa 4,15 (https:// www.sefaria.org/Mishneh_Torah%2C_Prayer_and_the_Priestly_Blessing .4.15?lang=bi&with=all&lang2=en).

Mark, Zvi (2009): Mysticism and Madness. The Religious Thought of Rabbi Nachman of Bratslav, London/New York: Continuum.

Pleshoyano, Alexandra (2010): "Etty Hillesum und Julius Spier: A 'Spirituality' on the Fringe of Religious Borders." In: Klaas A. D. Smelik/Ria van den Brandt/Meins G. S. Coetsier (eds.), Spirituality in the Writings of Etty Hillesum. Proceedings of the Etty Hillesum Conference at Ghent University, November 2008, Leiden/Boston: Brill, pp. 43–74.

Rilke, Rainer Maria (2004 [1957]): Die Gedichte, Frankfurt a. M.: Insel Verlag.

Schrijvers, Piet (2018): "Etty Hillesum in Jewish Contexts." In: Klaas Smelik/ Gerrit Van Oord/Jurjen Wiersma (eds.), Reading Etty Hillesum in Context: Writings, Life, and Influences of a Visionary Author, Amsterdam: Amsterdam University Press, pp. 315–331.

Smelik, Klaas A. D. (2018): "A Short Biography of Etty Hillesum (1914–1943)." In: Klaas Smelik/Gerrit Van Oord/Jurjen Wiersma (eds.), Reading Etty Hillesum in Context: Writings, Life, and Influence of a Visionary Author, Amsterdam: Amsterdam University Press, pp. 23–30.

Weil, Simone (2009 [1950]): Waiting for God, transl. by Emma Craufurd, New York: Harper Perennial.

Wiesel, Elie (1996): "Prayer and Modern Man." In: Gabriel H. Cohn/Harold Fisch (eds.), Prayer in Judaism. Continuity and Change, Northvale, NJ/London: Jason Aronson, pp. 3–11.

Woodhouse, Patrick (2009): Etty Hillesum: A Life Transformed, London: Bloomsbury.

Woodhouse, Patrick (2017): "The Influence of the Work of Rainer Maria Wilke on the Mind and Heart of Etty Hillesum." In: Klaas A. D. Smelik/Meins G. S. Coetsier/Jurjen Wiersma (eds.), The Ethics and Religious Philosophy of Etty Hillesum. Proceedings of the Etty Hillesum Conference at Ghent University, January 2014, London/Boston: Brill, pp. 285–298.

Literary Aspects of Philosophical Writing: The Case of Maimonides' Guide of the Perplexed

Michael Zank

The *Guide of the Perplexed* is a unique work in the long and complex history of Jewish books. As Maimonides puts it in the introduction, "[w]hat I register here is recorded in no book extant in our nation in our present age of exile."[1] Its literary form certainly has no parallel in medieval writing. Rather than a straightforward exposition, the work is "poetic" in the broadest sense of the word: it is carefully written and meant to be read with great care. As Maimonides admonishes the reader, "[t]o get the most out of this work and leave nothing behind, review the chapters against one another. Don't just focus on the main point of each chapter, but pay attention to each term used in the argument, even those not central to that chapter's theme. For the argument of the work is not laid out randomly but carefully and exactingly so as to omit no issue that needs clearing up." What precisely the message and meaning of the work is continues to be debated.[2] The elusiveness of the book's doctrine seems very much bound up with its literary form. It is this relationship between philosophical content and literary form of the *Guide* that I want to investigate.[3]

---

1 Here and in the following, I quote the *Guide of the Perplexed* from a pre-publication version of Lenn Goodman's new translation of the *Guide* unless stated otherwise. I am grateful to Prof. Goodman for making his translation available to me.

2 This essay builds on papers by the same title that I read at a Starr Fellows Seminar at Harvard University in 2021, at the 2022 AJS Annual Conference in Boston. I thank the members of the Spring 2024 BU Center for the Humanities Fellows Seminar for their comments on a further draft of this study. All remaining errors and shortcomings are entirely mine.

3 What I offer here is a preliminary investigation. The full argument will need to be made from a close reading of the *Guide*, which I hope to present in form of book tentatively titled "Maimonides and His Modern Readers".

The overall purpose of the treatise, as its title suggests, is to help its intended reader to find his way out of a state of perplexity. This is how this state of perplexity is described:

> [T]he specific purpose here is to arouse intellectually a religious, morally and spiritually mature person who is settled of mind and committed to the Torah's truth, who has studied and absorbed the philosophical sciences. Human reason draws such a person invitingly to its domain, but he is troubled by the surface sense of certain biblical expressions. Resisting what he still takes (or was taught) is the meaning of its multivalent, metaphorical, or ambiguous words, he hangs back, perplexed and confused. Should he follow his reason, reject what he took those words to say, and presume that he has shed core biblical precepts? Or should he hold fast to what he took those words to mean and fight reason's sway, dig in his heels and resist, feeling injured by reason, as though it had sullied his faith, retain his fanciful beliefs, yet remain deeply troubled by anxiety and disquiet.

It is this state of "anxiety and disquiet" in a conscientious person of faith that is meant to be remedied by means of what the treatise has to teach. The purpose of the writing is, thus, therapeutic, a remedy for an unhappy state of the soul, much as ancient Stoic philosophy was meant to achieve in its practitioners an untroubled state of mind. But the *Guide* is written for a soul troubled by a condition that was unknown to the ancients. He is disquieted by the seeming contradictions between the literal meaning of words of Scripture and the concepts of reason acquired by the study of science and philosophy. That both, Torah and philosophy, are to maintain their validity, that both are sources of knowledge and therefore must be brought into agreement with one another so as to resolve the "perplexity" of the troubled soul, distinguishes the situation for which Maimonides writes from that of the ancient Stoics.

Maimonides is aware of this difference between his own situation and that of the ancients. In *Guide* I, 31 he writes:

> Alexander of Aphrodisias says that there are three causes of disagreement about things. [...] However, in our times there is a fourth cause that he did not mention because it did not exist among them. It is habit and upbringing. For man has in his nature a love of, and inclination for, that to which he is habituated. [...] In a similar way, man has love for, and the wish to defend, opinions to which he is habituated and in which he has been brought up and has a feeling of repulsion for opinions other than those. [...] All this

is due to people being habituated to, and brought up on, *texts that it is an established usage to think highly of and to regard as true* [...]. (Maimonides 1963: 66–67, emphasis added)

The perplexity in question doesn't arise from what Leo Strauss (1997: 386–388) called the "natural difficulties" of philosophizing alone, so that the difficulties could be remedied by philosophical means. This explains why the *pharmakon* or remedy provided by the *Guide* in no way resembles a traditional philosophical treatise.

What Maimonides does in the *Guide* is often seen as a repetition of the project of Philo of Alexandria (cf. Cortest 2017; Harvey 2000). In this view, Maimonides basically reinvents allegorical interpretation all over again, much as Philo did before him, without having direct exposure to Philo's writing or to those of Philo's Christian heirs, such as Origen of Alexandria. But even though both authors take recourse to figurative interpretations of Scripture, there are major differences between them with regard to their philosophical sources and hence to their respective purpose. Philo is a Platonist and strives to show that Moses anticipated the insights of Platonism. For Philo, Moses himself was a philosopher – indeed the greatest philosopher of all. The tone of voice of Philo's writings is apologetic, as he writes for an audience convinced of the greatness of Plato but not necessarily persuaded of Moses' superiority. Maimonides, on the other hand, is not an avowed Platonist, and his agreement with Aristotle's natural philosophy is limited to what Aristotle teaches with regard to the sublunar realm. When it comes to astronomy, the part of science that the medieval philosophers regarded as essential to metaphysical arguments, Maimonides – much like his Andalusian contemporaries – was skeptical of the Ptolemaic worldview and believed that Aristotle had been groping in the dark. For this reason alone, Philo and Maimonides were not operating under similar conditions and they were in the same position neither with regard to the philosophical tradition nor with regard to the Torah and its character as understood by the communities of their respective readers.

Even if one does not equate his project with that of Philo, Maimonides still stands for a tradition that imbued the Scriptures with philosophical depth. Some modern critics of Maimonides, foremost among them Baruch Spinoza, went to great length in their attacks on this approach. For Spinoza, Maimonides was guilty of substituting the "ravings of the philosophers," namely of Plato and Aristotle, for the plain sense of Scripture. Maimonides appeared to Spinoza as not just mistaken but as dishonest. As Spinoza argued in the *Trac-*

tatus Theologico-Politicus, the words of ancient prophets had no deeper meaning but were well-intentioned attempts to impose a moral and political order on an unruly people. Prophecy was varied by individual style and marked by the life-world of each individual prophet, time-bound and practical in concern and orientation, political-theological in nature, and unrelated to the pursuit of intellectual perfection, of which those prophets were entirely innocent. There was no shred of philosophical doctrine contained in their proclamations, and the Laws of Moses were merely the new taskmaster imposed on a liberated slave people who hadn't shed their slave mentality. It wasn't – as one might speculate in light of Plato's *Laws* – a free law for a free people. Maimonides, one of few thinkers Spinoza mentions by name and criticizes explicitly, was not a careful reader of Scripture but one of those who bent its text to his will. His was the approach to giving the Scriptures timeless meaning that Spinoza meant to defeat once and for all (cf. Wolfson 1934).[4] For him, naturalizing prophecy and historicizing the Law of Moses meant giving modern man a chance to conduct his political affairs without the interference of religious power.

But there are other ways of reading Maimonides. In the attempt to read Maimonides afresh, I am aided by considerations of the literary aspects of philosophical writing more generally – that is, the problematic relationship between the appearance of truth in our minds and the linguistic or symbolic forms in which it invariably appears to us. Spinoza believed, with Descartes, that rational arguments about God, Nature, and human thriving could be stated as clearly and distinctly as geometric demonstrations and that therefore philosophical investigations could proceed with the same compelling force. And yet his own major philosophical work, the *Ethica, more geometrico demonstrata*, engendered completely opposite interpretations. With Hannah Arendt's *Life of the Mind*, leaning on Kant's distinction between *Verstand* and *Vernunft*, one may distinguish between the rational and the reasonable. The rational concerns what can be stated clearly and distinctly, like a mathematical equation, while the reasonable concerns those squishy questions of meaning that remain elusive and forever bound to speech and its interpretation, speech and more speech. Where does Maimonides' *Guide* come to rest in this regard? Is it a mere restatement of the neo-Aristotelian doctrines he might have

---

4   As Leo Strauss argued, Spinoza also shared the goal of Stoic philosophy but, in contrast to Maimonides, he found biblical belief in a creator god itself a troubling proposition, cf. Strauss 1965.

shared with his Andalusian compatriots in the form of a forced interpretation of prophetic riddles and parables, or is there more to learn from the *Guide* and its complex literary form?

The challenge to read Maimonides more carefully links, in my mind, with the larger, more universal confluence between literary form and philosophical content. More than merely engaging questions of genre, style, and the employment of short forms such as aphorisms, metaphoric speech, riddles, or parables,[5] I am interested in general problems of saying and meaning (cf. Hegel 1979), problems that Maimonides would have been keenly aware of through his attention to the logic of negation and its employment in theological speech (*apophasis*), not necessarily in pursuit of a mystical "unsaying" but perhaps for the sake of drawing the attention of his intended reader to the ways in which human thought is intertwined with human speech.[6]

The *Guide* as a Case for a Larger Issue

One might approach the Maimonidean work as a particularly intriguing case of a more common and perhaps pervasive issue, illuminating the vaunted, though often neglected, relationship between philosophy and writing – something that we might call the *literary aspects of philosophical writing*.[7] This is not the same as asking whether the *Guide* was concealing a dangerous doctrine – as the medieval French rabbis who banned the book feared it did –, a doctrine that, while hidden under a veneer of conformity with conventional beliefs, might undermine piety and devotion to the Law. This medieval interpretation was echoed by Leo Strauss in a 1941 essay called "Persecution and the Art of Writing," where he broadened the suspicion of hidden nonconformity to argue that true philosophers always take recourse to a certain "art of writing" that

---

5   Cf. e.g. Maimonides' Commentary on Mishnah Sanhedrin X:1: "[...] they [the sages] were speaking by way of a riddle and a parable – since this is the way of great wise men" (Maimonides 2020: 10:1, 14).

6   On the neo-Platonic tradition of negative theology, cf. Armstrong 1977. On Maimonides as part of a Jewish "maieutic" tradition, cf. Kavka 2009.

7   Cf. Jaeger 1923: 4: "[B]esonders die Fachphilosophie und die Literaturphilologie sind stets geneigt, die Form als etwas Literarisches zu betrachten [...]." Jaeger's critical comment supports my thesis, namely that the form of philosophy is not just a literary "mask" that can be dropped but something essential to understanding the content or intent of serious works of philosophy.

keeps the multitude in the dark while communicating matters that only a careful reader may discern between the lines.[8] In contrast to Strauss, I want to use the case of Maimonides to interrogate, indeed question and challenge, the conventional distinction between philosophical writing and literature.[9] To see philosophy as the other of literature rather than on a continuum of literary forms, or to conceive of philosophy as pure thought, even a "scientific" endeavor, and not also as a product of language and the imagination, seems insufficiently reflected.[10] While this insight is certainly not new, it has yet to receive the attention it deserves in the field of Jewish philosophical studies.[11]

The question is not whether philosophical writing and literature are on a continuum of modes of speech but where on that continuum they fall and how literary form and philosophical content are related in each case. Some texts penned by literary authors are also profound works of philosophy.[12] In other cases, philosophical authors ably draw on literary forms such as dialogue to give expression to philosophical thought.[13] There are also cases where poetry,

---

8   Strauss believed that this "art of writing" had first been cultivated by Plato. He believed that Maimonides was a Platonist in this regard, someone who understood the reasons why the true opinion of a philosopher must be concealed to all but the most discerning readers, cf. Strauss 1941; Zank 2004; Diamond 2002.

9   Josef Stern similarly takes on the idea that the *Guide* was meant to convey a specific doctrine, albeit one concealed under a thick layer of dissimulation (cf. Stern 2013). On Stern and his conclusion that Maimonides' philosophy is best understood as skeptical of true knowledge, cf. Pollock 2013.

10   Analytic philosophy arose as an antidote and corrective to the language dependency of all metaphysics. Cf. Stewart 1878: 112 (cited in Patton, 2011).

11   This investigation builds on studies related to problems of taxonomy and classification that I explored in previous publications, cf. Zank 2007, 2017, 2021.

12   Eminent modern examples include Voltaire's *Candide*, Rousseau's *Emile*, Jonathan Swift's *Gulliver's Travels*, and Johann Wolfgang Goethe's *Wilhelm Meisters Lehrjahre*, a classical *Bildungsroman*. One might argue that any nontrivial poem or novel is driven by some inherently philosophical problem. More's *Utopia* paved the way for the modern novel as a projection of possible societies, both utopian and dystopian. But even this has its antecedent in the Atlantis myth recounted in Plato's *Timaeus*.

13   There is the form of philosophical dialogues pioneered by Plato, emulated by Cicero, and renewed by Enlightenment philosophers such as David Hume. Closer to Maimonides' time, we might recall Ibn Tufayl's philosophical desert island novel, *The Epistle of Hayy Ibn Yaqzan*, which was the model for Daniel Defoe's Enlightenment novel, *Robinson Crusoe*, and of course Judah Halevi's *Sefer ha-Kuzari*. Modern authors of influential philosophical plays and novels include Rousseau, Goethe, Lessing, and Jacobi. Kierkegaard's use of pseudonyms, by which he "stages" his philosophical and theolog-

fact, fiction, allusive suggestions, and rational arguments are inextricably enmeshed with one another. An eminent example of this might be the great debate on Lessing's "Spinozism" between Jacobi and Mendelssohn, which involved private and public letters, publications and counter-publications. It hinged on a, perhaps invented (cf. Altmann 2007),[14] account of a conversation between Lessing and Jacobi, and ultimately concerned the philosophical views of a playwright who never publicly espoused any.[15] The original conversation between Jacobi and Lessing revolved around a poem by J. W. Goethe, the famous "Prometheus."[16] If this seems a remote and largely forgotten case of an entanglement between philosophy and literature, it should be recalled that the debate compelled European thinkers and writers to take another, rather consequential look at Spinoza (cf. Förster/Melamed 2015; Folkers 1998; Goldenbaum 2009). Philosophy, I would argue, may be propelled by thought but thinking itself can be stimulated by the literary imagination.

Maimonides: Bio-bibliographical Background

The author of the *Guide of the Perplexed*, Moses Maimonides (1138–1204), was a scholar and physician whose legal, medical, and philosophical writings were of great renown in the Arabic, Latin, and Hebrew scholarship of the medieval world. His pathbreaking comprehensive systematic codification of Jewish law, the *Mishneh Torah*, remains foundational to rabbinic legal culture, and thereby to Jewish communal life, even today (cf. Twersky 1949). He was the first to formulate, in *Thirteen Articles of Faith*, a Jewish creed articulating what Jews believe in that were eventually adopted into the prayer books of the entire Jewish diaspora (cf. Kellner 1986). His influence straddles the traditional ethno-linguistic

---

    ical explorations, is another case to be considered. Nietzsche, a master of the philosophical aphorism, uses the prophetic mode of speech in Zarathustra. The examples could be multiplied.

14   More generally on Jacobi and the question of philosophy as a "manner of writing," cf. Ortlieb 2010.

15   On Lessing and the question of belief, cf. Kerber 2021; Allison 1966.

16   Namely, "Prometheus." Mendelssohn found the poem immature and disturbing, cf. Jacobi 2004. Poetry and philosophy intersected in Hölderlin's contributions to the formation of German idealism and Novalis' Spinozist influence on the Romantic movement.

divide between Sephardic/North African Jewries and the Ashkenazic communities of Northern and Central Europe and their respective offshoots. Wherever there is a Jewish community around the globe, the name of Maimonides (aka Rabbi Moshe ben Maimon (Rambam), R. Musa ibn Maimoun (Maimouni), Al ra'is Musa al yahudi) is revered. Works that found wide circulation include his medical treatises (cf. Bos 2022; Stroumsa 1993) that were based on his extensive practice in Egypt, where he treated the illnesses and diseases of the Fatimid and Ayyubid elites he served, as well as caring for the poor of the community whose recognized leader he was. He had already made a name for himself as a young man with a public letter that urged rabbinic forbearance for Jews who had yielded to forced conversion under the radical Almohads that swept the Maghreb and invaded Moorish al Andalus, the home of Maimonides' family and his own.[17] His turn of mind bore the imprint of that of his father and his circle, who were heirs to the brilliant civilization of Umayyad Al Andalus, where Hebrew and Arabic poetry flourished, where the works of Greek philosophers Plato and Aristotle and of their commentators circulated in Arabic translation, and where the genius of the Baghdad "renaissance" flourished and provided the standard curriculum of logical, mathematical, astronomical, legal, and theological-metaphysical works to be studied before one could be considered a learned man.[18] It is characteristic for Maimonides that he subscribed to the oft-repeated dictum that one ought to accept the truth, no matter the source (cf. Mühlethaler 2014).

The initial response to Maimonides' halakhic works was mixed (cf. Kanarfogel 2023). The leadership of the Talmudic academies in Baghdad feared the impact of a concise and systematic exposition of the law as competition to their authority and expertise, which was expressed in *responsa* to legal queries. Maimonides' often apodictic legal decisions also raised eyebrows among his contemporaries in Southern France. Among the Muslim authorities of his time the suspicion circulated that Maimonides, while residing in Fez, had converted to Islam but reverted to Judaism later on – a severe crime in Islamic law. Some of

---

17   For biographical background, cf. Halbertal 2015. For cultural context, cf. Stroumsa, 2012.

18   I write "man" to indicate that there prevailed, in those days, a culture of male dominance that was not just unquestioningly accepted by Jews and Muslims but also subtended by the neo-Platonic ontology that coded the mind as male and the body as female. The "human" form one ought to strive toward was considered something entirely disembodied.

his Jewish opponents suspected that his belief in the resurrection of the body, while included among the *Thirteen Articles of Faith*, was not genuine, forcing him to compose an apologetic essay on Jewish eschatological beliefs, the coming of the Messiah, the resurrection of the dead, and the world to come (cf. Halkin/ Hartman 1993). But none of these controversies were as consequential as the response to the translation of the Judeo-Arabic *Dalalat al-ha'irin* into Hebrew, which brought it into circulation among the Jews of France, who were completely unfamiliar with the Aristotelian thinking it referenced and uncomfortable with the self-evident importance the Andalusian school attached to philosophical inquiry (cf. Stroumsa 2019). The *Guide* was banned, as was Greek wisdom (*hokhma yevanit*) in general, as detrimental to Halakhic zeal and mystical devotion to the Torah. This fierce opposition did not prevent the book from being circulated and studied, including in its Latin version (cf. Hasselhoff 2005), but it assured that the *Guide* led a marginal life among devout Ashkenazic Jews until it was rediscovered, printed, and diligently studied among Jews touched by the spirit of the European Enlightenment of the 17th and 18th centuries.[19] Moses Mendelssohn attributed his hump to the study of Maimonides' work on logic (*Millot ha-higayon*), and Solomon Maimon, a student of Kantian philosophy, honored the great medieval rationalist by his choice of name and included a detailed outline of the *Guide* in his famous memoir (cf. Maimon 2020). In North Africa and Yemen, the *Guide* was revered as a mystical treatise, largely owing to the influence of Maimonides' son Abraham (cf. Lobel 2021).

On the *Guide* and Its Intended Readers

The ostensible aim of the *Guide* is to resolve the perplexity or confusion that arises in the mind of one for whom the Torah and the Prophets hold utmost authority and who has also acquired a basic education in mathematics, logic, and astronomy. Maimonides addresses Joseph b. Judah directly as his immediate correspondent, but he says that he also writes for those who, like him, are bewildered by the contradictions between the statements of the prophets whose veracity they accept on faith, and the truths they have acquired by virtue of their study of the sciences. A further source of confusion arises from the – to

---

19   As a Sephardic Jew, Spinoza was aware of the *Guide*, which he refers to with appreciation in his *Ethica* and criticizes in his *Theological Political Treatise*. Similarly, the *Guide* enjoyed a lively reception in early modern Italy, cf. Nadler 2019; Motzkin 2011a.

Maimonides sophistical – arguments for the existence, oneness, and incorporeality of God proffered by the rhetorical arts of the *mutakallimun*.[20] The book that arose out of this correspondence stirred anxiety among those who feared that it promoted the study of science and philosophy at the expense of devotion to the Mosaic Law. While this fear of libertinism may have been stirred by the behavior of some of its superficial readers, it is difficult to see how it could arise from a careful reading of the *Guide*, a book that shows how the authority of the Torah can be maintained while seriously engaging with questions of apodictic and demonstrable truth.[21]

The book does not teach Aristotelian or Platonic philosophy but presupposes exposure to science and philosophy amongst its readers to a degree that causes confusion and perplexity. But it may be too narrow to think of the text as only addressed to the type of ideal (or rather less than ideal) reader Maimonides primarily wishes to reach.

According to Leo Strauss, the "Epistle Dedicatory" offers an answer to the question for whom, or for what type of person ("the perplexed"), the *Guide* has been composed (cf. Strauss 1963).[22] The need to answer this question arises, for Strauss, from the fact that it seems neither entirely addressed to the vulgar nor to the elite. The vulgar are told not to bother with the treatise as it would merely confuse them, and members of the elite may not need it in order to know what there is to know. When addressing the work to his absent pupil, Joseph, Maimonides describes his excellences and deficiencies. Joseph is described as possessing "passionate desire for things speculative and especially for mathematics." He "had an excellent mind and a quick grasp." He showed interest in "things divine as well as in an appraisal of the Kalam." On the other hand, Maimonides felt compelled to admonish him to proceed in an orderly, systematic manner rather than "impatiently or unmethodically." In particular, Joseph had "turned to divine science without having studied natural science" (Strauss 1963: xviii). It appears from what follows in Strauss' essay, that Maimonides is primarily concerned with this deficient order of study (divine sci-

---

20 Cf. *Guide* I:71 (Maimonides 1963: 179–183).

21 Scholars have argued that Maimonides' belief that the prophetic revelations represented philosophical/scientific truth in popular form was conventional at the time he wrote, cf., e.g., Berman 2008. I think this is too schematic an approach which overlooks that science, especially Ptolemaic astronomy, was under careful reconsideration at the time of Maimonides, especially in Al Andalus, cf. Saliba 2019.

22 Strauss' copious writings about Maimonides are now conveniently collected and annotated by Kenneth H. Green, cf. Strauss/Green 2013.

ence before natural science) and writes the *Guide* to make up for it. The *Guide* thus seems to be written with the aim of redirecting the mental orientation of someone interested in divine science toward attending to the connection between natural and divine science, the former being the condition for the latter. At the same time, the *Guide* "does not itself transmit natural science" (*Guide* II 2). This leads to the conclusion (Strauss 1963: xix) that the intended reader of the *Guide* "stands at the point where speculation branches off from acceptance of authority," even if it is the authority of Maimonides. One might conclude from this that placing divine science before natural science leads to another variant of idolatry, whereas placing natural science before divine science is another way of seeking "the apple of gold in a filigree of silver."

While written for readers who had great interest in "divine science" and some, though not complete, knowledge of "natural science" (in the Aristotelian sense), Maimonides risked the dissemination of his work among readers who had no background in "natural science" and therefore had no idea that "divine science," properly understood, needed to be grounded in "natural science." What do we make of the fact that Maimonides supervised a translation of his writing that was addressed to readers who had not been exposed to the philosophical literature that circulated in Arabic but not, at that time, in Hebrew? It seems as if Maimonides wrote for different kinds of readers, just as he says the Torah addresses different readers at the same time, while entirely speaking "in the language of human beings." The most basic statement we can make in this preliminary orientation is that the work offers a guide to interpreting the prophetic language of Scripture without forcing a reader to take the first sense of its words that comes to mind as their intended sense.[23] The words of Scripture themselves are turned into prompts for thought guided by a few basic assumptions, namely, the existence, the oneness, and the incorporeality of the deity (cf. *Guide* II, Intro and Chapters 1 and 2). In order for Scripture to function in this way, the literal sense of words that suggest otherwise must be distinguished from other meanings that are lexicographically actual and attested in biblical linguistic usage rather than merely allegorical.[24] In other words, there

---

23 Contrasting this principle, Rashi and his successors insisted in their commentaries that the plain sense of the words of Scripture never loses its meaning and significance. See Rashi's introduction to his commentary on the Torah, now easily accessible in Michael Carasik's translation of the *Miqra'ot G'dolot* (JPS), cf. Carasik 2015.

24 In this regard, Maimonides is not simply repeating methodologically what Philo of Alexandria had already done. In terms of his interpretive method as well as his mode

Philosophy and Jewish Thought

are real possibilities of meaning that require the reader to become active in deciding the most appropriate sense of the terms in question where they occur in prophetic speech. Thought and judgment must be activated based on multiple types of knowledge and put to use in the mind of the reader to achieve a state of mind that sets one on the path toward human perfection, not necessarily through recourse to science or philosophy, but through becoming habituated to reading actively and mindfully.

Literary Characteristics of the *Guide of the Perplexed*

Even the most superficial reader of the *Guide* will be struck by the fact that it is an odd book.[25] The manner of its exposition of matters pertaining to the language of the prophets is obscure, confusing, and intentionally cryptic.[26] The work deals with the ruses and parables by which the prophets teach about recondite matters of ultimate concern that are indicated by the rabbinic terms *Ma'aseh bereshit* and *Ma'aseh merkavah*. The former pertains to the exposition of Genesis 1 or the story of creation, which Maimonides summarily identifies with the subject of physics or "natural science" in the Aristotelian sense of the term; the latter pertains to the exposition of Ezekiel 1, the vision of the divine chariot, which Maimonides summarily identifies with the subject of metaphysics, "divine science," or "theology."[27] One may argue that the manner of Maimonides' exposition in the *Guide*, especially the obscure organization of the work, arises from the need to circumvent the rabbinic stricture against the public exposition of those two critical chapters. The author found it needful

---

of exposition, Maimonides (pace H. A. Wolfson) is therefore not to be embedded in a single trajectory that begins with Philo and ends with Spinoza, cf. Wolfson 1977.

25 Postmodern readers are perhaps more likely than typically modern ones to appreciate "disorganization" as an organizing principle of certain types of literature. Cf., e.g., Kleymann 2021.

26 No analysis of Maimonides can ignore his acknowledged and unacknowledged debt to prior thinkers. The originality of his thought may even be an optical illusion that will dissipate the more studies bring to light the views he shared with others. Cf., e.g., Pessin 2016. The literary form of the *Guide*, however, remains a unique product of its author's imagination.

27 The neo-Aristotelian tradition combined genuine Aristotelian doctrine with the neo-Platonic doctrine of emanation. More accurately, because of a false attribution of an Arabic version of the Enneads of Plotinus, the neo-Aristotelians of the Middle Ages considered neo-Platonic ontology genuinely Aristotelian. Cf. Adamson 2022.

to write about matters that were legally forbidden from being made the subject of writing, and his "art of writing" was the means to heed the letter of the law while suspending it because of the need of the hour.[28] But there are other or additional possibilities to account for the deliberate obscurity of the work. Maimonides felt the need to write about something that was not just forbidden to write about, but that he deemed necessary to put in writing because it involved a long-forgotten insight into the relationship between true knowledge and prophetic speech, between truth and language, that he believed to have recovered and feared would be lost if it was not preserved all over again. At the same time, the insight he wished to impart was not simply a hidden doctrine. If I am not mistaken, the *Guide*, much like a Platonic dialogue,[29] was written to stir the reader to acquire a new habit of reading and thinking.[30] The genre of the *Guide* – a book as unique in Jewish literature as is the Torah itself – is didactic, but it is also akin to poetry in that it alludes rather than articulates. Its effect was to be mimetic, or it was to have no effect at all. If his *Mishneh Torah* repeated the legal content of Written and Oral Torah in clear and distinct utterances (i.e., without recourse to poetic speech), the *Guide* performed a repetition of the most important characteristic of prophetic speech by using the imagi-

---

28   Cf. Mishneh Torah, Hilkhot Yesodey Hatorah 4:10-13. The "need of the hour" was invoked by the rabbis of the Mishnah when they decided to transgress the law against writing down the Oral Torah.

29   The analogy with Plato I see concerns attention to literary form, indirect communication, and the instilling of certain habits of mind in the reader, the awakening of the reader to critical thinking, much as Goethe understood Plato. See *Plato als Mitgenosse einer christlichen Offenbarung* (1796): "Gewiß, wer uns auseinandersetzte, was Männer wie Plato im Ernst, Scherz und Halbscherz, was sie aus Überzeugung, oder nur diskursive gesagt haben, würde uns einen außerordentlichen Dienst erzeigen und zu unserer Bildung unendlich viel beitragen; denn die Zeit ist vorbei da die Sibyllen unter der Erde weissagten; wir fordern Kritik und wollen urteilen ehe wir etwas annehmen und auf uns anwenden" (Goethe 1895: 140).

30   The emphasis on the right kind of habits and the need for habituation are an inheritance of Aristotelian ethics. That Maimonides was aware of the detrimental effect of the wrong kind of reading habits is clear from *Guide* I:31 where he considers habituation to taking revealed texts as ultimate authority, to be accepted without thinking, an obstacle to philosophizing that was unknown to the Ancients.

nation in the service of reason,[31] to stir in the reader the activity of thinking, even of thinking critically.[32]

As a written text, the *Guide* is a substitute for speech. As a *philosophical* text it is writing about speech and its relation to thought. As a *Jewish* philosophical text, it is a writing about prophetic speech that aims at action, namely, action of the limbs as well as action of the heart, which is the seat of the intellect. Maimonides both *employs* the imagination and writes about the role of the imagination in prophecy, drawing attention to the distinction between intellect and imagination. Without the imagination we cannot begin to know, or say, what we mean by that distinction. Caught in the seemingly inescapable echo chamber of saying and meaning, Maimonides *gestures* toward an "ascent" from one to the other.[33] The speech delivered in the Guide is *performative* in ways reminiscent of classical Aristotelian poetic theory; it remains incomplete, unless it causes a certain responsive action in the mind of the reader. As a philosophical dialogue with the intended reader, it aims at a certain *mimesis*, though not of emotional identification, *anagnorisis*, or *catharsis*, as in Greek tragedy, but of the intellect.

---

31   *Guide* II:34. The prophecy of Moses, according to Maimonides, was distinguished from all other ranks of prophecy by the subordination of the imagination to the intellect or reason. Maimonides expressly refrains from elaborating on this ultimate rank of prophecy. Cf. Motzkin 2011b.

32   I am aware of importing Arendtian and Kantian tropes that might strike the historically sensitive reader as anachronistic. I hope to justify this terminology in the larger version of this project, a reading of Maimonides in light of his modern readers, especially Spinoza, Maimon, Cohen, and Strauss.

33   In this connection, we must consider Maimonides' psychology, as laid out in "Eight Chapters," where he makes clear that "the soul is a unit" that manifests in different activities but cannot be divided into actual parts, even if the physicians speak in this manner. It is only in speaking about the soul that we take recourse to parts of the soul or multiple souls, such as the appetitive, nutritive, perceptive, imaginative, and rational soul. This implies that thought and imagination are really classifications of types of activities of the soul, not distinct entities, or hypostases. The soul is one, and the human soul is human *in potentia* or *in actu*, depending on how we think and act as human beings.

Strauss's Political-Philosophical Interpretation of Maimonides' "Art of Writing"

Maimonides undoubtedly employs some of the tensions between saying and meaning for rhetorical purposes, i.e., to avoid conveying in writing opinions on matters whose public exposition the law prohibits. But he also draws attention to the limitations of language and hence to tensions inherent in the characteristics of language. In other words, some things are sayable but should not be said, and some things are knowable but cannot be put in plain language. Among the modern authors who took the consideration of Maimonides' instructions on how to read his treatise as a prompt to consider some of the larger implications for philosophical writing was Leo Strauss. Strauss believed to have rediscovered an element of style buried and largely forgotten in the wake of the Enlightenment, namely "exoteric" writing.[34] He suggests that a philosopher's meaning may (and even *must*) be concealed, though perhaps in plain sight and on the surface of a text rather than in a presumed elusive depth.[35] Or it might be communicated indirectly and "between the lines." This heuristic assumption suggested for Strauss the opposite of the hermeneutical rule formulated by Kant in regard to Plato, namely, that one ought to understand an author better than he understood himself. In contrast, according to Strauss, to understand an author better than he understood himself, one must first and foremost understand him as he understood himself.[36] This observation arises for Strauss from his reading of Maimonides and his Arabic philosophical predecessors, and it paves the way for his conception of Platonic

---

34 The importance, in Strauss' mind, of Lessing points to the fact that the German dramaturgist and playwright renewed an earlier philosophical awareness for the necessity of careful writing that addressed multiple audiences at the same time. If Strauss was right, Lessing practiced this art even though it seemed to have been rendered obsolete by the Cartesian principle of writing "clearly and distinctly".

35 Note the spatial metaphors, which are common in this type of discourse. To what extent is our thinking guided and limited by the metaphors we employ? Cf. Blumenberg 1960.

36 I retain the conventional gendering of generalization as "male," though here I draw attention to this pseudo abstractness as a marker of the embodied characteristics of philosophical storytelling. Using male gender feigns an abstract and universal characteristic of philosophical articulation but, at the same time, it undermines its claim to universality. This is an excellent example of the linguistic/semantic quagmire of philosophical communication.

political philosophy. Strauss also takes Maimonides to have been completely in control of any contradictions the *Guide* might contain, deploying them intentionally. Strauss thus casts Maimonides as a perfect author, imitating how Maimonides casts Moses, namely, as a prophet *sui generis*.[37] The purpose of Strauss' statements is to caution the reader not to attribute inadvertent errors to a competent author whom we ought to presume to be cognizant of the implications of what he or she writes. Strauss also seems to caution us to avoid the biographic and historical fallacies of substituting personal or historical context and sources of influence for a thinker's actual thought, which must be established, as far as possible, by a careful reading of the text itself. The presumption of perfect authorial control seems to clash with the modern critique of language. For the early Romantic critic J. G. Hamann,

---

37 There are tensions in the biography of Maimonides that are at odds with the persona he projects in his writings. In the *Guide* and elsewhere, Maimonides projects an image of himself as a calm, deliberate, dispassionate, objective, measured, and careful man. Yet he spent a year in a state of abject depression after his brother died in a shipwreck. Later in life, he was overwhelmed with responsibilities that made it impossible for him to write anything but medical treatises on the conditions he was treating at court, including indigestion and impotence. There is also the strange occlusion of his life as a convert to Islam. To be sure, he must deny the fact of his conversion to avoid punishment, potentially even death. But the fact that he carried a secret suggests that he was well versed in the arts of dissimulation when it was expedient. This is not to suggest a deficiency of character but to complicate our image of the man. Much like the famous midrash about the sheikh who had a picture of Moses painted and, upon viewing the portrait, could not believe that the man represented, a man full of vices and evil inclinations, could be the same prophet who had led the Israelites out of Egypt. The answer he is given is that this was indeed a truthful portrait of the man and his character traits but that the famous leader had had to conquer his vices and evil inclinations. So, too, in the case of Maimonides. We cannot simply extrapolate the personality from the persona on display in the writings. The first literary artifice to note is therefore the authorial persona "Maimonides," which should not be confounded with the man. Even Moses, after all, was compelled to wear a mask when speaking to the Israelites after the second period he spent on the mountain, when he spoke to the Holy One, Blessed be His Name, "face to face." If the *Guide* represents an *imitatio* of that famous ascent and descent that is its major subject, then we must expect its author to wear a mask of sorts as well. The problem intimated here – the need to distinguish between the authorial persona that appears in a text and the actual author – is an important bone of contention in literary theory, specifically the theory of the novel. The position I take here is closer to that represented by Käthe Hamburger (1957) than to the one found in Mikhail Bakhtin (1981a).

language is excessive in that it always exceeds the meanings we intend or are aware of. Critics of language, including Fritz Mauthner, disparage the idea that anything can be articulated as clearly and distinctly in any language as was previously thought (cf. Hartung 2013; Henne/Kaiser 2000; Fuchs 1990). For Strauss, however, to begin to study a careful writer of the past requires the assumption that there is no such thing as the unintended meaning of a carefully written text. There obtains, at least heuristically, a perfect agreement between meaning and speech.[38]

Clearly, this is an exaggerated claim when it comes to human authors, and perhaps even when it comes to divine ones.[39] Human authors are never fully in control of the meaning of their writing. The hyperbolic claim of complete authorial awareness is, it seems, either naïve and delusional or, if employed with a view to being challenged, rhetorical, part of a "mask" employed to deflect the beholder's gaze.[40]

Toward a Different Interpretation

Taking a different point of departure than Strauss, I want to draw attention to a more fundamental aspect of the tension between saying and meaning, one that was well articulated in the Cambridge school of "ordinary language" philosophy. The question was perceptively voiced, among others, by Stanley Cavell in essays published under the title "Must We Mean What We Say?" Cavell (2002: 69) raises the question whether poems can be paraphrased. Translating this question to our context, I would ask: Can the philosophical meaning of Maimonides be expressed in terms other than the ones he uses – that is, can it be extracted from, and restated without, its "Jewish" form? Can we have the

---

38 It is not clear to me how this maxim can be made to agree with Plato's skeptical view of all written communication.

39 The limitation of divine knowledge of particulars is a theme in Maimonides' *Guide* and elsewhere. Mendelssohn renews it in his writing about Spinoza. For Hegel's *Phenomenology of the Spirit*, our knowledge of particulars is the key problem.

40 On the trope of the "mask" of Moses as a representation of a specifically Jewish hermeneutic, cf. Bruckstein 2001. As to the "perfect authorship" of M., note that Alfred Ivry, in his recent monograph on M., denies the assertion of authorial perfection. Instead, he reads the *Guide* as an ad hoc composition. He explains contradictions in the text as indications that M. changed his mind on certain things over the course of writing it. Cf. Ivry 2016.

"golden apple" without its "silver filigree"? In raising this question, I am arguing for a return to a more Aristotelian than Platonic approach to reasoning represented in the *Guide*, similar to what H. G. Gadamer (1997: 244) suggested when speaking of Aristotle's "limitation of theoretical insight in the practical field."[41] Maimonides' "art of writing" seems to hover between Platonic and Aristotelian insights, but these insights are never presented in his writing without also attending to biblical and rabbinic metaphors. It is this peculiar webbing of discourses represented in the *Guide* that strikes me as most pertinent to the question of its literary form.[42] I proceed on the assumption that the manner of writing is significant for what Maimonides means to say, or rather for what his text is meant to do and accomplish in the mind of a careful reader.

In philosophical terms, awareness for the quirks and limits of language leads us to question the straightforward meaning of the correspondence theory of truth, a theory Maimonides explicitly professes (cf. David 2022). Does this theory mean what it says? If truth obtains when what we represent to ourselves in our minds corresponds to what obtains outside our minds, if thinking thus corresponds to being, but thinking cannot be done without recourse to language, how serious can one be about truth claims? If truth cannot but be communicated in words, how can we know that it corresponds to being, unless being itself appears in language? But the claim that God can be adequately expressed in human terms is denied by Maimonides. The correspondence theory of truth is therefore limited to things we can articulate with apodictic certainty.

Is there a kind of "pure" thought without recourse to speech?[43] Or can speech, critically employed, mediate access to being? Is speech a hint to truths that appear behind the veil of human language and points to something that is "beyond being"? Does truth appear in words, or is it something we can mean or communicate without saying it in words? According to Hegel, for example, the truth value of language is problematic because it only expresses generalities,

---

41 "So hat Aristoteles die Möglichkeiten theoretischer Einsicht im praktischen Felde eingeschränkt. Nun scheint mir das gleiche für die Hermeneutik zu gelten und damit für die 'Geisteswissenschaften' und für alles Verstehen überhaupt" (transl. MZ).

42 Daniel Weiss, in *Paradox and the Prophets*, makes a similar argument for the language of Cohen's *Religion of Reason*, drawing on Bakhtin's concept of "heteroglossia" (cf. Weiss 2012). On the neologism разноречие [raznorechie], literally "other-speech-ness," see Bakhtin "Слово в романе" [Slovo v romane] (cf. Bakhtin 1981b).

43 I prefer "speech" to "language," though language, in the sense of having words, is more closely related to reason, while "speech" may be associated with pre-rational signs and utterings, including the "speech" of animals and preverbal infants.

concepts, not actual things. The individual things are essentially ineffable. They can only be pointed to, but not said, and therefore vanish the moment we refer to them in speech.[44] But how do we "point" to a being that is not a thing? Whenever I speak about something, I obscure it. This is not merely a theoretical problem for Maimonides but also a practical one that ties into his Aristotelian concept of the human form. The entelechy of the human being, human perfection, lies in becoming an intellect *in actu*. Teaching, even in the lesser form of writing, is meant to trigger, in the student's mind, the very activity he means to foster. The closest parallel we have in classical western philosophy is Socrates, or rather the Socrates of Plato's early dialogues.

Thinking, which I believe is what the *Guide of the Perplexed* means to teach, is necessarily always not just about things and thinking about things but also about how things dis/appear in speech and about thought and experience as articulated and, indeed, constituted in and by speech. This is true also, and especially so, when a philosophical text engages with the boundaries between objects of "knowledge" and products of the "imagination," specifically when writing about prophets and prophecy, which is the main subject of the *Guide*. Of course, prophets and prophecy are the subject not just of the *Guide*, but also of some of the writings of Maimonides' predecessors, including al-Farabi.[45] But the *form* of the *Guide* by no means resembles that of their writings. It is utterly unique not so much in the philosophical problems it tackles than in its literary form. No interpretation of the *Guide* should be deemed adequate that does not account for the literary aspects of Maimonides' writing.

---

44 Rosenzweig famously challenged this reductionist conception of speech with regard to concrete beings. To augment and rectify it, he draws on second-person rather than third-person speech, which Hegel did not consider. Another way of relating directly to someone arises in *naming*. Far from abandoning the philosophical project of German idealism (see Pollock 2013), Rosenzweig thus *artfully* augments and completes what seemed to him fragmentary and incomplete. Rosenzweig does this by lacing references to artistic representation throughout the *Star's* argumentative structure. The overall project is classified, by Rosenzweig, as "narrative philosophy," as first postulated by Schelling. Rosenzweig is therefore an important witness to the *necessary* conjunction of the philosophical with the literary-aesthetic pursuit. Cf. also Benjamin Pollock's essay in this volume.

45 Pace Strauss, one ought to consider that "prophetology" – and hence political philosophy – was perhaps not the *main* subject of Arab philosophy before or after Maimonides. On the critique of Strauss and Straussian approaches to medieval "Muslim" philosophy, cf. Gutas 2002; Kaya 2014.

Bibliography

Adamson, Peter (2022): "The Theology of Aristotle." In: Edward N. Zalta/Uro Nodelman (eds.), Stanford Encyclopedia of Philosophy, Fall 2022 (https://plato.stanford.edu/archives/fall2022/entries/theology-aristotle/).

Allison, Henry E. (1966): Lessing and the Enlightenment: His Philosophy of Religion and Its Relation to Eighteenth-Century Thought, Ann Arbor: University of Michigan Press.

Altman, William F. (2007): "Exotericism after Lessing: The Enduring Influence of F. H. Jacobi on Leo Strauss." In: Journal of Jewish Thought and Philosophy 15/1, pp. 59–83.

Armstrong, Hilary (1977): "Negative Theology." In: The Downside Review, 95/320, pp. 176–189 (https://doi.org/10.1177/001258067709532002).

Bakhtin, Mikhail (1981a): Dialogic Imagination. Four Essays by M. M. Bakhtin, ed. by Michael Holquist, Austin/London: University of Texas Press.

Bakhtin, Mikhail (1981b [1934]): "Discourse in the Novel." In: Dialogic Imagination. Four Essays by M. M. Bakhtin, ed. by Michael Holquist, Austin/London: University of Texas Press, pp. 259–422.

Berman, Lawrence (2008): "The Ethical Views of Maimonides within the Context of Islamicate Civilization." In: Joel L. Kraemer (ed.), Perspectives on Maimonides: Philosophical and Historical Studies, Liverpool: Liverpool University Press, pp. 13–32.

Blumenberg, Hans (1960): "Paradigmen zu einer Metaphorologie." In: Archiv für Begriffsgeschichte 6, pp. 7–142.

Bos, Gerrit (2022): The Medical Works of Moses Maimonides: New English Translations Based on the Critical Editions of the Arabic Manuscripts, Leiden: Brill.

Bruckstein, Almut Sh. (2001): Die Maske des Moses. Studien zur jüdischen Hermeneutik, Berlin: Philo Verlagsgesellschaft.

Carasik, Michael (2015): The Commentators' Bible: The Rubin JPS Miqra'ot gedolot, Lincoln, NE: Jewish Publication Society/University of Nebraska Press.

Cavell, Stanley (2002): Must We Say What We Say?: A Book of Essays, New York: Cambridge University Press.

Cortest, Luis (2017): Philo's Heirs: Moses Maimonides and Thomas Aquinas, Boston: Academic Studies Press (https://doi.org/10.1515/9781618116314).

David, Marian (2022): "The Correspondence Theory of Truth." In: Edward N. Zalta (ed.), Stanford Encyclopedia of Philosophy, Summer 2022 (https://plato.stanford.edu/archives/sum2022/entries/truth-correspondence/).

Diamond, James Arthur (2002): Maimonides and the Hermeneutics of Concealment: Deciphering Scripture and Midrash in the *Guide of the Perplexed*, New York: State University of New York Press.

Folkers, Horst (1998): "Spinozarezeption bei Jacobi und ihre Nachfolge beim frühen Schelling und beim Jenenser Hegel." In: Philosophisches Jahrbuch 105/2, pp. 381–397.

Förster, Eckart/Melamed, Yitzhak (eds.) (2015): Spinoza and German Idealism. Cambridge/New York: Cambridge University Press.

Fuchs, Gerhard (1990): "Fritz Mauthners Sprachkritik – Aspekte ihrer Literarischen Rezeption in der Österreichischen Gegenwartsliteratur." In: Modern Austrian Literature 23/2, pp. 1–21.

Gadamer, Hans Georg (1997 [1979]): "Das Erbe Hegels." In: Jean Grondin (ed.), Gadamer Lesebuch, Tübingen: Mohr Siebeck, pp. 236–256.

Goethe, Johann Wolfgang von (1895 [1796]): "Plato als Mitgenosse einer christlichen Offenbarung." In: Werke, 32. Teil: Aufsätze zur Litteratur, Bd. 2: 1822–1832, ed. by Georg Witkowski, Stuttgart: Union Deutsche Verlagsgesellschaft, pp. 136–140.

Goldenbaum, Ursula (2009): "Der Pantheismusstreit als Angriff auf die Berliner Aufklärung und Judenemanzipation." In: Aufklärung, 21, pp. 199–226 (http://www.jstor.org/stable/24361786).

Gutas, Dimitri (2002): "The Study of Arabic Philosophy in the Twentieth Century: An Essay on the Historiography of Arabic Philosophy." In: British Journal of Middle Eastern Studies 29/1, pp. 5–25 (https://www.jstor.org/stable/826146).

Halbertal, Moshe (2015): Maimonides: Life and Thought, Princeton, NJ: Princeton University Press.

Halkin, Abraham S./Hartman, David (1993): Epistles of Maimonides: Crisis and Leadership, Philadelphia: Jewish Publication Society.

Hamburger, Käthe (1957): Logik der Dichtung, Stuttgart: Klett-Cotta.

Hartung, Gerald (2013): An den Grenzen der Sprachkritik: Fritz Mauthners Beiträge zur Sprach- und Kulturtheorie, Würzburg: Königshausen & Neumann.

Harvey, W. Z. (2000). "On Maimonides' Allegorical Readings of Scripture." In: J. Whitman (ed.), Interpretation and Allegory, Leiden: Brill (https://doi.org/10.1163/9789047400158_009).

Hasselhoff, Görge (2005): Dicit Rabbi Moyses: Studien zum Bild von Moses Maimonides im Lateinischen Westen vom 13. bis zum 15. Jahrhundert, Würzburg: Königshausen und Neumann.

Hegel, Georg Friedrich (1979 [1807]): "Einleitung." In: Werke, Bd. 3: Phänomenologie des Geistes, Frankfurt a.M.: Suhrkamp, pp. 68–82.

Henne, Helmut/Kaiser, Christine (2000): Fritz Mauthner – Sprache, Literatur, Kritik: Festakt und Symposion zu seinem 150. Geburtstag, Berlin/New York: Max Niemeyer Verlag.

Ivry, Alfred L. (2016): Maimonides' *Guide of the Perplexed*: A Philosophical Guide, Chicago/London: University of Chicago Press.

Jacobi, Friedrich Heinrich (2004 [1785]): Über die Lehre des Spinoza in Briefen an den Herrn Moses Mendelssohn, Hamburg: Meiner.

Jaeger, Werner (1923): Aristoteles: Grundlegung einer Geschichte seiner Entwicklung, Berlin: Weidmannsche Buchhandlung.

Kanarfogel, Ephraim (2023): "On the Citation of Maimonides in Medieval Ashkenaz." In: David Sclar (ed.), The Golden Path: Maimonides across Eight Centuries, New York: Yeshiva University Museum, pp. 133–139.

Kavka, Martin (2009): Jewish Messianism and the History of Philosophy, New York: Cambridge University Press.

Kaya, M. Cüneyt (2014): "In the Shadow of 'Prophetic Legislation': The Venture of Practical Philosophy after Avicenna." In: Arabic Sciences and Philosophy 24/2, pp. 269–296 (doi:10.1017/S0957423914000034).

Kellner, Menacham (1986): Dogma in Medieval Jewish Philosophy, New York: Oxford University Press.

Kerber, Hannes (2021): Die Aufklärung der Aufklärung: Lessing und die Herausforderung des Christentums, Göttingen: Wallstein.

Kleymann, Rabea (2021): "Verlockungen der Unordnung: Die Noten und Abhandlungen des West-östlichen Divans." In: Formlose Form. Epistemik und Poetik des Aggregats beim späten Goethe, Leiden: Brill/Fink.

Lobel, Diana (2021): Moses and Abraham Maimonides Encountering the Divine, Brookline, MA: Academic Studies Press.

Maimonides, Moses (1963 [1190]): The Guide of the Perplexed, Vol. I, transl. by Schlomo Pines, London/Chicago: University of Chicago Press.

Maimonides, Moses (2020 [1160–1168]): Commentary on the Mishnah (https://www.sefaria.org/Rambam_on_Mishnah_Sanhedrin.10.1.14?lang=en).

Maimon, Solomon (2020): The Autobiography of Solomon Maimon: The Complete Translation, ed. by Yitzhak Y. Melamed/Abraham Socher, transl. by Paul Reitter, Princeton, NJ: Princeton University Press.

Motzkin, Aryeh Leo (2011a): "On the Interpretation of Maimonides: The Cases of Samuel David Luzzatto and Ahad Ha'am." In: Yehuda Halper (ed.), Philosophy and the Jewish Tradition. Lectures and Essays by Aryeh Leo Motzkin [Studies in Jewish History and Culture 34], Leiden/Boston: Brill, pp. 125–142.

Motzkin, Aryeh Leo (2011b): "Maimonides and the Imagination." In: Yehuda Halper (ed.), Philosophy and the Jewish Tradition. Lectures and Essays by Aryeh Leo Motzkin [Studies in Jewish History and Culture 34], Leiden/Boston: Brill, pp. 37–50.

Mühlethaler, Lukas (ed.) (2014): "Höre die Wahrheit, wer sie auch spricht": Stationen des Werks von Moses Maimonides vom islamischen Spanien bis ins moderne Berlin [Schriften des Jüdischen Museums Berlin 2], Göttingen: Vandenhoeck & Ruprecht.

Nadler, Steven (2019): "The *Guide of the Perplexed* in Early Modern Philosophy and Spinoza." In: Josef Stern/James T. Robinson/Yonatan Shemesh (eds.), Maimonides' "Guide of the Perplexed" in Translation: A History from the Thirteenth Century to the Twentieth, Chicago: University of Chicago Press, pp. 365–384.

Ortlieb, Cornelia (2010): Friedrich Heinrich Jacobi und die Philosophie als Schreibart, München: Fink.

Patton, Lydia (2011): "Anti-psychologism about Necessity: Friedrich Albert Lange on Objective Inference." In: History and Philosophy of Logic 32/2, pp. 139–152 (http://dx.doi.org/10.1080/01445340.2010.541183).

Pessin, Sarah (2016): "The Influence of Islamic Thought on Maimonides." In: Edward N. Zalta (ed.), Stanford Encyclopedia of Philosophy, Spring 2016 (https://plato.stanford.edu/archives/spr2016/entries/maimonides-islamic/).

Pollock, Benjamin (2013): "Review of Josef Stern's The Matter and Form of Maimonides' Guide". In: Notre Dame Philosophy Reviews (https://ndpr.nd.edu/reviews/the-matter-and-form-of-maimonides-guide/).

Saliba, George (1999): "Critiques of Ptolemaic Astronomy in Islamic Spain." In: Al-Qantara: Revista De Estudios Arabes 20/1, pp. 3–25 (https://doi.org/10.3989/alqantara.1999.v20.i1.449).

Stern, Josef (2013): The Matter and Form of Maimonides' Guide, Cambridge, MA: Harvard University Press.

Stewart, J. A. (1878): "Review of Lange's *Logische Studien*." In: Mind 3/9, pp. 112–118.

Strauss, Leo (1963): How to Begin to Study *The Guide of the Perplexed*, Chicago: University of Chicago Press.

Strauss, Leo (1941): "Persecution and the Art of Writing." In: Social Research, 8:1/4, pp. 488–504.

Strauss, Leo (1965 [1930]): Spinoza's Critique of Religion, New York: Schocken Books.

Strauss, Leo (1997): Gesammelte Schriften, Bd. 2: Philosophie und Gesetz – Frühe Schriften, Stuttgart/Weimar: Metzler.

Strauss, Leo/Green, Kenneth Hart (2013): Leo Strauss on Maimonides: The Complete Writings, Chicago: University of Chicago Press.

Stroumsa, Sarah (1993): "Al-Fārābī and Maimonides on Medicine as a Science." In: Arabic Sciences and Philosophy 3/2, pp. 235–249.

Stroumsa, Sarah (2012): Maimonides in His World: Portrait of a Mediterranean Thinker, Princeton, NJ: Princeton University Press.

Stroumsa, Sarah (2019): Andalus and Sefarad: On Philosophy and Its History in Islamic Spain, Princeton, NJ: Princeton University Press.

Twersky, Isadore (1949): The Code of Maimonides, New Haven, CT: Yale University Press.

Weiss, Daniel (2012): Paradox and the Prophets: Hermann Cohen and the Indirect Communication of Religion, Oxford: Oxford University Press.

Wolfson, Harry Austryn (1934): The Philosophy of Spinoza, Cambridge, MA: Harvard University Press.

Wolfson, Harry Austryn (1977): From Philo to Spinoza: Two Studies in Religious Philosophy, New York: Behrman House.

Zank, Michael (2004): "Arousing Suspicion Against a Prejudice: Leo Strauss and the Study of Maimonides' *Guide of the Perplexed*." In: Görge K. Hasselhoff/Otfried Fraisse (eds.), Moses Maimonides (1138–1204): His Religious, Scientific, and Philosophical Wirkungsgeschichte in Different Cultural Contexts [Ex Oriente Lux: Rezeptionen und Exegesen als Traditionskritik, vol. 4], Würzburg: Ergon, pp. 549–571.

Zank, Michael (2007): "Zwischen den Stühlen? On the Taxonomic Anxieties of Modern Jewish Philosophy." In: European Journal for Jewish Studies (EJJS) 1/1, pp. 105–134.

Zank, Michael (2017): "Torah v. Jewish Law. A Genre-Critical Approach to the Political Theology of Reappropriation." In: Allen Speight/Michael Zank (eds.), Politics, Religion and Political Theology, and Politics [Boston Series in Philosophy and Religion 6], Dordrecht: Springer, pp. 195–221.

Zank, Michael (2021): "A Peripheral Field. Meditations on the Status of Jewish Philosophy." In: M. David Eckel/Try Dujardin/Allen Speight (eds.), The Future of the Philosophy of Religion [Boston Series in Philosophy and Religion 8], Cham: Springer, pp. 179–189.

Authors

Beniamino Fortis holds a PhD in Philosophy. He studied in Venice, Florence, and Berlin. His research interests are in picture theory, aesthetics, and contemporary Jewish thought. Recently, he has published his second monograph *Tertium Datur. A Reading of Rosenzweig's 'New Thinking'* (2019) and edited the collective volume *Bild und Idol. Perspektiven aus Philosophie und jüdischem Denken* (2022). His current research is focused on the topic of idolatry between Jewish studies and philosophy.

Massimo Giuliani (Ph.D., Hebrew University of Jerusalem) is a professor of Jewish Thought at the University of Trent; of Jewish Culture at the University of Urbino; and of Jewish Philosophy at the Italian Rabbinical College of Rome. He is on the academic boards of the Maimonides Foundation (Milan), the Rosmini Center (Rovereto), and several academic journals. Among his books: *Theological Implications of the Shoah* (Peter Lang 2002); *Il pensiero ebraico contemporaneo* [on Contemporary Jewish Thought] (Morcelliana, 2003); *Rileggere Primo Levi* [Re-reading Primo Levi] (Quodlibet 2015); *La giustizia seguirai* [Justice shalt thou follow; on ethics and halakhah] (Giuntina 2016); *La filosofia ebraica* [A History of Jewish Philosophy] (La Scuola 2017); *Le terze tavole* [on the Jewish interpretations of the Holocaust] (EDB, 2019); *Le corone della Torà* [on Jewish hermeneutics] (Giuntina, 2021); *Il conflitto teologico* [on the theological conflict between Jews and Christians] (Morcelliana 2021); *Antropologia halakhica* [on Rav J. Soloveitchik's thought] (Belforte 2022).

Benjamin Pollock is the Sol Rosenbloom Associate Professor of Jewish Philosophy at the Hebrew University. Since 2017 he is also the director of the Franz Rosenzweig Minerva and since fall 2020 the chair of the Department of Jewish Thought. His field of research is modern Jewish philosophy, especially in the

German context, from the Enlightenment through the 20th century. His first book, *Franz Rosenzweig and the Systematic Task of Philosophy* (Cambridge University Press, 2009), was awarded the Salo W. Baron Prize for Outstanding First Book in Jewish Studies by the American Academy of Jewish Research, and the Jordan Schnitzer Award for Best Book in the Field of Jewish Philosophy and Jewish Thought 2009–2012, by the Association for Jewish Studies. His *Franz Rosenzweig's Conversions: World Denial and World Redemption* (Indiana University Press), appeared in the summer of 2014.

Silvia Richter studied medieval and modern history, philosophy and Jewish studies at the University of Heidelberg and the Hochschule für Jüdische Studien Heidelberg, where she submitted her Ph.D. thesis in 2011 on the topic "Language, Philosophy and Judaism in the Work of Emmanuel Levinas and Franz Rosenzweig" under the supervision of Prof. Ephraim Meir. In 2012 she worked as a scientific coordinator at the Mémorial de la Shoah in Paris, France. From 2013 to 2021 she worked as a research assistant at the Guardini Chair (Guardini Professur für Religionsphilosophie und Theologische Ideengeschichte) at Humboldt University of Berlin. Since January 2022 she is scientific coordinator at the Martin Buber Chair at Goethe University in Frankfurt/Main. Furthermore, in the summer semester 2024, she holds the deputy professorship for Jewish Philosophy at the Hochschule für Jüdische Studien Heidelberg.

Ellen Rinner studied art history, modern German philology, and philosophy at Freie Universität and Humboldt Universität in Berlin and at Sorbonne Université in Paris. From 2018 to 2022, she was a research assistant at the Selma Stern Center for Jewish Studies Berlin-Brandenburg and a member of the research group "The Ban on Images and Theory of Art" ("Bilderverbot und Theorie der Kunst"). Since 2022, she has been a research assistant at the Chair for Transcultural History of Judaism at the Department for Cultural History and Theory at Humboldt Universität. Her forthcoming dissertation focuses on the influence of Jewish cultural traditions on Aby Warburg's Kulturwissenschaft.

Christoph Schmidt is born in Helsinki/Finland, grew up in Cologne/Germany and finished Jesuit School in St.Blasien. Since 1977 he lives in Jerusalem, where he finished his studies in Judaism, Comparative Literature and Philosophy with a PhD thesis on Adorno's "Hermeneutics of Shock". Since 1994 he is teaching first at the Department for German literature, since 2005 he is associate professor and teaching as well at the departments of philosophy and comparative religion, since 2015 as full professor. Schmidt's publications deal with the problem of political theology in the context of Jewish, Christian and secular modernity. Forthcoming is his book on "The Two Bodies of the Subject – Political Theology between Feuerbach and Kierkegaard".

Mario Cosimo Schmidt studied composition, music theory, social sciences and philosophy in Leipzig and Paris. He lives in Leipzig as a composer, music theorist and publicist and is lecturer for music theory at the Hochschule für Musik, Theater und Medien in Hannover and the Hochschule for Music in Nuremberg. His theoretical works are mainly dedicated to questions about the philosophy of music, aesthetics, critical theory and Judaism. Numerous articles about these topics where published. In addition, he also works as a composer and sound artist. Several compositions for all kinds of instrumentation where premiered. He was Fellow at the Ernst Ludwig Ehrlich Studienwerk and the Selma Stern Zentrum Berlin.

Lars Tittmar studied philosophy and sociology at the University of Hamburg and the Humboldt-Universität Berlin. From 2018 to 2022 he was a research assistant at the Selma Stern Center for Jewish Studies in Berlin and a member of the research group "The Ban on Images and Theory of Art" ("Bilderverbot und Theorie der Kunst"). In 2023 he was a research fellow at the Franz Rosenzweig Minerva Research Center in Jerusalem. His research interests are Frankfurt School Critical Theory, social philosophy, philosophy of history, utopian thinking, aesthetics and the work of Jean Améry. He did his doctorate research in philosophy at Freie Universität Berlin and his forthcoming dissertation is focusing on the relation between utopian thinking and the ban on images in the philosophy of Ernst Bloch, Walter Benjamin and Theodor W. Adorno.

Michael Zank is professor of religion, Jewish studies, and medieval studies at Boston University, where he directed the Elie Wiesel Center for Jewish Studies from 2013 to 2022, and teaches courses in the sacred literature, history, and philosophy of the Abrahamic religions. He is the author, among others, of a brief history of Jerusalem (2018) and *Jüdische Religionsphilosophie als Apologie des Mosaismus* (2016). His current research centers on Maimonides and his modern readers, esp. Baruch Spinoza, Hermann Cohen, and Leo Strauss.

www.ingramcontent.com/pod-product-compliance
Lightning Source LLC
Jackson TN
JSHW010045260125
77759JS00004B/80